IF IT'S A QUESTION OF
LATINO HISTORY, CULTURE, OR CURRENT
AFFAIRS . . . FUN, FACT, OR FASCINATION . . .
YOU'LL FIND THE ANSWER IN

EVERYTHING YOU NEED TO KNOW
ABOUT LATINO HISTORY

- What happened at the Bay of Pigs and why did Cuban Americans blame President Kennedy?
- How did the drug trade engulf Colombia?
- Real power or paella in the sky: How much political clout do Latinos really wield?
- Who was Che Guevara?
- What was so great about the Incas, and what did they do with all that gold?
- What were the Zoot Suit Riots?
- Why is there a Cadillac named Eldorado?
- Does bilingual education mean we'll all be speaking Spanish soon?

All this and much more, including a comprehensive listing of Latino-related Internet addresses and additional readings.

Himilce Novas is the author of six previous books and has written for the *New York Times*, the *Christian Science Monitor*, *Connoisseur*, and *Cuisine*. She is also the host of a popular Santa Barbara radio show. She teaches American literature and lectures widely on Latino history and culture.

HIMILCE NOVAS

EVERYTHING YOU NEED TO KNOW ABOUT

LATINO

HISTORY

Revised Edition

ⓟ

A PLUME BOOK

PLUME
Published by the Penguin Group
Penguin Putnam Inc., 375 Hudson Street, New York, New York 10014, U.S.A.
Penguin Books Ltd, 27 Wrights Lane, London W8 5TZ, England
Penguin Books Australia Ltd, Ringwood, Victoria, Australia
Penguin Books Canada Ltd, 10 Alcorn Avenue,
Toronto, Ontario, Canada M4V 3B2
Penguin Books (N.Z.) Ltd, 182–190 Wairau Road, Auckland 10, New Zealand

Penguin Books Ltd, Registered Offices: Harmondsworth, Middlesex, England

First published by Plume, an imprint of Dutton NAL,
a member of Penguin Putnam Inc.

First Printing, October, 1994
First Printing (Revised Edition), October, 1998

1 3 5 7 9 10 8 6 4 2

Copyright © Himilce Novas, 1994, 1998
All rights reserved.

Excerpt from *How the García Girls Lost Their Accents* © 1991 by Julia Alvarez.
Published by Plume, an imprint of Dutton Signet, a division of Penguin USA Inc.
Published in hardcover by Algonquin Books. Reprinted by permission of Susan
Bergholz Literary Services, New York.

 REGISTERED TRADEMARK—MARCA REGISTRADA

LIBRARY OF CONGRESS CATALOGING IN PUBLICATION DATA
Novas, Himilce.
Everything you need to know about Latino history / Himilce Novas. — Rev. ed.
p. cm.
Includes bibliographical references and index.
ISBN 0-452-27991-7
1. Hispanic Americans—History.   I. Title.
E184.S75N69   1998
973'.0468073—dc21   98-4354
CIP

Printed in the United States of America
Set in New Baskerville and Pabst

Designed by Steven N. Stathakis

Without limiting the rights under copyright reserved above, no part of this publication may be reproduced, stored in or introduced into a retrieval system, or
transmitted, in any form, or by any means (electronic, mechanical, photocopying,
recording, or otherwise), without the prior written permission of both the copyright owner and the above publisher of this book.

BOOKS ARE AVAILABLE AT QUANTITY DISCOUNTS WHEN USED TO PROMOTE PRODUCTS OR
SERVICES. FOR INFORMATION PLEASE WRITE TO PREMIUM MARKETING DIVISION, PENGUIN
PUTNAM INC., 375 HUDSON STREET, NEW YORK, NEW YORK 10014.

For my mother and father, Herminia del Portal and Lino Novas Calvo, who had the courage to seek a new world and bring me to a new America, and for Rosemary Silva, whose help with this book made the journey joyous.

Acknowledgments

I wish to express my gratitude to the staff and the librarians of the Library of Congress, the New York Public Library, the Library of the Hispanic Society, the University Research Library at UCLA, and the Davidson Library at the University of California at Santa Barbara for their generous assistance in my research. I am indebted in particular to Erminio D'Onofrio, documents librarian at the New York Public Library, for his advice in locating materials and for his computer wizardry. I also wish to thank the Museo del Barrio in New York City and the Spanish History Museum in Albuquerque for their commitment to chronicling the history of the Spanish influence in America and preserving Hispanic culture and arts of the past and present. I owe special thanks to Deb Brody, my editor, for her harmony, wisdom, and art. For their enlightening commitment to unearthing Latin American and Latino voices for a new generation of Americans, I owe special thanks to Lorraine Elena Roses, professor of Spanish and director of Latin American studies at Wellesley College and S. Jill Levine, a professor of Spanish at the University of California at Santa Barbara.

Finally, friends and supporters deserve special acknowledgment. I am indebted to Theresa Mantenfel for countless years of warm friendship and emotional quarterbacking. Special thanks go to Lan Cao for years of loyal friendship and for reminding me that a writer writes. My heartfelt thanks also go to Gail and Steve Humphreys, Bill Campbell, Fran and Ted Halpern, Marilyn Gilbert, Nathan Rundlett, Carol Storke, Michael Smith, Penny and Terry Davies of the Earthling Bookstore in Santa Barbara, Henry Bloomstein and Jackie Green, Wendy Carlton, Marlyn Bernstein, everybody at the American Program Bureau, Charlie Carrillo, Carmen Alea Paz, and Guillermo Cabrera Infante. I also say *¡saludos!* to all the Latinas and Latinos who happily shared their knowledge of their culture, folklore and history during my many years of research.

Contents

Contents

Introduction

Latinos, also known as Hispanics, comprise the fastest growing ethnic minority in the United States. In 1990 the U.S. Bureau of the Census counted approximately 22.3 million Latinos. This figure represents a dramatic rise as only a decade earlier Latinos numbered 7.4 million. The Bureau of the Census estimates that if the Latino population continues to expand at its present rate, by the year 2000 there will be 31 million Latinos; by 2015, 44 million; and by 2050, 81 million.

Latinos have also been measured in terms of their economic clout. In 1997, the Latino consumer market weighed in with an estimated buying power of $228 billion—up from $205 billion in 1995. To meet the demand for goods and services, the number of Latino-owned businesses in the United States has risen exponentially in the last decade. Mainstream businesses, realizing that Latinos represent a gold mine at the cash register, have contributed many more advertising dollars to this ethnic group than ever before. As Latinos have grown in visibility economically, corporate America has awakened to the realization that they have a lot to contribute in the board room as well. The number of Latinos in the top echelons of major American corporations—from the late Roberto C. Goizueta, CEO of the Coca-Cola Company, to the family-owned and -operated Bacardi International Limited—is mounting.

Latinos have achieved prominence in every profession— the arts, science and technology, politics, law, finance, and sports. In the post–*I Love Lucy* decades (after long years when Desi Arnaz and maybe Charo and Xavier Cugat were among the only truly recognizable "Latins" around), Latinos have become household names: Antonia Novello, U.S. surgeon general during the Bush administration; Henry Cisneros, former mayor of San Antonio and HUD secretary under Clinton; Texas congressman Henry B. González, who has been in politics for nearly fifty years and chaired the powerful House Banking Committee for over a decade; Joan Baez, Linda Ronstadt, Gloria Estefan, Jon Secada, Mariah Carey, and Selena, music superstars; Pancho Segura, Rosie Casals, and Mary Jo Fernandez, top professional tennis players; Anthony Quinn, Jose Ferrer, Rita Hayworth, Rita Moreno, Chita Rivera, legends of the stage and screen; and many, many others.

Still, in spite of the enormous demographic and social changes in recent years and the extraordinary number of Latinos who have contributed immensely to this nation throughout history, most Americans know very little about their Latino neighbors—about their culture, their rich history, or their dreams for the future.

The history of Latinos goes back as far as American history itself. In fact, you could say that without Latinos there would be no United States of America as we know it today. Ever since Christopher Columbus sailed with his Spanish crew under Queen Isabella and King Ferdinand's flag, men and women of Spanish ancestry have been coming to America's shores in pursuit of their dreams. Hernando de Soto, who discovered the Mississippi River, dreamed of finding hidden caves of gold in Florida. Francisco Vasquez de Coronado, who explored the West, thought he had found there a brave new world destined for Spanish conquest.

Then after the formation of the thirteen colonies, peoples with Spanish blood from Mexico, Cuba, Puerto Rico, Colombia, and other Spanish colonies in Latin America, began coming north to seek their destiny, or as is the case for the ancestors of many Mexican Americans and much later for Puerto Ricans, suddenly found themselves a part of the United States. As a result of the Spanish-American War, the Cuban Revolution and the Cuban Missile Crisis, a bloody dictatorship and authoritarian leaders in the Dominican Republic, the civil wars in Nicaragua, Guatemala, and El Salvador, and hundreds of other political upheavals from Tijuana to the Argentine pampas, Latinos have settled in the United States by the millions and in the process have slowly changed the face of the nation.

In spite of my own Latino roots, the Spanish education I received at home, and my very early years spent in Cuba, I began this project cherishing some of the same misinformation and stereotypes subscribed to by many with no real knowledge of Latinos. After all, I, too, moved through the American school system at a time when the "Anglo" perspective on history was the only valid one, and when the word "bilingual" was mainly used when referring to an especially gifted secretary.

I had virtually no exposure to Latino history in high school, and for my introduction to Latino culture I depended almost exclusively on mainstream American writers' observations of Latinos, rather than Latinos' commentary on themselves. For instance, my reading assignments in the New York City public schools included Stephen Crane's "A Man and Some Others," which offers a simplistic portrait of Latinos; John Steinbeck's *Tortilla Flat*, which while attempting to honor Mexican Americans paints a picture of them as lazy drunkards; and the works of Ernest Hemingway, Katherine Ann

Porter, Jack Kerouac, and countless others who wrote passionately about Latinos but often missed the key thread of their existence and presented naive, stereotyped images of them.

Regrettably, the works of Latino writers of the time, such as Piri Thomas's *Down These Mean Streets*, José Antonio Villarreal's *Pocho*, and Tomas Rivera's *And the Earth Did Not Devour Him*, among hundreds of others, were nowhere to be found in school libraries until recently—and even now many of these works are only on the shelves of libraries in urban areas with large Latino communities.

I have learned much in the process of unearthing my own roots during the last twenty-five years of study. In some cases I have been as surprised by what I have found as Columbus must have been when he first tasted a habañero chile.

Answering some basic questions about Latino history has been more an act of *abrir la puerta* (opening the door) to this rich and enduring culture than an effort to cover a vast and complex history in one fell swoop. I have also attempted to present historical facts and events fairly, from the perspective of those whose history they represent.

How to Read This Book

I have organized this edition of *Everything You Need to Know About Latino History* just as I did the first: in an engaging question-and-answer format that allows the reader to hone in on those topics of Latino history and culture that are of most interest to her or him. Of course, the book may also be read from cover to cover, so that all the fascinating pieces of Latino life fall in place.

The term "Latino" embraces a multitude of peoples from various corners of Spanish-speaking Latin America, each with its own history and culture. As in the first edition, I have divided the chapters according to the various Latino subgroups. I have devoted entire chapters to the largest of these subgroups in descending order of population, namely Mexican Americans, Puerto Ricans, and Cuban Americans. In this edition, Dominican Americans, whose numbers are growing rapidly, are also afforded their own chapter.

I have also expanded the commentary on Americans of Central American descent and have grouped their histories together in one chapter entitled "The Newest Immigrants," since their collective experiences in America are strikingly similar. Salvadoran, Guatemalan, and Nicaraguan Americans, whose communities are the largest, are the focus of this chapter, but Costa Rican, Honduran, and Panamanian Americans are also touched upon. Also covered in this chapter are Americans of South American descent, who, although they are relatively few in number, wield a disproportionate amount of clout and are exerting an influence on American life. This chapter zooms in on the larger subgroups: Colombian, Ecuadoran, Peruvian, and Argentinian Americans, but also briefly considers Uruguayan, Paraguayan, Chilean, Bolivian, and Venezuelan Americans.

This edition of *Everything You Need to Know About Latino History*, like the first, has four chapters that present background and cultural information on Latinos as a group, all of which has been updated. I have incorporated some new information in the boxes filled with fast facts about Latinos and have added a list of Internet addresses relevant to Latino history and culture—from music and cuisine to political organizations—for those who cruise the Internet.

As in the first edition, I have sought not to compile dates and details, but to air out American history just a bit and provide fresh perspectives on one of the richest and most invigorating cultures of all time. In examining Latinos' place in the American landscape, I have shattered a few myths and taken a poke at some stereotypes so that the truth may be known about a marvelous people who have made valuable contributions to this country and who continue to shape American life.

—HIMILCE NOVAS
Santa Barbara, California
February 1998

1990 Latino Population, by State

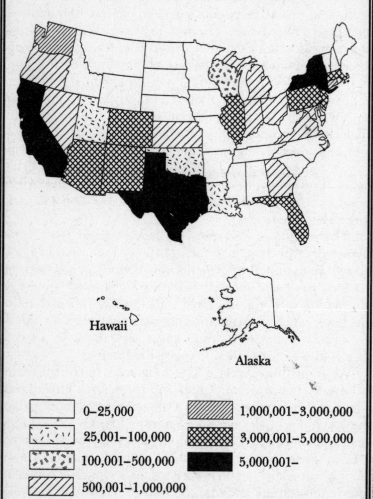

Hawaii

Alaska

0–25,000	1,000,001–3,000,000
25,001–100,000	3,000,001–5,000,000
100,001–500,000	5,000,001–
500,001–1,000,000	

Source: 1990 U.S. Census

© Claudia Carlson

UNO

Latino : Sí y No

What's in a name?

Why has there been a panic over "Hispanic"?

Are Brazilian Americans Latinos?

Why is it so difficult to count Latinos?

Mexican Americans: As many as the stars in the night sky?

Puerto Ricans: Why aren't they considered immigrants?

Cuban Americans: What makes them different?

Dominican Americans: What brought them to the United States in recent decades?

Americans of Central and South American descent: Why are they the new Latinos?

What's in a name?

When it comes to the term "Hispanic," you can say a great deal. "Hispanic" is derived from *España*, Spain, the country that led the conquest (as in *conquistadores*) of the New World. But Hispanics are more than just the descendants of New World Spanish conquistadors and settlers. As it turned out, the Spanish encountered many different native peoples, known generally as Amerindians, in the Americas, and to a large extent, intermarried and interbred with those they conquered. Add to that all the peoples the Spanish eventually brought from Africa to the Americas as slaves (with whom they also mixed), and you get the whole enchilada known as Spanish-speaking Latin Americans, the "relatives" of Hispanics.

Over the centuries many peoples from Spanish Latin America have made their way to the United States to forge a brand-new life or found themselves citizens due to shifting American borders. For the sake of clarity, Spanish Latin America is comprised of Cuba, Puerto Rico, the Dominican Republic, Mexico, Nicaragua, Costa Rica, Guatemala, El Salvador, Honduras, Panama, Venezuela, Colombia, Ecuador, Peru, Bolivia, Chile, Argentina, Uruguay, and Paraguay. All residents of the United States who originated from these countries, or whose ancestors did, are known as Hispanics. The U.S. Bureau of the Census also includes Spanish Americans, those whose forbears came directly from Spain, among Hispanics, but many scholars limit the definition to those of Spanish Latin American origin.

Perhaps no other ethnic group in the United States is as diverse in its culture, physical appearance, and traditions as the Hispanics. Most other ethnic groups have been categorized by country of origin—the Irish from Ireland, the Ukrainians from Ukraine, and so on. Hispanics, with roots in the eighteen sovereign nations and one U.S. Commonwealth (Puerto Rico) listed above, each with its own distinct culture, history, indigenous language(s), religions, culinary traditions, and individual philosophies, are classified by their own or their ancestors' mother tongue, Spanish, in the name of simplicity.

In Latin America people do not refer to themselves as Hispanic. Each Latin American country is a marvelous melting pot of diverse peoples, many of whom speak ancient indigenous languages in addition to Spanish, and thus "Hispanic" is not an appropriate appellation. National identity takes precedence, thus Mexicans call themselves *Mexicanos*, Puerto Ricans *Puertorriqueños*, Cubans *Cubanos*, and so on. For the recent immigrant from Latin America, the realization that he or she is no longer viewed by the larger society as Nicaraguan, Mexican, Cuban, or Colombian, but as part of the collective called Hispanics, is often startling. The majority of Hispanics, new immigrants and fourth- or fifth-generation Americans alike, identify first and foremost with the subgroup to which they belong, be it Mexican or Cuban, while a small percentage refer to themselves first and foremost as Hispanic or as American.

No matter how they view themselves individually, Hispanics as a whole have benefited greatly from the rise of a pan-ethnic consciousness or solidarity among the subgroups. As a large united front, Hispanics have managed to acquire the political clout necessary to effect positive change and fight the discrimination and injustices that have at times run rampant in American society.

Why has there been a panic over "Hispanic"?

Many Americans with roots in Spanish Latin America consider "Hispanic" merely a bureaucratic government census term, and prefer the pan-ethnic term "Latino" or "Latina" (depending on gender). Novelist **Sandra Cisneros,** author of such books as *The House on Mango Street* (1984) and *Woman Hollering Creek and Other Stories* (1991), is so adamantly against the term "Hispanic" that she refuses to let her work appear in anthologies that mention the word. She insists that "Hispanic" smacks of colonization: "It's a repulsive slave name," she declared in an interview published in the *New York Times.*

However, "Latino" has not been popular across the board either. **Enrique Fernández,** editor of *Más,* a Spanish-language entertainment magazine, believes that he speaks for many when he says that "Hispanic" is preferable to "Latino," since "Latino," taken back to its roots, refers to an even older empire—the one that took over Spain.

Others remain unperturbed and impartial when it comes to the "Hispanic-Latino" debate. **John Leguizamo,** the Puerto Rican–Colombian American writer, actor, and creator of the one-man show *Spic-o-rama,* which ran in New York in the early 1990s, has said that he used to call himself "Spanish" (a term that until recently was used for Puerto Ricans in New York City), but now prefers "Latino," although he does not consider "Hispanic" offensive. "Now 'wetback, greasy spic' that's derogatory," he once told an interviewer.

Are Brazilian Americans Latinos?

No. Brazilian Americans have roots in Brazil, a South American country that was conquered by the Portuguese and not the Spanish. On April 22, 1500, a Portuguese navigator by the name of **Pedro Álvares Cabral** landed at Pôrto Seguro, Brazil, and claimed the region for Portugal, in keeping with guidelines established by the pope in the Treaty of Tordesillas signed in 1494. Portugal would rule Brazil for about the next three hundred years. Historians have speculated that Spanish explorers may have sighted and even visited the coast of Brazil before the Portuguese put up stakes.

While Brazilian Americans are of Portuguese, not Spanish, ancestry, and therefore do not qualify as Latinos, many see themselves as part of a larger pan-Latin American diaspora and have forged close ties with the Latino community.

Why is it so difficult to count Latinos?

According to the U.S. Bureau of the Census, in 1990 Latinos numbered approximately 22.3 million, constituting nine percent of the American population. This figure represents a whopping increase of 7.4 million from 1980 and 15.5 million from 1960. The Bureau of the Census estimates that, given the current birth rate, the Latino population will rise to 31 million by the year 2000, 44 million by 2015, and 81 million by 2050. By the year 2005, Latinos are projected to surpass African Americans as the nation's largest minority group. The rapid growth in the Latino population is attributed to their tendency to have larger families (2.5 children on average as compared to 1.8 children for non-Latino Caucasians) and an increase in immigration.

Contrary to popular belief, most Latinos are U.S. citizens, but some are legal resident aliens with green cards. An unknown number are undocumented—mostly workers who slip across the border illegally to earn a measly sum in the fields and factories that they send back home to keep their families afloat. Since the U.S. government cannot calculate just how many undocumented workers there are in the United States, it is impossible to arrive at an accurate count of Latinos.

In the 1980s, the U.S. government attempted to improve the lot of undocumented workers. The Immigration Reform and Control Act of 1986 granted amnesty and the opportunity to obtain American citizenship to thousands of undocumented workers. However, many who would have qualified for amnesty did not obtain it because the law required them to show proof that they had been living and working in the United States before January 1, 1982. In many instances, their employers refused to step forward on their behalf and validate their claims for fear that the government would impose stiff penalties upon them for knowingly hiring illegal aliens. It was one of those damned-if-you-do and damned-if-you-don't situations that creep up in our history from time to time.

The mid-1990s brought an intense wave of antiimmigrant sentiment that embraces America to this day. Life became nearly unbearable for undocumented workers in California in 1994, when the state's Republicans, led by Pete Wilson, championed Proposition 187, a measure that would deny them access to federal programs such as Medicaid, welfare, and food stamps, prevent their children born in the United States from obtaining U.S. citizenship, attending public schools, and receiving government-sponsored health care. The measure passed at the polls, but is currently tied up in the courts.

The general antiimmigrant sentiment in America also fostered the passage of a new immigration law which took effect on April 1, 1997. The law gives immigration officers the right to refuse entry to a foreigner at the border or at airports with no right to appeal, as well as the power to deport undocumented immigrants and bar them from reentering the United States for several years, even if they present the proper documentation. Many Latinos and Latin American leaders feared that there would be a mass deportation after the passage of this law, but that did not take place. Latino residents with American-born children feared that the law would break up their families.

FACTS AND FIGURES

1. In 1990, New Mexico had a higher percentage of Latinos in its population (38.2 percent) than any other state. California came in second with 25.8 percent.

2. More Latinos (34.4 percent in 1990) call California home than any other state.

3. 55 percent of Latinos are bilingual (as of 1997).

4. Miami, Florida, has more Latino-owned businesses than any other metropolitan area.

5. In 1990, approximately 72 percent of all Latinos lived in metropolitan areas.

6. Half the Latino population of Miami and Los Angeles is foreign-born, but only one-quarter of Latinos in New York City were born outside of the continental United States.

7. In 1991, nearly one-half of first- and second-generation Latinos in New York City tied the knot with a person of a different national origin.

8. Latino men intermarry at a greater rate than Latina women.

9. In 1996, 14 percent of the children in the United States were Latino. By 2020, 20 percent of the nation's children will be Latino.

10. Between 1972 and 1992 the number of Latino students in America's public schools doubled.

11. In 1990, 72 percent of Latinos identified themselves as Roman Catholic.

12. In 1997, the Latino consumer market had an estimated buying power of $228 billion—up from $205 billion in 1995.

13. As of 1997, 80 Latinos or their families had fortunes of at least $25 million.

14. California boasts the greatest number of affluent Latino families in the nation.

15. In 1996, 72 percent of Latinos voted Democrat in the presidential elections.

Mexican Americans: As many as the stars in the night sky?

The majority of Latinos—approximately 12,110,000, according to 1990 U.S. census reports—are of Mexican origin. While many Americans believe otherwise, the majority of Mexican Americans—67 percent—were born in the United States. The states with the largest Mexican American population include, in descending order, California, Texas, Illinois, Arizona, New Mexico, and Colorado. In 1990 over six million Americans of Mexican ancestry resided in California, and nearly four million in Texas. More people of Mexican descent call Los Angeles home than any other city in the world except Mexico City.

These census figures do not take into account the population known as Hispanos, the descendants of residents of the region of Mexico annexed by the United States under the Treaty of Guadalupe Hidalgo after the Mexican-American War (1846–1848). Although Hispanos, some of whose ancestors were here before the Pilgrims sighted Plymouth Rock, live mostly in New Mexico, many have been largely assimilated into the non-Hispanic population of the United States. Hispanos are the direct descendants of the Spanish *conquistadores* and *mestizos*, or those of mixed Spanish and Amerindian blood.

Due to the Hispano assimilation, it is virtually impossible to ascertain how many Latinos of Mexican origin make their home in the United States. This matter is further complicated by the scores of undocumented Mexican workers and *mojados* ("wetbacks") trying to piece together a living in the underground.

Puerto Ricans: Why aren't they considered immigrants?

Because they aren't—not on their island and not on the isle of Manhattan, either.

Puerto Ricans are American citizens by birth, thanks to the Spanish-American War (1898), the annexation of Puerto Rico, and its subsequent status as a U.S. Commonwealth (*Estado Libre Asociado*). Thus their movement to and from Puerto Rico is considered part of the internal migration of Americans and not immigration, as is the case for Mexicans, Cubans, Salvadorans, and all other Latinos. In some years as many as five million Puerto Ricans travel between the island of Puerto Rico and the continental United States, many in search of employment and higher wages.

Mainland Puerto Ricans comprise the second largest Latino group, but trail far behind Mexican Americans in number. According to the 1990 U.S. census, Puerto Ricans number about 2,652,000 on the U.S. mainland. Since the early days of Puerto Rican settlement in the continental United States, New York City has been the number one destination. Nowadays about 900,000 Puerto Ricans reside in the city. Other states with a significant Puerto Rican population include New Jersey (320,000), Florida (247,000), Massachusetts (151,000), Pennsylvania (149,000), Connecticut (147,000) and Illinois (146,000).

Puerto Ricans are the second youngest group of Latinos,

after Mexican Americans, with 38 percent under the age of twenty-one. Only about ten percent are older than fifty-five. Of mainland Puerto Ricans, 57 percent were employed in 1993, as opposed to 66 percent of Mexican Americans. One-half held professional, managerial, technical, and administrative support jobs, as opposed to one-third of Mexican Americans. In 1993 more than 53 percent of mainlanders had graduated from high school. However, when the second generation of Puerto Ricans on the mainland was considered separately, their educational level approached the national average, and their occupational status was seen as advancing at a steady pace.

Cuban Americans: What makes them different?

Cuban Americans number a little over one million, according to the 1990 U.S. census. The majority, about 64 percent, live in Florida, particularly Miami, where they have transformed the city, with their love of enterprise and distinct Latin rhythms, into a chic, cosmopolitan metropolis and a center for international business. New Jersey, New York, and California are each home to between 70,000 and 80,000 Cuban Americans, and a small number are scattered across the rest of the country. Cuban Americans have long identified with European refugees who came to our shores fleeing Nazism, communism, and other totalitarian regimes, and like those refugees of old, Cubans have actively pursued the American dream.

In 1993, 72 percent of Cuban Americans were foreign born. Most foreign-born Cubans came to the United States in the 1960s and 1970s as refugees from the communist revolution led by **Fidel Castro,** who seized the reins of power in 1959. In 1980, another group of Cubans, known as the Marielitos because they departed Cuba from the port of Mariel, reached the United States as part of a seven-week airborne and seaborne exodus from Cuba. Their journey to American shores and subsequent resettlement were aided by the U.S. government. In 1994, many thousands of Cubans reached America's shores during the rafter refugee crisis, but in 1995 the U.S. government passed measures to stanch the flow of Cubans from the island to the United States.

The first wave of Cuban Americans who came by the hundreds of thousands in the sixties and seventies are now largely middle class. Of all Latinos, Cuban Americans enjoyed the lowest unemployment rate in 1993 and have the most formal education (although some Americans of South American descent are close behind). Their assimilation into the American mainstream has been more rapid than that of other Latinos, whose main reason for immigrating has not been political but economic, and whose communities include fewer Caucasians than the Cubans'.

Since Castro's revolution forced Cubans to flee the island, three generations of Cuban Americans have forged lives for themselves in the United States. Some members of the older generation still profess the desire and determination to return someday to their homeland. But those who have been raised in the United States, such as singer and songwriter **Gloria Estefan,** merely say they hope one day to visit a democratic, prosperous Cuba.

Dominican Americans: What brought them to the United States in recent decades?

According to the U.S. census, Dominican Americans numbered approximately 506,000 in 1990. Over half call New Jersey and New York home, and New York City boasts the largest Dominican population outside of Santo Domingo. The Dominican American community is centered in the Washington Heights section of New York. Massachusetts, Florida, and Puerto Rico also have small Dominican American communities.

From 1930 until 1961, the Dominican Republic experienced one of the most violent dictatorships in world history. The nation suffered tremendously under the rule of dictator **Rafael Trujillo,** who answered dissent with genocidal massacres and terror inflicted by his secret police. Few managed to escape Trujillo's Dominican Republic.

After Trujillo was assassinated in Santo Domingo in 1961, the Dominican Republic experienced a power vacuum, and in 1963 a civil war broke out that sent the U.S. Marines rushing to the Caribbean nation and Dominicans fleeing to America's shores. Despite the fact that the Dominican Republic endured a series of bumbling authoritarian leaders in the decade after the civil war, living conditions improved thanks to an economic boom. By 1978 the boom was a thing of the past. Hyperinflation, a collapsing infrastructure, and unemployment swiftly became permanent fixtures on the Dominican landscape, and in the 1980s the number of Dominicans emigrating to the United States skyrocketed. The 1990s have seen no break from the awful conditions that besiege the Dominican Republic. Having lost all hope for a prosperous future and a stable life, Dominicans have left their nation in unprecedented numbers in the 1990s. In 1996, the first democratically elected leader took power. Only time will tell if conditions will improve enough to stem the tide of emigration.

Americans of Central and South American descent: Why are they the new Latinos?

About 78 percent of all Americans of Central American descent have roots in El Salvador, Guatemala, and Nicaragua. In 1990 the U.S. Bureau of the Census counted approximately 565,000 Salvadoran Americans, 269,000 Guatemalan Americans, and 203,000 Nicaraguan Americans. (There are roughly 131,000 Honduran Americans, 100,000 Costa Rican Americans, and 92,000 Panamanian Americans.) About 50 percent of Americans with roots in Central America reside in Califor-

nia, though a significant number also live in New York and
Florida. Los Angeles has the largest Guatemalan and Salvadoran communities outside of Central America. These are
poor communities, but the people are extremely hardworking and they have great aspirations to acculturate and learn
English.

Of all Americans of Central American origin 79 percent are foreign born, as emigration from Central America
on a large scale is a fairly new phenomenon. Civil war in
El Salvador and Guatemala in the 1970s unleashed the first
large wave of Central American immigration. In the 1980s
both countries were led by authoritarian governments that
sent their citizens racing over the border in record numbers.
That same decade civil war broke out in Nicaragua and
Nicaraguans streamed into the United States. As a result
of authoritarianism in El Salvador and Guatemala, and civil
war in Nicaragua, about half of all Central Americans came
to the United States in the 1980s. Now that combat has ceased
in El Salvador, Guatemala, and Nicaragua, the approximately 300,000 refugees from these countries not yet granted
political asylum in the United States could face deportation due to the immigration law passed in 1997. But not without a fight. In June 1997, a federal judge blocked efforts,
on the part of the INS and the Justice Department, to deport about 40,000 Central American legal immigrants living
in Florida, Georgia, and Alabama. The case will be heard
in 1998.

About three out of every four Americans of South Ameri-
can descent have roots in Colombia, Ecuador, and Peru. The
1990 U.S. census reported approximately 379,000 Colombian
Americans, 191,000 Ecuadoran Americans, and 175,000 Peruvian
Americans. There are about 69,000 Chilean Americans, 48,000
Venezuelan Americans, 38,000 Bolivian Americans, 22,000
Uruguayan Americans, and 7,000 Paraguayan Americans. Of
Americans who are of South American origin 75 percent were
born outside of the United States, and about one third of all

South Americans entered the United States in the 1980s. Most Americans of South American origin call California, Florida, and New Jersey home. As a group they are well educated and have enjoyed as much success as Cuban Americans.

DOS

Roots

If Columbus was Italian, why do Latinos celebrate Columbus Day?

Did Columbus really discover America?

What was Columbus really in search of?

What did Columbus first lay eyes on when he reached America?

What was Columbus's most amazing feat?

So who were the native peoples Columbus encountered in the Americas?

Who else lived in the Americas before Columbus got there?

THE MESOAMERICAN PEOPLES: THE MAYA, THE AZTEC, THE INCA

Why is it said that the Maya were conquered but never defeated?

What are the Halls of Montezuma, anyway?

Why did they call them the heart-eating Aztec?

Besides the halls, what else did the Aztec have to brag about?

How did Mexico get its name?

Are there any Aztec left?

What was so great about the Inca, and what did they do with all that gold?

Are potatoes a gift from the Inca?

Why were the Inca really not Inca at all?

How did the Inca get so big?

How did the Inca lose their empire, and where are they now?

Why is there a Cadillac named Eldorado?

THE "SPANISH" IN "HISPANIC"

Hispanics have Spanish roots, but where do the
Spanish come from?

Are Latinos the descendants of people from all over
Spain?

What is the Spanish "lisp," and where did it really
come from?

Why do Latinos have two last names?

Why do Spaniards say "Olé"?

Who were the Moors, and how did they manage to
dominate Spain?

Why did the Jews settle in Europe, and how did they
fare in Moorish Spain?

Who were the Marranos?

What role did Queen Isabella and King Ferdinand
play in the reconquest of Spain?

What was the fate of the Moors and the Jews in
Spain after the reconquest?

How bad was the Spanish Inquisition?

What else happened in 1492?

THE AFRICAN PEOPLE

Why do more Latinos have African roots than
Anglos?

If Columbus was Italian, why do Latinos celebrate Columbus Day?

Columbus Day is known among Latinos as *El Dia de la Raza*, meaning "the Day of the Races," or the day celebrating the union of two races or ethnic groups—the Spanish and the Amerindians. Among Mexican Americans in contemporary society, *la raza* means "the people," that is, the Chicanos, and is an expression of solidarity. Columbus Day is an official holiday throughout Latin America, Spain, and Latino America, and Latinos celebrate it with much fanfare.

Given the murders, rapes, pilferage, and other atrocities the Spanish committed against the native peoples of the Americas, it may seem puzzling that the day the Spanish and the Amerindians came together is celebrated. But Latinos are a product of both cultures since they are the direct descendants of the Spanish *conquistadores* or the Iberians who later settled the Americas. They pay homage to their Spanish ancestry on Columbus Day with floats and spectacles that proudly reenact the bravery and daring of the Spanish explorers who sailed perilous and uncharted seas and who were, after all, the first to "discover" and conquer the New World.

Christopher Columbus is called **Cristobal Colón** in Spain, and although he originally came from Genoa, Italy, hardly anyone in Spain considers him anything but Spanish. Columbus's voyage was commissioned by **King Ferdinand** and **Queen Isabella** of Spain, and he sailed under the Spanish flag and commandeered a crew that was mainly Spanish.

Did Columbus really discover America?

Christopher Columbus, of course, is credited with discovering America, and without him there might not be an America at all—certainly not as it exists today. But the America he discovered was not the land mass we know today as the United States, but rather the Caribbean islands and other regions of Latin America that comprise the ancestral lands of Latinos.

Since you cannot really discover a land that's already populated with advanced ancient civilizations, Columbus could more accurately be said to have discovered a route from Europe and northern Africa to the Americas. It was all an accident, as we know, since Columbus believed his course would take him to the Far East—and, by the way, died thinking he *had* found a route to Asia.

It is also certain that Columbus was not the first European to cross the Atlantic. The Vikings reached the New World around 1000 A.D., and evidence suggests that both the English and the Portuguese may have landed in Newfoundland and Labrador during the fourteenth century.

What was Columbus really in search of?

Columbus was ostensibly in search of two things. The first was gold, gold, and more gold so that he could satisfy the Spanish crown's insatiable desire to transform Spain into the greatest and most powerful country in the world (which, incidentally, he did). The second was to meet the Grand Khan, or Emperor of China, about whom Columbus's hero, **Marco Polo,** had written extensively.

This second goal, to meet the Chinese emperor, is what truly motivated Columbus to cast himself headlong into a perilous voyage and, quite possibly, into the abyss. In his *Lettera rarissima* of July 7, 1503, addressed to **Ferdinand** and **Isabella**, Columbus quotes Marco Polo as having said that "the emperor of Cathay some time since sent for wise men to teach him one religion of Christ." It was Columbus's wish to be that wise man who could teach the religion of Christ to the "heathen" Chinese emperor.

But Columbus's grand aspirations did not stop there. He believed he could procure enough gold in Asia and enough political clout with the Spanish crown to enable him to organize a crusade to liberate Jerusalem from the Arabs and transform it into a Christian city. Just before he set sail, Columbus made Queen Isabella promise him that, should he find a westward route to the Far East, she would fulfill this desire. The queen agreed, but later changed her mind, feeling that she had enough on her plate—namely a whole New World with which to contend.

What did Columbus first lay eyes on when he reached America?

All in all, **Christopher Columbus** made four voyages to the New World. In his first foray into the Americas, he made landfall on an island in the Bahamas on October 12, 1492. Columbus christened the island San Salvador. This was the first of thousands of names the Spanish gave the New World, from Amarillo, Texas, to San Diego, California, in an effort to claim the land for all time.

Some days later Columbus sailed from San Salvador to Cuba and delegations from his ship went ashore to seek the court of the Emperor of China and demand gold. In December, Columbus journeyed east to Hispaniola (present-day Haiti and the Dominican Republic). He sent thirty-nine of his men ashore to remain on the island while he sailed back to Spain to tell the queen of his remarkable discoveries.

When Columbus returned to Hispaniola, he found that his men had been killed for looting the native settlements and raping the women. This event marked the beginning of a tumultuous relationship between the Spanish and the native peoples scattered across the Caribbean, Mexico, Central America, South America, and North America.

What was Columbus's most amazing feat?

In the end, **Columbus** proved to be a poor administrator and as a result was taken back to Spain a prisoner in shackles. He was out of favor with **Queen Isabella** for his inept handling of the Spanish settlements in the West Indies. Columbus died in Valladolid, Spain, on March 20, 1506, while pressing his claims in court.

Many contemporary historians attribute Columbus's greatness not only to the fact that he introduced Europe to a brave new world, but to his ability, despite major errors in his navigational computations, to find his way back and forth between Europe and the West Indies again and again.

So who were the native peoples Columbus encountered in the Americas?

The native peoples who first greeted **Columbus** and his alien-looking crew when they made landfall in the Bahamas were the Arawak, who inhabited not only the Caribbean but also South America. The Arawakan groups living in the Greater Antilles were the Taino and Siboney. It is not known how many Taino and Siboney inhabited the Caribbean islands at the time of Columbus's arrival, but judging from the records of **Friar Bartolomé de las Casas,** the first ordained Roman Catholic priest to travel to the New World, an estimated thirty to fifty thousand Taino called the Caribbean home in 1492. The Taino and the Siboney enjoyed a highly developed social and economic system, based on farming and fishing. They were peaceful and disciplined peoples, who carried out elaborate harvest ceremonies and held naturalistic beliefs in bush spirits that foretold the coming of messiahs.

Just a short time before the Spanish conquistadors reached the Caribbean, the Carib, fierce native warriors, had driven the Arawak off the Lesser Antilles. The Spanish subdued the Carib, forcing them to convert to Catholicism and adopt Spanish ways along with the Antillean Arawak. Hundreds perished from overwork at the hands of the Spanish and from the diseases the Europeans brought with them for which the native peoples had no immunological defenses.

The Taino, Siboney, and Carib are the ancestors of many

of the peoples of Cuba, Puerto Rico, the Dominican Republic, and South America. However, since they either succumbed to the harsh conditions imposed by the Spaniards or were forced to adopt Spanish values, their culture and traditions faded and are not readily apparent in the Caribbean today. The gentle Siboney and Taino spirit must still live on in many of the peoples of Latin America with Arawak genes, as well as in Latinos who walk the streets of New York, Miami, Los Angeles, and places in between.

Who else lived in the Americas before Columbus got there?

Aside from the Arawak, three highly advanced indigenous cultures were thriving in the Americas at the time of the Spanish "invasion." These were the Aztec of central Mexico; the Maya, who still live on their ancestral lands of Yucatán in southern Mexico and in Guatemala; and the Inca of the Andean highlands and the west coast of South America.

In addition, the Spanish had a great deal of interaction with the Seminole Indians of Florida and the Pueblo (Spanish for *town*) of the southwestern United States, descendants of the prehistoric Anasazi peoples, including the Hopi of northeastern Arizona and the Zuni of western New Mexico and the Rio Grand pueblos.

THE MESOAMERICAN PEOPLES: THE MAYA, THE AZTEC, THE INCA

The two main cultures that dominated Mexico and Central America before the Spanish *conquista* were the Maya and the Aztec. Their civilizations are known as Mesoamerican, or Middle American. The cornerstones of the Mesoamerican civilizations are believed to have been laid by the Olmec, who prospered from 1150 B.C. to 500 A.D. along the southwestern gulf coast of Mexico in the states of Tabasco and Veracruz. The highly evolved intellectual life of the Olmec gave rise in ensuing centuries to the extraordinary scientific and artistic accomplishments of the Maya and Aztec.

Why is it said that the Maya were conquered but never defeated?

The Maya, descendants of the Olmec, flourished in southern Mexico, especially in the present-day states of Chiapas, Tabasco, Campeche, Yucatán, and Quintana Roo, as well as in Belize, Guatemala, and Honduras between 1500 B.C. and 1000 A.D. At its peak, about two million people may have dwelt in the vast Mayan empire, with about a hundred thousand alone living in Tikal, the largest population center.

The Maya, who spoke a language related to Chol, Yucatec, and Chortu, were the first peoples of the New World to keep historical records. Their written history began in 50 B.C., when Spain and the rest of Europe did not yet exist as national or cultural entities. The Maya recorded their history not on parchment but on jade, human bones, pots, stone monuments, and the walls of their impressive palaces. Their inscriptions tell the story of great Mayan queens and kings right up to the sixteenth century, when the Spanish changed the course of their history forever.

The Maya were the most advanced of all the pre-Columbian civilizations in the Americas in the areas of architecture, sculpture, painting, mathematics, and astronomy. They are particularly known for their monumental architecture, including pyramids that tourists climb to this day. On many of the monuments, Mayan lords, who ruled as divine kings, are depicted wearing the masks of the gods. Their temples were pantheons filled with gods and goddesses who jealously ruled over their subjects.

The Maya's skill in mathematics was extraordinary; they formulated the first system of numeration by position that includes the concept of zero. With their mathematical erudition, the Maya were able to create an accurate calendar. They also enjoyed a rich literary and artistic life. In 1502, only a few years after **Columbus** and his son **Ferdinand** had moored their ships off the coast of Honduras, a young nobleman from Quiche penned the *Popol Vuh*, a sweeping epic of Mayan civilization that is the most important surviving work in Mayan literature in the Latin alphabet. (The text was written in the Quiche language using Spanish orthography.) The Maya (and other native peoples of the Americas) learned Spanish quite readily. For a people who claimed to have superior intellectual powers, the Spanish were seldom able to master the languages of those they conquered.

By the time the conquistadors reached the Americas, the Mayan civilization was already in decline, racked by war and famine, and by divisions among the various city-states. The Spanish took advantage of this internal strife and, in 1542, established their own capital at Mérida in Yucatán, on the site of the Mayan city Tiho.

Even though the Maya intermarried with the Spanish, their culture survived intact on the shores of the Apasion-Usumacinta river system in Central America, in the highland plains encircled by volcanoes, and in the lowland forests of that magical region. Today many there speak a version of their ancestral language and worship the same gods as the Maya of old. It is said that the Maya's roots went so deep and their bond to their mother earth was so great that, although they were seemingly conquered, in the end they were never truly defeated.

The faces of the Maya are reflected in the faces of millions of people in Mexico, Central America, and the United States, and their pyramids continue to loom tall, a constant reminder of their noble ancestry.

What are the Halls of Montezuma, anyway?

At the time that the conquistadors set foot in the New World, the Aztec had achieved the most advanced civilization in the Americas. **Montezuma II,** also known as **Moctezuma II,** was the Aztec emperor who ruled over Tenochtitlán (what is present-day Mexico City) and the valley of central Mexico when **Hernán Cortés** (1485–1547) first arrived on November 8, 1519. And Montezuma had halls, all right.

Tenochtitlán was a magical city situated on an island in the middle of Texcoco Lake. Three wide causeways led to huge white palaces and elaborate pyramids and temples. During his reign from 1502 to 1520, Montezuma II lived in a lavishly decorated palace, surrounded by obsequious nobles and thousands of slaves who catered to his every whim. The place was neat as a pin and ran as efficiently as a Swiss watch as order and harmony were divine requirements and every effort was made to keep the emperor happy. Montezuma II came from royal lineage (he was believed to be directly descended from the gods), and as such his subjects owed him endless homage.

On the other side of town, though, life was quite different for the drones. Floating island farms called *chinampas*, made of mud dredged up from the lake bottom by slaves, surrounded the city. Farmers lived in wattle-and-daub huts and looked on the Halls of Montezuma from afar with wonder and reverence. They led simple lives and worked hard.

Unlike previous Aztec rulers, who had been great warriors and leaders, Montezuma II was more interested in Aztec religion and prophecy and the good life than in preserving his great empire and saving his people from certain domination. He was certainly unprepared for Hernán Cortés and the Spanish Conquest. At first, Montezuma was unsure whether the Spanish were gods or men. But after consulting soothsayers and uncovering omens, he concluded that the conquistadors were, categorically, white gods, and that his reign was up. Rather than battle the Spaniards, Montezuma II tried everything else to entice them to leave—from gifts of gold chests and jeweled boxes to sorcery. When none of his stratagems worked and he was unable to either buy the Spanish off or to make them magically disappear, Montezuma II invited Cortés to enter the island capital of Tenochtitlán and was instantly taken prisoner. Their emperor's actions enraged the Aztec people, who fought the Spaniards with enormous daring. They managed several successful ambushes that kept the white men at bay, but eventually the Spanish and their weapons prevailed, and what is present-day Mexico City fell under Spanish domination. Montezuma II perished under mysterious circumstances; presumably he was killed by his own people in reprisal for his unspeakable betrayal.

As for his halls, the Spaniards, who were horrified by the Aztec religious rites involving human sacrifice, ruthlessly destroyed Montezuma II's temples. Later, the Spanish missionaries who ventured to the New World to convert the native peoples to Catholicism completed the desecration of the Aztec temples by burning the records and smashing the idols.

Why did they call them the heart-eating Aztec?

The Aztec religion included hundreds of gods that ruled not only over certain days, but even over certain hours of the day. The Aztec gods personified the forces of nature, and many of the Aztec religious ceremonies were centered around appeasing the gods by performing rites that often involved human sacrifice.

For instance, at the dedication in 1487 of their great pyramid temple Huitzilopochtli, the Aztec sacrificed twenty thousand captives as an offering to the gods. The captives were led up the steps of the high pyramid, where priests slit open their bodies and tore out their hearts, considered the most precious organ to offer the gods. During some religious ceremonies, the Aztec ate the flesh of their human sacrifices in an act they believed would imbue them with the virtues of their victims.

Besides the halls, what else did the Aztec have to brag about?

The Aztec could be said to have been brilliant imitators rather than privileged originators. They managed to absorb the cultures of earlier, more advanced peoples, including the Toltec, Zapotec, and Maya. They learned from the Maya how to calculate the solar year. They learned architecture and engineering from the Toltec, then built magnificent temples, as well as the remarkable city of Tenochtitlán, which left **Hernán Cortés** thunderstruck.

All over the territory that constitutes Mexico, the Aztec were admired for their art, ingenuity, and great technological and agricultural advancements. Their chief crops, which they bartered using cacao beans as change, included pears, tomatoes, corn, beans, chiles, squash, and cotton—all of which they grew with a high degree of uniformity harvest after harvest.

How did Mexico get its name?

The Aztec, who spoke Nahuan or Nahuatl, which is related to the languages of the Pima and Shoshone tribes of the western United States, referred to themselves as the Mexica people— thus, the whole of Mexico is really named after them. They were originally nomadic farmers who in the twelfth century began wandering the great expanse known as Mesoamerica. By the thirteenth century, the Aztec had settled in the valley of central Mexico, founding Tenochtitlán around 1342. When the Spanish reached the New World, Aztec rule extended from the Gulf of Mexico to the central Cordilleras and southward into what is now Guatemala.

Are there any Aztec left?

Neither **Juan de Grijalba,** the Spaniard who first glimpsed Mexico in 1581, nor **Diego Velázquez,** who was in charge of the Mexican expedition, nor **Hernán Cortés,** who actually dethroned **Montezuma II,** nor the Spanish settlers who followed them, was able to completely destroy the Aztec. Many of the native peoples and *mestizos* living in Mexico today, as well as countless Mexican Americans, are the descendants of the proud Aztec people. Aside from their obvious genetic legacy, the Aztec left a wealth of wisdom, artistry, and folklore that lives on in the hearts and minds of their heirs.

SOME PLACES WHERE YOU CAN RELIVE LATINO HISTORY

1. **The Arizona Historical Society Museum**   Tucson, Arizona

This museum chronicles the history of Arizona from the arrival of the Spanish settlers to the present day. It houses a rich collection of Spanish and native artifacts.

2. **The Spanish History Museum**   Albuquerque, New Mexico

The Spanish History Museum traces Spain's involvement in America, particularly in the Southwest, through exhibits, lectures, and tours.

3. **De Soto National Memorial Park**   near Bradenton, Florida

This small park commemorates the arrival of Spanish explorer Hernando de Soto's expedition in Florida in 1539. U.S. park rangers dressed as Spanish soldiers of the period show young visitors the fine points of the crossbow and allow them to try on Spanish armor.

4. **Castillo de San Marcos National Monument**   St. Augustine, Florida

---

On this site stands a massive fort built of shell rock, which the Spanish began erecting in 1672 to protect St. Augustine from invasion. The fort is strategically situated at the entrance to St. Augustine harbor.

5. **Cabrillo National Monument**   San Diego, California

This monument, with a visitors center and museum, commemorates the "discovery" of California by the Spanish explorer Juan Rodríguez Cabrillo. On September 28, 1542, Cabrillo and his crew sailed into San Diego Bay and claimed all the surrounding land for the Spanish crown.

6. **The California Missions**   coastal California

The twenty-one Franciscan missions that dot the California coast from San Diego up to Sonoma were founded between 1769 and 1823 by Spanish Franciscan friars. The mission system was established to bring Catholicism to the native peoples of California as well as to settle the land.

7. **Columbia State Historic Park**   Columbia, California

Columbia is one of many towns that sprang up during the heady days of the California Gold Rush that began in 1848. In a few years the town yielded $87 million in gold, but by 1860 all the gold that was easiest to find had been mined, and Columbia's population plummeted from ten thousand to five hundred citizens. In 1945 a historic park was established in Columbia, where you can tour replicas of a miner's cabin, a livery stable, a firehouse, and a church.

8. **The Mexican Museum**   San Francisco, California

The collection at the Mexican Museum encompasses pre-Hispanic art and colonial art, as well as Mexican and Mexican

American fine arts and folk arts. One of the missions of the museum is to collect and exhibit the works of contemporary Mexican and Mexican American artists, many of whom have been overlooked by mainstream galleries and art museums.

9. **The Alamo**   San Antonio, Texas

Called the shrine or cradle of Texas liberty, this is the state's biggest attraction. The chapel and barracks are all that remain of the original mission and fort where a small band of Texans battled a Mexican army of thousands for five days before resigning to defeat.

What was so great about the Inca, and what did they do with all that gold?

Spanish conquistador **Francisco Pizarro** reached Peru in 1532 and immediately succumbed to gold fever. He saw hundreds of productive gold fields, which the people of the Cuzco valley mined daily. But to the Spaniard's amazement, the citizens of the Incan empire, which stretched from the Pacific coast of South America across the Andes to the Atlantic, and from Ecuador three thousand miles southward to central Chile, did not consider gold a commodity at all. Unlike the Europeans, whose economies were based on the gold standard, the Inca relied on a system of barter.

The worship of the sun was at the core of the Incan religion. The Incan emperors were considered divine beings directly descended from the sun god. And gold symbolized the sun. Consequently, the precious metal was used exclusively by the Incan emperors and the elite for decorative and ritual purposes. They sported gold brooches, buckles, and headdresses, and even had knives, plates, and entire walls made from gold. While gold was not currency for the Inca, they held it in as high esteem as the Spanish.

Gold, however, is not the only reason these extraordinary people are famous. The Inca developed amazing methods for irrigating thousands of miles of valleys, and built roads and bridges throughout their territory. They created a highly organized political system that kept the vast region prosperous no matter what the sun or rain gods did in any particular season. For instance, if crops failed in one locality, the government records would show where the harvest had been more abundant, and the shortage would be made good by drawing on public warehouses in those districts. When it comes to the arts, few cultures on earth have approximated the accomplishments of the Inca. They practiced every style of hand-weaving known today, and their jewelry, exhibited in museums around the globe, is simply breathtaking. The Inca were also great architects. Among the most superb examples of Incan architecture are the 143 granite ceremonial buildings and houses which comprise the remote city of Machu Picchu. Built at the end of the fifteenth century, the site was not discovered by the Spanish and thus remained intact—unlike Cuzco, the Incan capital, which the conquistadors destroyed almost completely.

Are potatoes a gift from the Inca?

The Inca were the first to grow potatoes, native plants of the Andean region. Some of the varieties of potatoes that later found their way to Europe, especially to Ireland, were first cousins of those cultivated by the Inca. The Inca also grew quinoa (a highly nutritious grain), corn, sweet potatoes, and cassava (known to most Latinos as *yuca*, not to be confused with yucca, a tropical New World plant with white flowers). In agriculture and for transportation, the Inca relied not upon horses like the Spanish, but upon llamas, which made just as fine beasts of burden and mounts, and were much hardier in the higher altitudes.

Why were the Inca really not Inca at all?

Originally the term "Inca" referred strictly to the ruler of the people, the divine emperor, as well as to a few individuals who lived in the valley of Cuzco. However, the Spanish used the term to refer to all the inhabitants of the dozens of kingdoms in the Tawantinsuyu region that were politically and economically tied to the Inca. These inhabitants spoke many different languages, but Quechua was the official language of the empire. It is still spoken by many of the indigenous peoples of South America. Nowadays Quechua can be heard on American streets as many Latinos with roots in Ecuador, Peru, and Bolivia pepper their Spanish with words from the ancient tongue.

How did the Inca get so big?

The Inca were big as in powerful, but they were short in stature by contemporary American standards; an Incan man stood an average of four feet tall. For that matter, most of the Spanish *conquistadores* were pretty short, too. (Check out the Spanish armor at the Metropolitan Museum of Art in New York City.)

The beginnings of the Incan empire are shrouded in mystery, because Incan mythology and history are closely intertwined. The Spanish recorded Incan history just as it was conveyed to them, but the Inca may have told them more fiction than fact. The Incan empire started out as a series of small kingdoms, just like many others that thrived in the Andes around the fourteenth century. **Manco Capac** is believed to be the founding ruler of the Incan empire, although he may have been fictional. The Inca were fierce fighters and, apparently, were able to conquer and then rapidly develop their enormous territory by great military might, as well as sophisticated political strategies of "divide and conquer."

How did the Inca lose their empire, and where are they now?

When the conquistadors first stepped foot in the New World, the legendary **Atahualpa** was the Incan emperor. Unlike **Montezuma II** of Mexico, Atahualpa was someone to be reckoned with. He was not about to hand over his treasures and sacrifice his people to the greedy conquistadors without a valiant struggle. In the end, though, the Spanish captured and killed Atahualpa to show the Inca that their emperor was, in fact, a man of flesh and blood who had not feet of gold but of clay.

Atahualpa's treacherous half brother, **Manco Inca Yupanqui,** collaborated with the Spanish in the capture of Atahualpa. The Spanish then installed him as a puppet ruler, but they mistreated him, and finally in 1536 Manco Inca Yupanqui fled Cuzco for Vitcos, a city on the edge of the jungle, where he built a fortress from which to begin reconquering his land. The Spanish proved too mighty, and eventually Manco Inca Yupanqui was forced to negotiate a surrender in exchange for his life. Other Incan nobles continued the guerilla effort against the Spanish. They won an impressive number of skirmishes and left a trail of decapitated Spaniards along the Andean mountainsides, but they lost the war when the last Incan leader, **Tupac Amarú,** was captured and executed in 1572.

The Incan regional capitals were immediately transformed into Spanish towns bearing Spanish names, and most of the Inca were forced into slavery—principally as gold miners and laborers who filled the Spanish galleons and the king's coffers to the brim.

As with most of the indigenous populations conquered by the Europeans, the Inca and their culture could not be entirely erased. Incan language, religious beliefs, artistic and culinary traditions, and even philosophy are kept alive by the descendants of the Inca, including those who live in Lima, Peru; Quito, Ecuador; and Coral Gables, Florida.

Why is there a Cadillac named Eldorado?

"El Dorado" is Spanish for "the gilded one." In the sixteenth and seventeenth centuries, the Spanish conquistadors learned of a South American Chibcha Indian legend that told of a land swimming in gold somewhere between Bogotá, Colombia, and Lima, Peru.

The legend probably stems from a ritual the Chibcha performed in the highlands of Colombia that involved anointing a new chief with resinous gums and decorating him with gold dust as an offering to the earth gods, while the people threw gold bars and jewelry into the water. This ritual of the Man of Gold, or El Dorado, had died out before the Spanish arrived in the sixteenth century, but stories of a city of gold, also called El Dorado, buried somewhere in the deep, persisted.

The Spanish organized expeditions in search of El Dorado from around 1569 until 1617. One of the most important expeditions was led by **Gonzalo Jiménez de Quesada,** who conquered the Chibcha and founded the city of Bogotá. The search for El Dorado spread from the Bogotá highlands all the way into the deep valleys of the Amazon and Orinoco rivers. The Englishman **Sir Walter Raleigh** also got into the act and actually led two expeditions, one in 1595 and another in 1617, in search of the fabled city of gold.

Although El Dorado was never found, the search for it resulted in the exploration and conquest of much of northern South America. El Dorado has come to connote a golden dream, which is probably how the Cadillac automobile got its name.

THE "SPANISH" IN "HISPANIC"

Hispanics have Spanish roots, but where do the Spanish come from?

Obviously, the Spanish come from Spain, a country that occupies about five sixths of the Iberian Peninsula (the last sixth is Portugal, the British possession of Gibraltar, and the microstate of Andorra). The Canary Islands off the northwest coast of Africa, the Balearic Islands in the western Mediterranean, the enclaves of Melilla and Ceuta in northern Morocco, and three island groups near the Moroccan coast also belong to Spain. In all, Spain comprises an area about the size of Iowa, Illinois, and Missouri combined.

The Spanish enjoy one of the oldest and most diverse cultural and ethnic heritages in Europe, and thus can be said to come from many different places. They are descended from the Carthaginians, Celts, Romans, Vandals, Visigoths, and Moors. Also, a large number of Jews settled in Spain, particularly in the south, as the result not of an invasion, but rather a migration, and contributed vastly to Spanish society.

When **Columbus** sailed the ocean blue there was no such thing as a typical Spaniard, nor is there such a thing today. Spain is divided into five distinct autonomous regions—Castile, Andalusia, Galicia, the Basque Country, and Catalonia—and regional devotion runs deeper than national pride.

The Castilians on the Meseta Central are considered by most foreigners to be "real" Spaniards. The reason for this is that Castilian Spanish, *Castellano*, is the official state and literary language.

The people of Andalusia on the sunny southern coast, who, in addition to *Castellano*, speak the Andalusian dialect, are known for their gaiety and love of horses and dance. They have Jewish and Moorish blood, and have incorporated both cultures, particularly the Arabic culture, into their daily lives.

In the lush, rainy northwest corner of Spain, a region known as Galicia, live the Galicians (*Gallegos*) whose roots are Celtic or Gaelic like the Irish. (The name Galicia is derived from the Gallaeci, or Gauls, a Celtic race that inhabited the area when it was conquered by the Romans around 137 B.C.) And like the Irish, the Galicians are thought of as a hardworking, frugal, and somewhat melancholy lot. To this day, many Galicians play the bagpipes, dance the Spanish jig, and wear kilts on certain festive occasions, in homage to their proud Celtic ancestors.

Catalonia, the region hugging the northeastern Mediterranean, breeds brisk, industrious, and artistic people, who speak Catalan, a language related to the Provençal of southern France, as well as Spanish. Three of the greatest artists of the twentieth century hailed from Catalonia: **Pablo Picasso, Salvador Dalí,** and **Joan Miró.**

Basque country (which is comprised of three provinces along the Bay of Biscay and part of Navarre) seems almost a world away from the rest of Spain. The Basque people speak Basque (or *Euskera*), which is unrelated to any other European language and whose origins remain a mystery. Ethnic nationalism runs deep in the Basque country, and the Basques have long sought to sever ties with the rest of Spain. Euskadi Ta Askatasuna (ETA), a small Basque terrorist group founded in 1959, has been attempting to secure independence through violent means, but most Basques condemn its actions.

Are Latinos the descendants of people from all over Spain?

Spaniards from all five regions in Spain conquered and later settled the New World. Thus the different flavors of each region were added to the prodigious melting pot—or, more accurately, distinctive stew of the Americas—which gave rise to the Americans known as Latinos.

What is the Spanish "lisp," and where did it really come from?

The Castilians, as well as Spaniards from other regions in Spain, pronounce the letter c like "th" when it precedes the vowels i and e and are thus said to "lisp." For instance, "San Francisco" is pronounced "San FranTHisco." The "th" sound in Spanish, contrary to popular opinion in the United States, cannot be traced to a Spanish king who lisped, but is an example of the Greek influence on Latin, and later on its first cousin, Spanish.

The "th" sound, like some wine, did not travel well and was completely dropped in Latin America, where c is pronounced like s before the vowels i and e as it is in Andalusia and other areas of Spain. This does not mean that Latin Americans do not speak Castilian Spanish—they do, and not only that, it is the official language of all the Spanish-speaking Latin American countries. Thus there is no such thing as, say, the Cuban or Puerto Rican language. However, Cubans and Puerto Ricans (and each Latino group) speak Spanish with their own unique accent and pepper their speech with words that the indigenous peoples of the Americas and the African slaves lent to New World Spanish centuries ago.

Why do Latinos have two last names?

In Spain, every newborn is given both the father's last name and the mother's maiden name. Thus if María's father's surname is Pérez and her mother's maiden name is López, María's full name will be María Pérez López. When María becomes a mother, she will pass on her father's name to her child. Thus if María's husband has the surname González, the baby will have González Pérez as a surname. And so the patriarchal line prevails. The Spanish and Latin Americans still adhere to the two-surname tradition, but most Latinos drop their mother's name.

Why do Spaniards say "Olé"?

"Olé" is the Spanish adaptation of "Allah," the Arabic word for God. So when Spaniards cry *"Olé!"* at a bullfight, they are saying "Praise Allah!" even if they really mean *"Viva . . ."* which is Spanish for "Long live . . ." or "Live . . ." or, even, in some circles, "Man alive!" In a sense, no single word could be said to encapsulate as much Spanish history as that three-letter word *"Olé"*—seven centuries of history involving the Moors, to be precise.

Who were the Moors, and how did they manage to dominate Spain?

The Visigoths ruled Spain from 415 to 711 A.D. In the seventh century, Arab armies swept across Northern Africa, and conquered the Berbers, giving rise to a new mixed race called the Moors (Muslims). The Moors crossed the Straits of Gibraltar into Spain in 711, and overthrew the Visigoths at the battle of Guadalete. Thus began seven centuries of Muslim domination in Spain, evidence of which can be found in Spanish, Latin American and Latino culture, music, art, architecture, and philosophy to this day. For instance the numerical combination seven-eleven, which is also the year the Moors made their way to Spain, is considered lucky to Latinos. It was certainly lucky for the Moors—as seven hundred years, by anyone's calculations, is a very long winning streak.

The Moors left their stamp on all of Spain except the northern regions that were controlled by Christian kingdoms. With their ingenious methods of irrigation, they transformed the arid coastlands and southern hills of Spain into lush, palatial gardens. They rebuilt the old Roman cities along Arabic lines, with mosques and elegant courtyards complete with fountains. Ceramic tiles, fine silk, beautifully crafted leather goods, and metalworks became the trademarks of Moorish Spain.

The Moors transformed the city of Córdoba, in Andalusia, into a glorious caliphate that emerged as a center of learning. Scientists, mathematicians, philosophers, and writers flourished there and in other regions of Moorish Spain.

Why did the Jews settle in Europe, and how did they fare in Moorish Spain?

After the destruction of Jerusalem in 70 A.D., many Jews settled in North Africa or in Mediterranean cities. Later they made their way to other parts of Europe, especially Spain. Spanish Jews and their descendants are known as Sephardim. Their customs, rituals, and Hebrew pronunciation differ somewhat from those of Ashkenazic Jews, who settled in other European countries.

The Christian Visigoths nearly wiped out the Jews of Spain. When the Moors conquered Spain, they established more liberal policies with regard to the Jews and did not oppose new Jewish immigration. Spanish Jews, who wrote and spoke mostly in Arabic, were financiers, tradespeople, and philosophers who excelled at the art of rhetoric. They were also scholars who produced important legal works and biblical commentaries, and writers who penned beautiful Hebrew poems. Among the Jewish scholars of the eleventh and twelfth centuries were **Solomon Ibn Gabirol, Judah ha-Levi,** and the great **Maimonides.** Jewish literary tradition, music, and philosophy became deeply embedded in Iberian culture.

Around the twelfth century, a fanatical Arabic sect from North Africa known as the Almohads seized control of Moorish Spain, and the Jews faced certain death if they did not either convert to Islam or escape Spain. Many Jews fled to northern Spain, where Christian rulers were organizing efforts to reconquer the Iberian Peninsula. The Christians of the north found useful allies in the Jews—at least for a while, until a new era of Christian fervor.

Who were the Marranos?

Eventually, Christian fanaticism took hold of northern Spain to the same extent that Almohad zeal gripped the south. In 1391, Spanish Christians massacred thousands of Jews and forced thousands of others to convert and be baptized. The converted came to be known as Marranos (Spanish for "swine"). Many Marranos achieved high positions at court and in the church, but many others were suspected of practicing Judaism in secret and persecuted. The persecution of Jews eventually culminated in autos-da-fe—burning heretics at the stake. As a result of these pre-Inquisition policies in Spain, Spanish Jews came to value highly the mystical doctrines of Cabala.

What role did Queen Isabella and King Ferdinand play in the reconquest of Spain?

A large one. With a little bit of dynastic fortune and an ounce of luck, **Isabella** acceded to the throne of Castile in 1474. When her husband, **Ferdinand II,** became the rightful heir to the throne of Aragon in 1479, the two most influential kingdoms of Spain outside the Moorish empire were joined. And, as luck would have it, both the queen and the king were savvy leaders committed to joint rule and the equal division of labor. Isabella loved governing internal affairs, while Ferdinand enjoyed tinkering with foreign policy. Together, the "Catholic Kings," as they were known, launched a massive *reconquista* (reconquest) of Spain, and in the process managed to create a monarchy that unified the country.

Under the banner of Catholicism, Isabella and Ferdinand both performed some of the most laudable feats and committed some of the most atrocious acts known to humanity.

What was the fate of the Moors and the Jews in Spain after the reconquest?

With **Isabella** and **Ferdinand** on the throne, the Moors were driven out of Spain and their lands were settled by the Spanish Christians. The final blow to Moorish rule came with the crown's conquest of Granada in 1492.

Once the last Moorish rulers fled to North Africa and Spain was newly unified, all professing Jews were forced to leave the country, unless they agreed to be baptized and earnestly practice Catholicism. Countless Jews left Spain or perished as a result of the Spanish Inquisition. Many stayed and managed to lead a peaceful life. Some rose to positions of power in all spheres of Spanish life, but especially in politics and finance. A few took an active role in the conquest of the New World. Around 1582, the Dominican friar **Diego Durán,** the son of a converted Spanish Jew, made the journey to Mexico at age six. Later he wrote *Historia de las Indias de la Nueva Espana y islas de la tierra firme*, in which he eloquently describes the glories of the Mesoamerican civilizations. It is an astounding historical text and one of the few remaining records of the Aztec people.

How bad was the Spanish Inquisition?

Bad. The song in *My Fair Lady* goes: "I'd prefer a new edition of the Spanish Inquisition/than to ever let a woman in my life." It is an example of Anglo Saxon flippancy on the part of an Englishman who obviously (a) did not understand history, or (b) needed a sex therapist in the worst way.

At the behest of **Queen Isabella** and **King Ferdinand, Pope Sixtus IV** endorsed the creation of an independent Spanish Inquisition in 1483, presided over by a high council and a grand inquisitor: the infamous **Tomás de Torquemada.** Torquemada's main concern was eliminating, by any means necessary, all Marranos (converts from Judaism) and

Moriscos (converts from Islam) who were suspected of religious infidelity. He relied on sophisticated instruments of torture, massacres, mass burnings at the stake, book burnings, and other means to bring about the swift destruction of the "foreigners" within newly unified Spain.

Thanks to the Spanish Inquisition, the Jews and Moors of Spain would have to wait until 1967 before the country's Jewish synagogues and Muslim mosques once again opened their doors.

What else happened in 1492?

Just as 1492 saw the fall of Granada, the final defeat of the Moorish Empire, and the reunification of Spain, it also marked **Columbus**'s first voyage to the Americas. In many ways the Inquisition that gripped Spain carried over to the New World: the native peoples were subjugated and ultimately forced to convert to Catholicism. All who were not Catholic (the only kind of Christian the king and queen recognized) were considered less than human and were treated as such.

THE AFRICAN PEOPLE

Why do more Latinos have African roots than Anglos?

The Spanish conquistadors exploited the Arawak, Maya, Aztec, and Inca as a labor force from the very start, and before long the native peoples succumbed to exhaustion and disease. The Spanish were in desperate need of laborers to work in agriculture and mining, and so they resorted to importing slaves from Africa, a practice begun by the Portuguese, who transported the first shipload of African slaves to the Americas in 1502. (Slavery had been a common practice in Africa by this time, where African slave traders bartered human beings for weapons, metal, cloth, and liquor.)

The Spanish and the Portuguese were not the only Europeans to engage in the African slave trade. The Dutch, French, and English also brought African slaves to their colonies. In fact, slavery became such big business that the great shipping companies of Europe bid against each other for the right to transport Africans to the New World colonies. Only the best "specimens" were brought to the Americas—and even then hundreds of thousands did not survive the terrible voyage across the waters, which they spent shackled in extremely close quarters with barely enough water, food, or air to sustain them.

It is estimated that as many as fifteen million Africans were transported to the New World between the sixteenth century and the nineteenth century. When the slave trade reached its peak in the eighteenth century, about six million Africans had been carried to North America and Latin America. In 1807, England abolished the slave trade and persuaded Spain, France, and Portugal to follow suit. However, much illegal slave trading went on in the Americas well into the nineteenth century.

Most of the African slaves brought to the Spanish colonies came from eastern Nigeria, the Gold Coast, and the Congo basin. Despite the odds, they managed to preserve many of their religious and cultural traditions. Over time their gods, their art, their music, and their foods entered the mainstream, and nowadays it is difficult to determine where one culture ends and the other begins. Even African words and phrases such as *kimbombo*, Yoruban for okra, made their way into colonial Spanish, especially in the Caribbean, and now enliven the everyday speech of Americans with roots in the region.

As to the reason for a greater *mestizaje* (racial or ethnic mixture) in the former Spanish colonies, there are three prevalent theories. The first is that the ratio of Africans to Caucasians and native peoples was greater in the Spanish colonies than in the English colonies. The second theory says that the Spanish conquistadors and settlers were apt to leave their wives at home in Europe when they first ventured across the ocean. The English, as well as the Dutch, Germans, and other settlers of North America, on the other hand, preferred to bring their families along with them and had less of a desire to stray. The third theory is that the Spaniards found the African peoples generally pleasing in their physiques and personalities, and they were far less concerned about mingling with peoples of another race than the English. Which, of course, is not to say that the English did not interbreed with Africans, as a cursory glance across North America reveals.

TRÉS

Mexican Americans

Who are the Chicanos?

Who are the Anglos?

Who are the gringos?

THE *CONQUISTADORES* IN MEXICO

How long did it take the Spanish to conquer Mexico?

Did Mexico become Spanish right away?

How did the Spanish rule in Mexico?

What role did women play in the conquest, and was there such a thing as a conquistadora?

Who was La Malinche, how did she help the Spanish conquer Mexico, and why do some historians call her the first Mexican feminist?

NORTHERN EXPOSURE, OR HOW NEW MEXICO CAME TO BE KNOWN AS *NUEVO MEXICO* AND CALIFORNIANS AS *CALIFORNIOS*

What did the Spanish want with New Mexico?

What was Cabeza de Vaca's spiritual awakening all about?

What was the Northwest Passage, and what role did Sir Francis Drake play in the Spanish Conquista of the Southwest?

Besides the Pueblo peoples, who were the first real settlers of the Southwest?

THE SPANISH SETTLEMENT OF TEXAS AND CALIFORNIA

Parlez-vous Texan? No way!

Who were the Californios?

MEXICO VS. SPAIN

Where did Spain go wrong? (Don't blame it all on the Spanish Armada!)

So what was the defeat of the Spanish Armada all about?

What was the Grito de Dolores?

THE ANGLO CONNECTION

When did the Anglos and the Mexicans first meet?

What was the Santa Fe Trail?

How did the Santa Fe traders open the doors to Anglo expansionism?

What exactly was Manifest Destiny?

HOW TEXAS WAS WON—OR LOST

Who was Stephen F. Austin and why is he called the father of Texas?

Why should we remember the Alamo?

Why do Mexican Americans cringe when they hear "Remember the Alamo"?

What role did African Americans play in Texas history?

THE MEXICAN WAR

Just why did the American republic fight with Mexico?

How did the phrase "a Mexican standoff" come to be?

If all Zachary Taylor had was a small volunteer army, how did the United States win the war?

What is the Treaty of Guadalupe Hidalgo?

What was wrong with the Treaty of Guadalupe Hidalgo?

How did the Anglos treat the new American citizens?

What was the Gadsden Purchase, and why did Mexicans say they needed it like a hole in the head?

CALIFORNIA DREAMING

What was the Bear Flag Revolt, and how did the Californios feel about joining the United States?

Was the California constitution drafted exclusively by Anglos?

What was the California Gold Rush, and how did Mexico miss out on it by a couple of days?

What role did Latinos play in the success of California mining?

Allá en el rancho grande: What happened to the Mexican American rancheros during the Gold Rush and after?

DESPERADOS AND THE MEXICAN REVOLUTION OF 1910

What is a desperado, anyway?

Was Pancho Villa a desperado?

What was the Mexican Revolution all about, and how did the United States get involved?

How did the Mexican people fare during the Mexican Revolution?

What did the Mexican Revolution have to do with U.S. Congressman Henry B. González becoming chairperson of the House Banking Committee?

A TIME OF TROUBLES: MEXICAN AMERICA IN THE 1920s, 1930s, AND 1940s

When did the United States begin policing the border with Mexico?

Why do Mexican Americans say the country was built on their backs?

What's a barrio, and what's a colonia?

Chicano go home? Why were Mexicans and Mexican Americans repatriated?

What was the Bracero Program?

Why did Texas pass a law declaring that all Mexicans were white?

What brought an end to the Bracero Program?

What was the Sleepy Lagoon Case?

What were the Zoot Suit Riots?

Mojados: *Illegal or undocumented?*

What was "drying out the wetbacks"?

What was the El Paso Incident?

Who are the commuters?

IDENTITY, ACTIVISM, AND *VIVA LA RAZA*

How have Mexican Americans served their country?

How did Mexican American activism get its start?

Who was César Chávez?

What is the Chicano Movement?

MEXICAN AMERICAN WOMEN: REVOLUTIONARIES, THINKERS, HEALERS, AND MOTHERS

What exactly is machismo?

Is there such a thing as macha?

What's a curandera?

What's a partera?

So who are the notable women in Mexican and Chicano history?

CULTURAL HERITAGE: A MOVABLE FIESTA

Who are some of the great Mexican American writers of today?

Chicano mural painting: When is art on a wall not graffiti?

How many holidays do Mexican Americans celebrate?

Why do Mexican Americans celebrate Cinco de Mayo?

What's a charreada?

What are mariachis?

What's a piñata party?

Did Montezuma II eat tacos?

Are tacos, burritos, gorditas, and fajitas the Mexican national dishes?

Is chocolate really Mexican?

How is New Southwestern Cuisine different from traditional Mexican cooking of the Southwest?

What are pulque, mescal, and tequila?

The history of Mexico and that of the United States are so inextricably linked that these nations have been compared to

Siamese twins who, before enduring a radical and painful separation, shared the same heart. When we speak about Mexican Americans, we do not mean an ethnic minority who merely crossed our borders and then by slow assimilation became part of the great American mosaic. We refer to a minority group that actually established roots within the boundaries of the present-day United States long before the English built a settlement at Jamestown. As the saying goes among *Tejanos*, Texans of Mexican origin: "We never crossed a border. The border crossed us."

Who are the Chicanos?

"Chicano" is an abbreviated form of *Mexicano*, the Spanish word for "Mexican," and was originally a pejorative term used by both Anglos and Mexican Americans to refer to unskilled workers in America born in Mexico, particularly recent immigrants. But since prejudice seldom makes fine distinctions, all Mexican Americans, no matter how many centuries their families have lived in the territory that is the United States, have often been labeled "Chicanos."

When **César Chávez** organized a labor revolt in the 1960s, Mexican Americans began to forge a positive identity and fight for their rights, and in the process they claimed racial slurs like "Chicano" as their own in order to strip away their negative content. Many Mexican Americans began calling themselves "Chicanos" to assert their ethnic pride and show their solidarity with *la raza*—the people.

Who are the Anglos?

To Mexican Americans, the term "Anglo" referred originally to Americans of Anglo-Saxon descent. Today "Anglo" is more broadly defined as Americans who are neither African American, Latino, Native American, Asian, or brown. Italian Americans and Hungarian Americans qualify as Anglos, even if they do not have a drop of Anglo-Saxon blood coursing through their veins.

Who are the gringos?

"Gringo" is the Latin American word for a foreigner of English or Anglo American descent. The term is used interchangeably with "Anglo" by some Mexican Americans, but it seems to be slowly falling into disuse in America. Theories abound as to how "gringo" entered the Spanish language. Some historians have argued that it evolved from a phrase Mexicans oft repeated during the Mexican War to the American soldiers who were clad in green uniforms—"green go" home or "green go" away.

THE *CONQUISTADORES* IN MEXICO

How long did it take the Spanish to conquer Mexico?

In February 1519, approximately two years after the Spanish conquistadors began their exploration of Mexico, Spanish explorer **Hernán Cortés** and his 509 men dropped anchor off the coast of the Yucatán near what is now Veracruz. About three years later, the Spanish had conquered the Aztec, the most powerful empire in Mexico. For all intents and purposes, Mexico was in the hands of the Spanish.

The swiftness of the takeover can be attributed in part to the belief of Aztec emperor **Montezuma II** that the Spaniards were gods and that their conquest had been divinely preordained to punish the Aztec for having subdued and enslaved the Toltec and other indigenous peoples. But the conquistadors owed their success to several advantages they had over the Aztec. For one, the brave Aztec warriors with their wooden clubs and spears were no match for a Spanish army equipped with cannons, harquebuses, and horses. The Spanish also unwittingly introduced biological warfare, as they had brought with them smallpox and other European diseases which the native peoples succumbed to by the thousands. Finally, the native peoples of Mexico were themselves divided into many warring factions, among them the Tlaxcaltecs, whom the Spanish enlisted as powerful allies against Montezuma II.

IMPORTANT DATES IN MEXICAN AMERICAN HISTORY

1519	Spanish conquistadors defeat the Aztec of Mexico.
1810	Father Miguel Hidalgo unleashes the Mexican movement for independence from Spain with his *Grito de Dolores* (Cry of Dolores).
1821	Mexico wins its independence from Spain.
1848	The Treaty of Guadalupe Hidalgo is signed.
1910	The Mexican Revolution, a long, bloody civil war, commences.
1924	The U.S. Border Patrol is created.
1943	Discrimination against Mexican Americans turns brutal during the Zoot Suit Riots in Los Angeles.
1962	César Chávez launches the National Farm Workers Association.

Did Mexico become Spanish right away?

In principle, yes, but in practice, no. While **Hernán Cortés** swiftly conquered the Aztec, razing their prize city Tenochtitlán (Mexico City was later built at the site), the rest of Mexico fell slowly under Spanish dominion. The Maya in the South, for instance, were difficult to subdue, and the Spanish left them alone for quite a while. Similarly, the Chichimec of the north continued in their traditional ways almost uninterrupted by the Spanish.

How did the Spanish rule in Mexico?

With two goals in mind: to Christianize the "heathens" of the New World and to fill Spain's coffers with gold and more gold.

The Spanish conquistadors and early colonists, aided by armies of missionaries, imposed Catholicism on the native peoples from the very start. In fact, Catholic friars accompanied **Cortés**'s expedition. The Spanish confiscated the native peoples' gold, often telling them that Spaniards suffered from a strange disease that only gold could cure. They also put the Amerindians to work mining for gold, and later, silver. This was their chief occupation at the beginning of the conquest. Later they would be put to work cultivating the land and supplying the colonists with exquisite foods, beautiful women, and comfortable lodgings built in the Spanish style.

Hernán Cortés gave the early Spanish colonists *encomiendas*, grants that afforded them ownership and control over native land and goods in perpetuity. As a means of establishing a labor pool, the *encomenderos* were given as many as 20,000 native peoples each to cultivate the land and supply clothing, food, and shelter. The native peoples worked for no pay, thus the institution of the *encomienda* essentially meant the codification of slavery. Atrocities committed against the enslaved Amerindians ran rampant; the *encomenderos* saw nothing wrong in forcing them to work with little rest, robbing them of their possessions, beating them badly, and even killing them. Many members of the clergy, such as **Friar Bartolomé de las Casas,** who was called the "defender of the Indians," objected strongly to the *encomiendas*. The native peoples took the matter into their own hands from time to time and revolted against Spanish control, but with little lasting success.

One of their most successful campaigns by the native peoples against Spanish domination took place in 1680. **Popé,** a distinguished Pueblo medicine man in New Mexico who practiced his own religion and called for an end to Spanish rule, led the Pueblo in a revolt against their oppressors. Hundreds of Spanish colonists and missionaries in northern New Mexico were killed in what is known as the Popé Rebellion. Once his people were free of Spanish domination, Popé set about to restore the old Pueblo way of life, even rinsing clean the Pueblo who had been baptized. In 1692, soon after Popé died, the Spanish again subdued the Pueblo.

As for the *encomienda* system, it proved so profitable that although it underwent reform to lessen the suffering of the native peoples, it was not dismantled entirely until 1786.

What role did women play in the conquest, and was there such a thing as a conquistadora?

To begin with, in the early days of the conquest Spanish women did not accompany the men to the New World the way Englishwomen did on the Eastern seaboard. This was a fundamental reason why the Spanish mixed with the native peoples, giving rise to the *mestizos*, or peoples of mixed race, not only in Mexico but throughout Latin America.

Both the Spanish and the native peoples of the Americas had patriarchal systems, and women, by and large, were treated as chattel. The following account, written on October 28, 1495, by **Michele de Cuneo,** who sailed with **Columbus** on his second expedition, is a fine example of how the Spanish treated Amerindian women from the very beginning.

It is also testimony of the universality of both sexism and racism:

> While I was in the boat, I captured a very beautiful Carib woman, who the aforesaid Lord Admiral gave to me, and with whom, having brought her into my cabin, and she being naked as is their custom, I conceived the desire to take my pleasure. I wanted to put my desire to execution, but she was unwilling for me to do so, and treated me with her nails in such wise that I would have preferred never to have begun. But seeing this (in order to tell you the whole event to the end), I took a rope-end and thrashed her well, following which she produced such screaming and wailing as would cause you not to believe your ears. Finally, we reached an agreement such that, I can tell you, she seemed to have been raised in a veritable school of harlots.

Not only is the nameless native woman taken hostage and raped, but, once subdued, she is called a whore. She was not only the object of a double rape—sexual and racial—but she, like the native peoples as a whole, once overpowered, is accused of liking and accepting the European "civilization" with the alacrity of a harlot.

Decades later, when Spanish women began making the journey to the Americas, they were held accountable for the enslavement, forced conversions, and brutalization of the native peoples by their husbands, brothers, and fathers, even though they played no active role. This is not to say, of course, that Spanish women did not share the belief in the white man's superiority to the native peoples, or that they did not disdain native religions and consider the infinitely sophisticated Amerindian cultures primitive. They did, of course, in the same way most Englishwomen did, holding with the general beliefs of European society on the whole, while not actively participating in the decimation of Native Americans.

Who was La Malinche, how did she help the Spanish conquer Mexico, and why do some historians call her the first Mexican feminist?

La Malinche, known as Malintzin to the Amerindians and baptized "Doña Marina" by the Spanish, played a vital role in **Hernán Cortés**'s conquest of Mexico.

An Aztec, La Malinche was sold as a slave to the Maya by her own family. When the Spanish conquistadors set foot in the Yucatán, the Maya offered her to them as a gift. The minute he set eyes on her, Hernán Cortés was enchanted with La Malinche and took her as his mistress, although he also "offered" her to one of his lieutenants and later married her off to another conquistador.

La Malinche informed Cortés of the Aztec's great wealth, much of it amassed in their capital city Tenochtitlán, which lay 560 miles inland. Cortés was determined to conquer the Aztec, by force if necessary, and La Malinche remained dutifully at his side until the conquistador achieved his aim with the fall of Tenochtitlán. According to **Bernal Díaz del Castillo,** a Spanish soldier who wrote a chronicle of the conquest, "Hernán Cortés could not understand the Indians without her." La Malinche spoke several indigenous languages, including her native Nahuatl and Maya, and picked up Spanish in a matter of weeks. She interpreted for Cortés not only the words of the native peoples but their psyche. During the fateful meeting between Cortés and **Montezuma II,** when the Aztec emperor was taken captive, La Malinche served as ambassador and spokesperson.

Some speculate that La Malinche persuaded Montezuma II that his reign was over and did not attempt to sabotage the campaign of the Spanish, not only because she was in the service of Cortés, but because she held a grudge against the Aztec for having sold her into slavery in the first place. Ever since they first sought independence from Spain in 1810, Mexicans have regarded La Malinche as a symbol of betrayal and servitude to the European invaders. The word *malinchista* means deserter and coward, among other things.

In the minds of some historical revisionists, La Malinche, who gave her original oppressors a taste of their own medicine, is the first Mexican feminist. Some also assert that since she wielded enormous clout with the Spanish, La Malinche may actually have saved thousands of native peoples from imminent death at the hands of the conquistadors.

Myths about La Malinche live on to this day in Mexico and Mexican America. One says that she drowned her son when Cortés insisted on taking the child back to Spain with him and leaving her behind. Supposedly, La Malinche still weeps over the tragic loss of her child. She has been called "La Llorona" (The Weeper), and rumors persist that her cries can be heard all across the American Southwest. In the late 1980s, a group of Chicano teenagers reported that they had heard La Llorona's cries over the line when they were talking to friends from telephone booths. Their mothers forbade them from using public telephones.

NORTHERN EXPOSURE, OR HOW NEW MEXICO CAME TO BE KNOWN AS *NUEVO MEXICO* AND CALIFORNIANS AS *CALIFORNIOS*

What did the Spanish want with New Mexico?

Upon informing Congress in May 1961 of U.S. intentions to pursue space exploration and put a man on the moon, **President John F. Kennedy** remarked: "We choose to go to the moon . . . and do the other things, not because they are easy, but because they are hard." The Spanish, too, launched their exploration of northern Mexico and beyond not because it was easy but because it was hard. As usual, however, there were political and military considerations as well.

All in all, it took the Spanish from about 1530 to 1800 to

complete their exploration and development of land north of what is now present-day Mexico. They settled New Mexico, Texas, and California, and they also claimed parts of Arizona, Colorado, Nebraska, and Oklahoma.

In June 1527, Spanish conquistador **Pánfilo de Narváez** set sail from Sanlúcar, Spain, for Florida with orders from **Charles V** to settle the land. Narváez made landfall near Tampa Bay in April 1528, and then set off with his men in search of gold. Plagued by starvation and unrelenting attacks from the native peoples, Narváez's expedition ended in complete disaster. **Álvar Núñez Cabeza de Vaca** was one of only four who managed to survive the ordeal. Shipwrecked on an island off the Texas coast, Cabeza de Vaca wandered for eight years across the present-day southwestern United States and northern Mexico before he finally met up with fellow conquistadors in Culiacán, Mexico. He brought them news that changed the course of history in the Southwest.

In dealing with the native peoples as he journeyed across the New World, Cabeza de Vaca had experienced a remarkable spiritual awakening that afforded him an entirely new outlook on life and on so-called "different" people. But his awakening was of no interest to the Spanish.

What did cause a great stir among the gold-hungry Spanish were the reports Cabeza de Vaca sent to the king of Spain in which he revealed that during his travails in Mexico and the Southwest he learned of the fabulous Seven Cities of Gold known as Cibola. Cabeza de Vaca's reports prompted **Fray Marcos de Niza** in 1539, **Francisco Vásquez de Coronado** in 1540, and **Hernando de Soto** in 1541, to launch their own explorations of the Southwest in earnest. None of them found Cibola or the fabled gold, but they did encounter a most charming land populated by the Pueblo Indians. But then, rich silver mines were discovered in Michoacán, Zacatecas, San Luis Potosí, and Guanajuato, and the Spanish left the idea of conquering the Southwest on the back burner for the next fifty years.

What was Cabeza de Vaca's spiritual awakening all about?

Shipwrecked, naked, and hungry, the mighty conquistador **Álvar Núñez Cabeza de Vaca** was taken captive by the Pueblo Indians inhabiting regions of present-day Mexico and Texas. The Pueblo believed the white man possessed divine powers, and they ordered him to heal the sick in exchange not only for food but for his life. At first, the conquistador argued that he was a soldier and could not perform such "supernatural" feats, but the Pueblo were not about to back down.

Faced with certain death, Cabeza de Vaca fell on his knees and prayed sincerely and earnestly for the recovery of the sick. Amazingly, the sick were healed. The Pueblo then escorted the Spaniard from village to village to perform his "miracles." In the process, Cabeza de Vaca was transformed from a bloody soldier to a mystic and a lover of the Pueblo people.

Cabeza de Vaca wrote to the king of Spain that in his encounters with the Pueblo he had learned to practice primitive Christianity and its lost element of healing—something which the strict priestly and hierarchical Catholic Church of his time deemed heretical. In fact, *iluminados,* or mystics, were burned at the stake by the Spanish Inquisition, along with the Moors and the Jews of Spain, for having unauthorized religious experiences.

Even more startling, perhaps, than his ability to heal and his bold confessions to the king was Cabeza de Vaca's newfound pacifism: "I said to Andres, 'if we reach Spain, I shall petition His Majesty to return me to this land, with a troop of soldiers. And I shall teach the world how to conquer by gentleness, not by slaughter.' "

What was the Northwest Passage, and what role did Sir Francis Drake play in the Spanish Conquista of the Southwest?

The Northwest Passage, a route from Europe to Asia through the northern extremities of North America, eluded European navigators for centuries. It was the carrot in front of the donkey for the English, French, and others who sought an easy route to China, bypassing the New World altogether. However, it would not be until the twentieth century that a Scandinavian navigator named **Roald Amundsen** was actually able to traverse the Northwest Passage by following the Canadian coast westward. This route has been judged impractical, since the northern waters remain icebound most of the year.

In the late 1570s, the famed English privateer **Sir Francis Drake** sailed through the Straits of Magellan, up the west coast of South and North America, across the Pacific, and around the world. The Spanish were sure that Drake had at long last found the mythical Northwest Passage, which in those days was believed to lie just north of Mexico. The Spanish crown immediately took measures to protect its territorial interests by at last settling the American Southwest. In 1598 **Juan de Oñate** led an expedition of several hundred colonizers into what is present-day New Mexico and founded San Gabriel de los Españoles (Chamita). It was nine years before the English would build a settlement at Jamestown.

In 1609, the Spanish established Santa Fe de San Francisco, the first permanent settlement near the Rio Grande, and in 1610 they erected the town of Santa Fe.

Besides the Pueblo peoples, who were the first real settlers of the Southwest?

Since **Sir Francis Drake** had not, after all, discovered the Northwest Passage, the only reasons the Spanish saw for settling the Southwest were, first, to exploit the mineral wealth of the region, and second, to Christianize the Pueblo. When New Mexico yielded little mineral weath, the Spanish took the latter mission very much to heart.

With the aid of native peoples and *mestizos* from the Mexican territory, Spanish settlers, soldiers, and missionaries pushed northward. Over the course of the next century, twenty-one missions would be established in the Southwest and numerous settlements would spring up along the Rio Grande.

The native peoples and *mestizos* played a vital role in settling the American Southwest, as the white ruling classes had an aversion to living in "uncivilized" frontier towns. By one of the many twists of fate, the wife of the first governor of the province of New Mexico, **Juan de Oñate,** was actually the great granddaughter of the **Emperor Montezuma II.**

THE SPANISH SETTLEMENT OF TEXAS AND CALIFORNIA

Parlez-vous Texan? No way!

In the 1670s and 1680s, a French explorer by the name of **Robert Cavelier, sieur de la Salle,** ventured to North America to explore and set up trading posts. La Salle was given the authority to govern the area between Lake Michigan and the Gulf of Mexico, but geography got the best of him. La Salle realized that the Mississippi had the potential to be a great inland trade route, and when he reached the mouth of the river in 1682, he claimed the entire Mississippi drainage basin, an enormous area, for France, naming it Louisiana after **Louis XIV.** He devised a plan to conquer part of Mexico and set out on an expedition to first fortify the mouth of the Mississippi and then head into Mexican territory. By a terrible miscalculation, La Salle's ships made landfall at Matagorda Bay in Texas instead of the mouth of the Mississippi which lay 500 miles east. La Salle set out on several journeys on foot in search of the Mississippi, but was stymied. He was murdered by his own men, who had long grown impatient and fearful when La Salle was unable to find the Mississippi and instead took them wandering around Texas. So began the French crown's efforts to get a piece of the rock known as North America.

France's burgeoning interest in colonizing North America alarmed the Spanish. To protect their investment in the Americas, the Spanish established a mission on the Neches River in Texas. The following year Texas was declared a Spanish province, and before long six missions and a presidio, or fortress, were erected. By 1718 San Antonio de Béxar, now known simply as San Antonio, was settled. San Antonio is also the modern hometown of **Henry Cisneros,** who served as the city's mayor from 1981 to 1988, and as **President Bill Clinton**'s Secretary of Housing and Urban Development during his first term from 1992 to January 1997. In 1997 he was named president and chief operating officer of Univision Communications, Inc.

Spanish expansion across Texas unnerved the French; it was too close for comfort and they worried that the Spaniards were eyeing the Louisiana territory. But the French were also fighting the French and Indian Wars (1689–1763), what amounted to a series of frontier attacks across North America as France and Britain struggled to build their empires. The British got the best of the French. As a way to prevent all of their beloved territory from falling into British hands, the French secretly ceded the area west of the Mississippi and the "Isle of Orleans" to Spain, while Great Britain was handed the area to the east of the Mississippi. In 1800 Spain retroceded the Louisiana territory to the French, who, questioning the feasibility of hanging on to so much land, sold the whole kit n' caboodle in 1803 to the Americans for a song—$15 million, to be exact.

Who were the Californios?

In the 1760s the Spanish crown received word that the Russians were coming—not to Spain but southward from Alaska toward the Northwest—and that the British had suddenly acquired a great yen for Pacific coast real estate. In typical fashion for a European empire in an age of expansion, the Spanish scrambled to settle Alta California, now known simply as California.

Gaspar de Portolá commanded the second expedition to Alta California, setting off from Baja California in 1769. Portolá's job was to extend Spanish dominion north to the Monterey Peninsula, which Spanish explorer **Sebastian Vizcaino** had discovered in 1602. On the way, Portolá established a small colony at San Diego Bay. Accompanying Portolá to San Diego Bay was a Franciscan missionary by the name of **Junípero Serra,** who remained behind to erect a mission at San Diego, while the rest of the party headed north. It was the first of twenty-one Franciscan missions Father Serra would establish by 1823 along the California coastline from San Diego all the way up to Sonoma. In addition to attracting flocks of tourists, many of the missions continue as religious institutions to this day.

The Franciscan missionaries in California sought to convert the native peoples, whom they also put to work in the fields and in raising cattle. The early Spanish-Mexican colonists who followed the missionaries into California were mostly Caucasians of Spanish descent, and *mestizos*, and were called *Californios*. Like the missionaries, the *Californios* took advantage of the state's abundant sunshine, gentle climate, and fertile soil, and pursued farming and cattle ranching.

MEXICO VS. SPAIN

In 1776, the thirteen English colonies declared themselves independent of Europe, giving birth to the nation called the United States in 1781. By 1810, the Mexican *criollos*, or creoles, those born to Spanish parents in Mexico, were ready to follow suit.

Early on, the American revolutionaries had turned to France and Spain for support in their campaign against British domination. The Spanish governor of Louisiana, **Bernardo de Gálvez,** sold munitions to the American rebels and permitted them to traverse Spanish Louisiana and use the port at New Orleans. Many of Gálvez's men were actually Mexican *criollos*, and most of the money to help the early American revolutionaries came from Mexico.

Where did Spain go wrong? (Don't blame it all on the Spanish Armada!)

Latinos, Latin Americans, and Spaniards tend to view the English and American explanation for the eventual decline of Spain as another example of native historical jingoism. For centuries, Anglo historians have argued that if the Spanish Armada had not been defeated by **Queen Elizabeth I**'s English "sea dogs" in 1588, under **Sir Francis Drake**'s command, Spain would not have gone downhill as a world power a century later.

The reasons for Spain's decline as an empire—and for England's loss of its colonies, for that matter—are much more complicated, and cannot be explained away by gloating over a single victory at sea.

As early as the seventeenth century, the Spanish economy had begun to collapse as a result of inflation caused in part by mismanagement and in part by the very wealth Spain had amassed from its colonies in the Americas. There were also incredible economic burdens due to governing more than half a hemisphere an ocean away.

The hardship imposed by the *encomiendas* as well as disease and the misuse of the land had reduced the native population of New Spain from eleven million or more in 1520 to a mere million a few decades later. Without laborers to mine the silver and ore deposits or cultivate the land, Spain could do little to reverse the recession that gripped its enormous empire. There were still more contributors to Spain's troubles in Mexico—as in the rest of the colonies: social unrest, racial tensions, and of course the chorus of voices calling for freedom.

So what was the defeat of the Spanish Armada all about?

Simply put, **Philip II,** king of Spain from 1556 to 1598, was a zealous Catholic who viewed the English Protestant Reformation with aversion. He also considered **Queen Elizabeth I,** a Protestant, not only a preposterous heretic, but a military threat. He figured Queen Elizabeth just might be fixing to stir up trouble in his colonies, so in a preemptive strike, he gave his fleet, the Spanish Armada (or "Armed Navy"), orders to sail up the English Channel and invade England. Elizabeth I reacted swiftly, turning her "sea dogs" loose on the Spanish Armada's 130 ships. The Spanish fought valiantly but were no match against the "sea dogs." Although the defeat of the Spanish Armada inflicted great psychological damage and cost a good deal of money, it did not by any means break the rich Spanish bank, or eclipse Spain's control of Mexico or its other New World colonies. It took another century and a great deal of political unrest to finally topple the Spanish empire—and the English had little to do with it in a larger sense.

What was the Grito de Dolores?

As the nineteenth century dawned, Spain's colonies—Mexico included—were getting really antsy. From the beginning of Spanish domination, the Mexicans had suffered social and economic injustice and had rebelled on numerous occasions. In 1541 the Zacatecas Indians had led a major uprising to protest the brutal treatment by the Spanish of the native peoples of Michoacán, Jalisco, Nayarit, and Sinaloa. The battle was fierce, and the Spanish, though they emerged the victors, lost hundreds of soldiers. The final skirmish, fought in the Mixton hills, near the city of Guadalajara, ended in the slaughter or enslavement of most of the native rebels. However, this act of suppression only fueled the flames of discontent and strengthened the native peoples' resolve to rid themselves of Spain.

The Mexican *criollos* were even more fervent in their resolve to end Spanish domination than the native peoples. To the Spaniards, place of birth meant everything, and thus even though the *criollos* were Caucasians with Spanish blood, they were New World progeny who could not be trusted to fulfill the demands of the crown. Thus they were considered second-class citizens, superior to the native peoples but inferior to those born in Spain, the *peninsulares*. At the hands of the Spanish, the *criollos* endured rampant discrimination, as well as "taxation without representation," which had also stirred grave discontent among the Americans in the English colonies. *Criollos* seldom got the best jobs or the choice parcels of land; these were reserved for the Spanish-born elite, who also had the final say in local government affairs.

By the time the nineteenth century dawned, the *criollos* had had enough of Spain. On September 16, 1810, **Father Miguel Hidalgo y Costilla,** a *criollo* pastor in the small Mexican village of Dolores, uttered the famous *Grito de Dolores* (Cry of Dolores), which ignited Mexico's revolution for independence. "Long live our Lady of Guadalupe!" he cried before the crowd assembled in the town square. "Down with bad government! Down with the Spaniards!"

The native peoples and *mestizos*, or those of mixed native and Spanish parentage, who had suffered terrible discrimination, also answered the call for social change in Mexico. Led by Father Hidalgo, fifty thousand natives and *mestizos* banded together as an army and marched toward Mexico City. Along the way, they pillaged the haciendas of wealthy *peninsulares*. Father Hidalgo's powerful army could have defeated the Spanish and taken control of Mexico City, but for some reason the pastor withdrew his troops before a final victory could be won, and on January 11, 1811, his army fell in defeat.

A close friend of Father Hidalgo's, the *mestizo* **Father José María Morelos y Pavón** took up the baton and waged guerilla warfare against the Spanish. While his forces battled on, Morelos called a congress, and with other leaders declared Mexican independence in November 1813. But it would not be so easy. In 1815 Morelos was captured and executed. In 1821 Spain finally recognized Mexican sovereignty and in 1824 a Constituent Congress proclaimed Mexico a federal republic with an elected president. Before the end of the decade, Spain attempted to reconquer Mexico by force, but the Mexican army under the leadership of **Antonio López de Santa Anna** defeated the Spaniards. In 1832 Santa Ana seized the reins of power. He would emerge as a major player in the Texas secessionist movement of 1836, in the Mexican War (1846–1848), and in the Gadsden Purchase in 1853, when he sold southern Arizona to the United States for ten million dollars.

THE ANGLO CONNECTION

When did the Anglos and the Mexicans first meet?

The westward movement of English-speaking people commenced not long after the thirteen colonies won their independence from England. With the exhortation "Go west, young man" ringing in their ears, the Anglo colonists settled the territory up to the banks of the Mississippi River between 1776 and 1800.

Then, when **Thomas Jefferson** purchased Louisiana—a territory of about 828,000 square miles (much larger than the modern state) which extended from the Gulf of Mexico to British North America and from the Mississippi River to the Rockies—from the French in 1803, the American Republic instantly doubled in size. The young nation was well on its way to consummating a dream in the making: Manifest Destiny, the eventual occupation of the entire North American territories.

In Thomas Jefferson's day, hats made of beaver fur were in high demand. The Upper Rio Grande in New Mexico was a prime habitat for beaver. Around 1790 mountain men from Kentucky began trespassing on Spanish Mexican land in New Mexico to trap beaver. They trapped without licenses and they traveled where they pleased. Sometimes their loot was confiscated, but no matter, they kept coming back for more. These frontier beaver trappers were grubby, bearded, and uncouth; they cussed and spat and picked fights willy-nilly. Often the native peoples and *mestizos* of New Mexico took perfumed cloths to their noses just to be able to stand next to the Anglo trappers. And so the relationship between the fledgling United States and Mexico got off to a rough start.

What was the Santa Fe Trail?

On the heels of the trappers came the merchants, who wanted to capitalize on the new, untapped market in New Mexico. These traveling salesmen needed to find a way to enter New Mexico without being spotted by Spanish Mexican authorities, who viewed them as interlopers.

By approaching New Mexico from the north rather than the east, the merchants were able to sneak into Spanish Mexican territory undetected with wagons laden with goods—from snake oil to women's underwear. In 1821 trader **William**

Becknell spread the news among the Anglos that Mexico was free from Spanish rule, the Mexicans had eased restrictions on commerce with foreign countries, and Santa Fe invited trade with the Americans. Beginning in 1822 caravans made the forty- to sixty-day trip to Santa Fe along the Santa Fe Trail on a regular basis. The head of the trail was in Independence, Missouri, where traders obtained wagons and loaded supplies, and it wound for 780 miles through rugged terrain. The Santa Fe Trail fell out of use in 1880 when the newly built Santa Fe Railroad reached its terminus in Santa Fe.

How did the Santa Fe traders open the doors to Anglo expansionism?

Overnight the Santa Fe Trail became the highway of opportunity. Business boomed for the Anglos. They had hit pay dirt in a territory badly in need of essential goods that the Mexican government could not supply. The first official American traders went with only $5,000 in goods, but by 1855, $5 million worth of merchandise had been transported to Santa Fe.

Merchandise was not all the Americans took to New Mexico. They also introduced exciting and innovative ways of looking at the world. Unlike the beaver trappers, these Easterners dressed well and were generally well-mannered, and the New Mexicans welcomed them with open arms. However, the Anglos also harbored certain prejudices that would soon surface and create a painful rift between the two countries. The Americans felt superior to the Mexicans of New Mexico, who they viewed as lazy and uncivilized—the same attitude the Spanish conquistadors had had of the indigenous peoples of the Americas three centuries earlier.

As more Anglos poured into New Mexico, and in some cases married and stayed for good, the Mexican government began to worry about the long-term effect of so much foreign influence in an area so far from Mexico City. In an attempt to turn back the clock, Mexican President **Antonio López de**

Santa Anna outlawed trade between Anglos and New Mexicans. But the people had grown accustomed to their new way of life and loved the excitement of the teeming marketplaces. They protested loudly, and Santa Anna was forced to rescind the law in 1844. The residents of New Mexico were beginning to feel separate from their government to the south. By then, however, the Anglo economic domination of New Mexico was a done deal. There was no going back.

What exactly was Manifest Destiny?

In the summer of 1845, an article appeared in the *United States Magazine and Democratic Review* that put into words what the citizens of the young American republic were already feeling. The anonymous author held that "our manifest destiny overspread the continent allotted by providence for the free development of our multiplying millions."

In a nutshell, Manifest Destiny was an Anglo version of the national supremacy theory and justified the desire on the part of the United States to extend its borders from sea to shining sea. The phrase took and so did the sentiment. Politicians from both the Democratic and Republican parties made mention of Manifest Destiny in articles and speeches everywhere, and felt as full of imperialist zeal and purpose as the Spanish conquistadors had.

In the 1830s and 1840s, the American republic would work especially hard at manifesting its destiny. Acquiring Mexican territory seemed like the next logical step in American expansion, although the more extreme exponents of Manifest Destiny spoke of pushing America's borders as far north as the Arctic Circle and as far south as Tierra del Fuego.

Several Mexican observers have remarked that, looked at from a different perspective, Manifest Destiny could have been called "Mexican Fate," since the country that suffered the most from this doctrine was Mexico.

HOW TEXAS WAS WON—OR LOST

Who was Stephen F. Austin, and why is he called the father of Texas?

Stephen F. Austin (1793–1836) was an American frontiersman with a special interest in Texas. His father, **Moses Austin,** had been granted permission by the Spanish in 1818 to settle Americans in Texas. As he lay dying, Moses Austin requested that his son Stephen be permitted to carry out his plan. In 1823, the Mexican government granted Stephen Austin permission to establish a settlement in Texas, provided he and his fellow American colonists obey Mexican law, become Mexican citizens, convert to Catholicism, and bar slavery on their lands.

Austin allotted each American family willing to farm land 117 acres and those who wanted to raise livestock 4,428 acres. The frontiersman took almost 100,000 acres for himself as a bonus for organizing the territory. The first group of Americans, three hundred strong, settled in the best lands along the Bernard, Colorado, and Brazos rivers. Within ten years the number of Americans living in Texas as Mexican citizens rose to about 50,000. Incidentally, the Anglo Texans did not always abide strictly by Mexican law. Many, including Austin, brought in hundreds of Africans to work the cotton fields as slaves.

The U.S. government also felt that Texas held promise, and in 1927 it offered Mexico $1 million for the territory. Mexico, alarmed at the Anglo Texans' behavior, and pressure from the United States to sell Texas, responded to the offer by imposing stricter controls on the Anglo Texans and passing anti-American legislation, such as a law that gave the Mexican government the right to tax American-owned ships plying the Rio Grande. Tensions mounted. The Mexicans finally had enough, and in 1830 **General Manuel de Meir y Terán** led his soldiers into Texas territory with the intent of expelling

Stephen Austin and all the Americans in his colony. His efforts failed, and the seeds of animosity between the Anglo Texans and the Mexican government were sown.

By 1832 Texas was in a state of chaos. Its citizens—both Anglos and Mexicans—believed that the only way to ease tensions was to establish a separate state within the Mexican federation. While Anglo and Mexican Texans had begun to view themselves as apart from other Mexicans, they did not want secession. Yet when they applied for statehood at an 1833 Mexican convention, **President Santa Anna** misinterpreted their petition as a request for independence. Even after the confusion was cleared up, Santa Anna was left fuming. He refused to grant the Texans any of their wishes and jailed Stephen Austin for eighteen months. Upon his release, Austin demanded in a speech that Texas be allowed to secede. It was the bugle call that heralded the beginning of Texas independence.

Why should we remember the Alamo?

Driven by independence fever, **William B. Travis,** one of **Stephen Austin**'s men, stormed the customs garrison at Anáhuac during the fateful summer of 1835. Some months later another group of Texans seized the garrison at Goliad, which contained valuable supplies. Finally, on December 5, Texan armies, with both Anglos and Mexicans in the ranks, raided a military supply depot at the Alamo mission, and San Antonio, the leading city in Texas, fell into rebel hands. A humiliated Mexican government was forced to agree to Texan demands for independence.

But not for long. In retaliation **President Santa Anna** organized an army numbering in the thousands and prepared to lead his forces in attacking Texas. The Texan rebels, believing that Santa Anna would strike through the city of Matamoros, withdrew most of their men from the Alamo garrison and stationed them in Matamoros. On March 6, 1936, Santa

Anna led his impressive army right into El Alamo territory, killing 182 Texans barricaded behind the mission walls.

The besieged Texan forces, under the command of William Travis, defended the fort valiantly for five days. Among the Texan heroes defending the Alamo garrison were frontiersmen **Davy Crockett** and **Jim Bowie.** According to Mexican American legend, though, Crockett was nothing more than a mercenary soldier whom the Mexicans captured and executed.

Santa Anna won a great victory with his preemptive strike, but he was unaware that an enraged Texan army, led by **Sam Houston** and armed to the teeth, was in hot pursuit of his men. Houston's army caught up with Santa Anna's soldiers at the San Jacinto River and Buffalo Bayou, shouting "Remember the Alamo!" When the smoke cleared on April 21, 1836, 600 of Santa Anna's men, but only six Texans lay dead on the battlefield. The Texans imprisoned Santa Anna for six months and later the Mexican government forced him out of office for humiliating his country. In 1853 he was restored to his office—a turnabout not uncommon in early Mexican politics.

The Texans had won independence and Texas became a state without a country under its newly elected president and war hero, Sam Houston.

Why do Mexican Americans cringe when they hear "Remember the Alamo"?

When **Santa Anna**'s forces stormed the Alamo and killed 182 Texans, Anglo hatred against Mexico and anything Mexican exploded with a vengeance, and the seeds of ethnic prejudice and intolerance that lay beneath the surface sprouted like prickly cactus across the Texas landscape. Suddenly Mexican Texans whose families had lived within the borders of Texas for untold generations were viewed as defenders of Santa Anna. The truth was that most had sided with **Sam Houston** and many had fought and died for Texan independence. The great majority had pinned their hopes on the Anglos, who they believed understood the needs of the vast, proud, and complicated land called *Tejas*. And yet, they became the enemy within. Before long, the phrase "Remember the Alamo!" was uttered as a warning to Mexican Texans that they better watch out.

What role did African Americans play in Texas history?

In March 1836, the United States, as well as Great Britain, France, Holland, and Belgium, recognized the Texas Republic as a sovereign nation. But even at the outset it was difficult for the young republic to survive on its own. For one, Mexico kept remembering the Alamo, too, and continually organized raids on Texan cities and towns, particularly Goliad, San Antonio, and Nacogdoches, which had a large Anglo population.

In addition, the Apache and other Native American tribes had declared war on the Anglo conquistadors, and their attacks claimed lives and valuable property. The Texas government also had serious financial troubles. The solution seemed clear to most Anglo Texans: join the United States. In September 1836, Texans voted for annexation.

But there was a hitch. At that moment in American history, the issue of slavery weighed heavily in the balance. The states were evenly divided on the issue, and since most of the Anglo Texans had come from Southern states and owned slaves themselves, Texas would tip the scale in favor of the slave states. Texans waged the battle for annexation for ten long years, thanks to abolitionists who kept Texas out of the republic. Finally on December 29, 1845, the U.S. Congress admitted Texas as the twenty-eighth state in the Union, with slavery permitted according to its state constitution. In 1861, Texas would secede from the Union, but was readmitted in March 1870, after ratifying the Thirteenth, Fourteenth, and

Fifteenth Amendments to the U.S. Constitution, which abolished slavery and protected the rights of former slaves and all people of color.

THE MEXICAN WAR

Just why did the American republic fight with Mexico?

In 1845 the Mexican government broke off diplomatic relations with the United States on the grounds that the annexation of Texas was an act of aggression aimed at Mexico. The Mexicans not only mourned the loss of Texas, they feared that the imperialistic Americans had other tricks up their sleeve—namely the acquisition of more of Mexico's territory. Their fear was perfectly justified as **President James Polk,** who steered a nation in the throes of Manifest Destiny, had publicly stated that the United States had every intent of acquiring California.

When, in 1845, President Polk sent a diplomat by the name of **John Slidell** to Mexico with an offer to buy California and New Mexico, part of which Texas claimed, for $25 million, an outraged Mexican government refused to negotiate. The United States reacted with the full zeal of Manifest Destiny. President Polk ordered **General Zachary Taylor,** who was stationed in Texas at the time with a volunteer army as a show of force against Mexico, to advance to the Rio Grande River.

How did the phrase "a Mexican standoff" come to be?

General **Zachary Taylor** reached the mouth of the Rio Grande in March 1846. The Mexican Army, instead of attacking the invader, decided to wait and see what General Taylor's men were up to. Both armies hunkered down on opposite sides of the river, measuring each other's military might, shouting insults back and forth, even joking. It was a war of nerves, with each side goading the other to make the first move, which finally happened when the sides clashed on April 25. It was from this military checkmate, or game of wait and see, that the phrase "a Mexican standoff" was coined.

If all Zachary Taylor had was a small volunteer army, how did the United States win the war?

At first, the Mexicans, led by **General Pedro de Ampudia,** were confident of a swift victory. Their army was three times larger and far better trained than the paltry U.S. volunteer army with adventurers, vagabonds, and escaped criminals in the ranks. But once the United States officially declared war on May 13, 1846, Congress authorized the formation of an army of 50,000 soldiers and appropriated $10 million for the war effort.

There was no contest. The fact that Mexico was torn by civil strife at the time and some of the states had refused to band together as a united front did not help matters for the Mexicans. On August 24, 1847—scarcely a year and a half after the Mexican standoff—Mexico accepted an armistice.

What is the Treaty of Guadalupe Hidalgo?

The Treaty of Guadalupe Hidalgo, signed on February 2, 1848, is the formal agreement that ended the Mexican War. By the terms of the treaty, Mexico handed over California, Utah, Nevada, and parts of Colorado, Wyoming, New Mexico, and Arizona—approximately 525,000 square miles of territory—to America. With the acquisition of this land, the map of the United States was almost complete.

By a single stroke of the pen, a large group of Mexican citizens right in their very own homes, found themselves smack in the middle of another country whose laws, political and social institutions, and fundamentally WASP traditions were alien to them.

A critical part of the treaty concerned the fate of these Mexicans who now lived in ceded American territory. They were given a year to decide whether they wanted to retain Mexican citizenship or become U.S. citizens. Nearly eight thousand Mexicans living in the new American territory opted to become American citizens, while about two thousand moved south of the Rio Grande, the new boundary between the two countries, in order to keep their Mexican citizenship.

What was wrong with the Treaty of Guadalupe Hidalgo?

A lot. For one, the Treaty of Guadalupe Hidalgo that the Mexicans signed was not the same treaty ratified by the United States, since most of the important paragraphs that did not suit certain U.S. senators were simply deleted without informing the Mexicans. Furthermore, the treaty failed to address the protection of social institutions that were a vital part of Mexican tradition.

How did the Anglos treat the new American citizens?

Article IX of the Treaty of Guadalupe Hidalgo specifically provided that Mexicans living in the new U.S. territories would have the right to retain their property. In utter disregard for Mexican tradition and the Treaty of Guadalupe Hidalgo, the Anglos who settled in the newly acquired territories in droves ousted Mexican grantees from the most desirable properties (those near water), and then claimed that they had the right to homestead vacant lands. The Mexican system of property laws, with its lack of surveys, dependence on verbal agreements instead of legally binding documents, and communal tradition, hindered the Mexicans in their attempts to retain ownership. Unable to produce written proof of ownership, deemed adequate by Anglo law, many lost their land and their homes.

What was the Gadsden Purchase, and why did Mexicans say they needed it like a hole in the head?

In 1853, the U.S. government sent **James Gadsden** to Mexico to settle minor territorial disputes between the two nations. What resulted was the Gadsden Purchase, which gave the United States the right to purchase a strip of land along the Gila River in southern Arizona and southern New Mexico. As fate would have it, this territory was inhabited by Mexicans who had moved there from the north, in the aftermath of the Mexican War, so that they could retain their Mexican citizenship.

The terms of the Gadsden Purchase covered a number of other issues, such as the right of Americans to cross the Isthmus of Tehuantepec and the reestablishment of commerce between the United States and Mexico. According to the terms of the Gadsden Purchase, the United States agreed to pay Mexico $5 million in claims for damages resulting from protests by native peoples over the loss of their ancestral lands to the U.S. government in return for the deletion of Article XI of the Treaty of Guadalupe Hidalgo, which made the United States liable for raids on Mexico perpetrated by native peoples.

On a positive note, the Gadsden Purchase reaffirmed the civil rights of Mexican Americans and guaranteed their land titles—a covenant which, not surprisingly, was not entirely heeded.

Mexico had no choice but to accept the terms of the Gadsden Purchase, for to reject them would have meant another costly war and another defeat. So, much as it was touted as the treaty that finally ended the Mexico-United States conflict, most Mexicans believed they needed the Gadsden Purchase like a hole in the head.

CALIFORNIA DREAMING

What was the Bear Flag Revolt, and how did the Californios feel about joining the United States?

Like Texas and New Mexico, California was experiencing a large influx of Anglo settlers by the 1840s. In 1826 **Jedediah Strong Smith** and other trappers made the first American journey overland to California, but the Americans did not settle in California in significant numbers until 1841. The very first Anglo settlers in the region joined the Spanish-speaking California society. Many married into *Californio* families and became Mexican citizens. But before long, a different breed of Anglos began arriving in California via the Oregon Trail. These newcomers brought their families, refused Mexican citizenship, and settled remote areas, far from Mexican supervision. They were inspired by Manifest Destiny and brought with them a spark for rebellion that rocked California just before the outbreak of the Mexican War (1846–1848).

That rebellion of 1846, known as the Bear Flag Revolt, was led by American explorer and soldier **John Charles Frémont,** who organized American settlers disgruntled by the way the Mexicans handled affairs in California. These settlers wanted to be backed by the mint and might of the U.S. government, and they had established the Bear Flag Republic at Sonoma that very same year.

When the Mexican War erupted, **Commodore John D. Sloat** seized control of Monterey and claimed California for the United States. Soon after, **Commodore Robert F. Stockton** appointed himself governor of California. The *Californios* in the north flew the Stars and Stripes, but those in the south resisted U.S. imperialism. It seems that the American government had put an insensitive captain by the name of **Archibald Gillespie** in command of California. Gillespie had no respect for Spanish Mexican tradition and imposed all sorts of restrictions on the *Californios*, which rubbed those in the south the wrong way. The southern *Californios* fought the good fight, but U.S. general **Stephen W. Kearny** and his army eventually got the best of them.

Peace was negotiated with the southern *Californios* under the Treaty of Cahuenga in 1847, and a united California cheered when the Treaty of Guadalupe Hidalgo was signed and the territory was officially handed over to the Americans. In 1850 California was admitted to the Union as a nonslavery state. While there was much proslavery sentiment on the part of southern Californians, the state remained in the Union during the Civil War (1861–1865) and was little affected by the devastating conflict.

Was the California constitution drafted exclusively by Anglos?

Many wealthy California ranchers of Spanish and Mexican descent had a great deal to do with laying the necessary groundwork for California's admission into the Union, and with fulfilling the tasks that statehood created. Among the delegates who helped draft the California state constitution were influential Mexican Americans such as **Pablo de la Guerra, Mariano Vallejo,** and **José Antonio Carrillo.**

What was the California Gold Rush, and how did Mexico miss out on it by a couple of days?

As fate would have it, just as the United States and Mexico were negotiating the Treaty of Guadalupe Hidalgo, the very gold that had eluded both the Spanish and the Mexicans for centuries turned up unexpectedly and in such incredible quantities as to change the course of American history.

On January 24, 1848, a contractor named **John Marshall,** who was building a sawmill for **John Sutter** in the Sacramento Valley of California, noticed some shiny yellow rocks along the millrace. He looked closer. What he had found was not just a few gold nuggets, but the mother lode, the richest gold-bearing territory the world has ever known.

Sutter and Marshall decided to keep their discovery a secret. They were greedy and wanted to horde all the treasure, but they also knew that the fate of a nation was at stake. They feared that if the news of gold got out, Mexico would never agree to surrender its territory—and they were probably right. After all, had not an entire hemisphere been conquered, settled, and resettled for gold?

A few days after the Treaty of Guadalupe Hidalgo was signed, word of gold spread like wildfire, not only across America, but around the globe. Newspapers ran enormous headlines detailing the discovery, and men from all over the world descended on California to claim their fortune. Virtually overnight, California's population exploded and San Francisco became a boom city.

What role did Latinos play in the success of California mining?

Ironically, the first miners to reach California were Peruvian and Chilean immigrants who sailed up the Pacific coast. It seems fitting that descendants of the Inca, whose culture both revered gold and had been destroyed for it, would be the first California prospectors.

Miners from the Mexican state of Sonora followed closely on the heels of the Peruvians and Chileans. Then Mexican Americans from all around the Southwest poured into California. After that Europeans and Anglo Americans from the East came to the state in droves, risking life and limb against warring Native American tribes, the elements, and the seemingly impassable mountains and plains.

The Anglo prospectors were strong, avaricious men with firm resolve, and they soon outnumbered the Spanish-speaking miners. But the Anglos knew nothing about panning for gold, and they turned for help to the Latin Americans and Mexican Americans, who taught them how to extract the precious metal from the rivers and streams with a flat-bottomed pan with sloping sides. They instructed the Anglos in the use of an *arrastra*—a mill that pulverized rock and made it possible to remove gold from quartz. And they showed them how to use mercury to refine gold—a process the Spaniards had devised to refine silver in northern Mexico three centuries earlier.

Having mastered gold mining at the feet of Latin Americans and Mexican Americans, the Anglos then decided that since California was American, all the gold belonged to them and not to the Mexicans, as they called all Spanish-speaking peoples, even the Peruvians and Chileans. The Latin American and Mexican American miners strongly objected, and they settled away from the Anglos in the southern part of the mother lode. The Anglos stayed in the north, but before long they began invading the southern mines. To discourage the Spanish-speaking miners, California passed a law taxing all foreigners heavily. The Latin American miners protested and revolts broke out all over the mines. The Anglos prevailed because they were in the majority and because, as the Mexicans put it, they "stopped at nothing." In the ensuing years, dozens of Mexican Americans and Latin Americans were lynched or otherwise murdered. Under such assault, many simply gave up their right to the gold and fled for their lives. Sadly, it was the first of many times that Mexican Americans would meet bald-faced discrimination without legal recourse.

Allá en el rancho grande: *What happened to the* **Mexican American** rancheros *during the Gold Rush and after?*

An old Mexican folk song that lives on among Latinos begins: *"Allá en el rancho grande, allá donde vivia . . ."* ("Back there on the big ranch, the place where I used to live . . ."). It's a song that romanticizes life on the *rancho*, or ranch, a landscape filled with handsome *rancheros* (ranchers) and *vaqueros* (cowboys), beautiful señoritas, big sombreros, and wide-open spaces.

During the Gold Rush, hordes of southern Californians rushed north to try their luck at a pot of gold, and many towns in southern California turned into virtual ghost towns. However, the *ranchos* of central and southern California flourished. An exploding California population meant that many people needed to be fed, and beef was the entrée of choice for most of the new and often nouveau riche citizens.

In the heyday of the *ranchos*, California ranchers, many of whom were *Californios*, could demand $100 a head for their cattle—not bad in the days when $100 bought a house. The *Californio rancheros* decorated their homes in the style of the early Spanish *hacendados* and ran their enormous ranches like small fiefdoms. They hired *vaqueros*, who wore *chaparreras* (a word Anglos shortened to chaps) and roped cattle with *la riata* (which the Anglos called a lariat). The Gold Rush was good to the *rancheros* and *vaqueros*, if not to their less fortunate compatriots who searched for gold.

But soon the tide turned. First the cattle ranchers in the Plains states undercut the Californians' prices, causing demand for California beef to dwindle in just a few years. In 1861, winter floods devastated southern California, killing many cattle. The floods were followed by two years of drought that also had a devastating effect on the cattle herds.

As if these catastrophes were not enough, the *Californio rancheros* had to deal with anti-Mexican laws that were put in place in the decade after the Mexican War. Whereas the Treaty of Guadalupe Hidalgo had rendered legitimate the land titles of Mexican Americans, the Federal Land Grant Act of 1851, drafted with California very much in mind, stipulated that all Spanish and Mexican land grants had to be presented for verification within two years, and those that were not would automatically be rendered null and void.

However, most land grants had not been recorded on paper, in keeping with Spanish and Mexican traditional protocol, and families had divided and subdivided their lands over the centuries for inheritance purposes. With no papers to show, many of those who had managed to keep their ranches after the Treaty of Guadalupe Hidalgo was signed now had to turn them over. Adding insult to injury, the California Supreme Court upheld an English law of riparian water rights—i.e., individuals, not communities, owned water rights, which meant that many a *ranchero* was forced to sell cheap or give up his land, because neighbors could dam up his water and parch his land as they pleased.

The writing was on the wall. Very few *rancheros* were able to survive and Anglo speculators bought up their property for a song. As a result, scores of Mexican Americans, who had previously been thriving landowners, became a homeless, bankrupt underclass overnight, forced to seek menial jobs across the vast American frontier.

DESPERADOS AND THE MEXICAN REVOLUTION OF 1910

What is a desperado, anyway?

The word "desperado" is a contraction of the Spanish *desesperado*, meaning "desperate one," and is defined as a desperate, dangerous criminal. In the frontier years of the mid to late 1800s, many desperados, both Mexican and Anglo, roamed the American Southwest.

One Mexican desperado who went down in history is **Joaquín Murieta,** although his existence has never been confirmed. The story goes that Murieta, who hailed from Sonora, Mexico, was a peaceful California gold miner until Anglos took away his gold-mine claim and murdered his brother around 1850. In a desperate attempt to avenge the injustices done him, other Mexicans, and Mexican Americans, Murieta robbed, ransacked, and killed anybody that got in his way. He was compared to Robin Hood, but his random acts of lawlessness only served to deepen the animosity Anglos felt for Mexicans. When it was suspected that Murieta was the one who raided Calaveras County, California, and set the devastating fire that consumed the mining town of Stockton in 1850, the state of California put a price on his head: $1,000, dead or alive. Some California rangers reported later that they had killed Joaquín Murieta, but his identity was never confirmed.

Another desperado was Mexican folk hero **Juan Nepomuceno Cortina,** whom Mexican Americans have likened to **Daniel Boone** and other intrepid frontiersmen. Born in Mexico, Cortina fought the Americans in the Mexican War, and then settled on a ranch he purchased near Brownsville, Texas. Cortina could not swallow the injustices the Anglos perpetrated against Mexicans in the United States after the war. When a Brownsville deputy sheriff unfairly arrested a *vaquero* (cowboy) on his ranch in 1859, Cortina apparently grew so enraged that he shot the sheriff and then freed all the prisoners at the local jail. Cortina became a scofflaw and an "avenging angel." Many hold him responsible for inciting dozens of riots, including the angry riots that broke out in El Paso in 1877 after Anglo profiteers tried to take the salt mines away from the Mexicans and Mexican Americans. This incident, known as the Salt War, cost many lives and caused thousands of dollars in damage.

Acts of destruction on the part of Mexican and Mexican American desperados who felt persecuted and disenfranchised after the Mexican War gave rise to armies of vigilantes in California, Texas, and the Southwest, and to the feared

Texas Rangers. The Texas Rangers became notorious for the "law and order" violence they perpetrated against Mexican Americans. Often they arrested or killed innocent citizens whom they took for desperados. The rangers created an atmosphere of antipathy and suspicion that some say still lingers in the hearts of many.

Was Pancho Villa a desperado?

Pancho Villa was a hero of the Mexican Revolution of 1910 in which Mexicans fought to depose dictator **Porfirio Díaz** (who had held power since 1884) and institute a pluralistic democracy that would return the land to the peasants and food to the people.

Like **Juan Nepomuceno Cortina** and **Joaquín Murieta** to the north, Pancho Villa became disgusted with the establishment and decided to take the law into his own hands. As a young man, he took to the hills and launched a career as both a guerilla fighter for democracy and a bandit who terrorized northern Mexico, robbing banks and trains and ransacking mining towns.

When the United States recognized **Venustiano Carranza** as president of Mexico, while several Mexican leaders literally battled each other for the post during the Mexican Revolution, Villa became enraged over U.S. intervention in the affairs of his country. In retaliation, he killed sixteen American engineers on board a train that had entered Mexico from the United States, and in early 1916, he attacked Columbus, New Mexico, slaughtering seventeen Americans. In a matter of days, U.S. general **John J. Pershing** and his large army was given the order to capture Pancho Villa and bring him to the United States to stand trial. The clever guerilla fighter who knew the difficult Mexican terrain like the back of his hand, slipped into hiding and Pershing's army came up empty-handed. Pancho Villa became a hero overnight.

What was the Mexican Revolution all about, and how did the United States get involved?

The Mexican Revolution of 1910 was a lengthy, bloody, and devastating civil war which changed Mexico forever. Precipitated by both class and racial struggle, it was in many ways like the Bolshevik Revolution in Russia that followed seven years later. By 1910 the rich of Mexico had grown richer (and so had foreign investors), and the native peoples and *mestizos*, who were at the bottom of the pecking order, had gotten poorer. Finally they said "*basta ya*," "Enough is enough," and revolted.

It was a complicated revolution, with many factions vying for power—some more liberal and inclusive, others more radical, virulent, and unforgiving. Much of the protest was waged against the Catholic Church. Native peoples and *mestizos* stormed Catholic churches and toppled religious statues, just as the early Spanish missionaries, seeking to convert the peoples of Mexico to Catholicism centuries before, had smashed images of the Aztec and Maya gods. Interestingly, when the Mexicans demolished statues of Roman Catholic saints, they often found figurines of Mexican gods encrusted in the plaster. It seems that rather than complete conversion, a kind of cultural and religious syncretism went on from the very beginning.

The revolution started in November 1910 when liberal leader **Francisco Madero** organized a revolt against dictator **Porforio Díaz.** A year later Díaz resigned and Madero became president. In 1913 Madero was overthrown by his general, **Victoriano Huerta,** and then murdered. Huerta proved to be just another dictator and the people, led by **Emiliano Zapata,** a native peasant who had backed Madero, and **Pancho Villa,** revolted. They destroyed railroads and most of the nation's crops and livestock, unleashing a food shortage which led to mass starvation and uncontrollable epidemics. All hell broke loose south of the border.

In response U.S. President **Woodrow Wilson** ordered an arms blockade against Mexico in 1913. It was the eve of World War I and the United States feared that Germany might meddle in the hemisphere and take advantage of the chaos in Mexico. U.S. involvement in Mexico escalated in April 1914 when a battalion of marines who had landed in Tampico, Mexico, to pick up supplies were arrested by the Mexicans. **Admiral Henry T. Mayo** demanded an apology from the Huerta government, but when the Mexican dictator refused to comply or even salute the American flag, President Wilson sent a fleet to Veracruz and the United States prepared to invade Mexico and declare war.

At the eleventh hour, Argentina, Chile, and Brazil interceded and war between Mexico and the United States was averted. Huerta resigned, **Venustiano Carranza** was named president, and the United States saw no reason for further overt hostility against the Mexican people. Civil war erupted again in 1914, but Carranza got the country under control by 1915, although his foes Pancho Villa and Emiliano Zapata continued their raids on both sides of the border until the Mexican Revolution ended in 1917.

How did the Mexican people fare during the Mexican Revolution?

Terribly. Over a million Mexicans died, and countless people suffered political persecution and violence, losing their homes, their possessions, their financial well-being, and their hope.

The misery caused by the Mexican Revolution unleashed the first significant wave of Mexican *immigration* (not absorption due to shifting borders) to the United States. Between 1910 and 1930, nearly ten percent of Mexico's citizenry fled their homeland in search of a brighter future. Most of the refugees (about 700,000) chose to forge a new life in the United States. By the hundreds of thousands they walked endless miles to the promised land of the American Southwest, Texas, and California. They waded across the shallow Rio Grande, belongings and babies on their backs, seeking refuge from the devastation. Many were upper-middle and middle class; many were poor, uneducated peasants.

The Mexicans who fled the revolution and went to work in America had a positive impact on the nation's economy. They also enriched the country's cultural heritage and nurtured future generations of leaders in all walks of life who would not only reshape Mexican American communities but the nation as a whole.

What did the Mexican Revolution have to do with U.S. Congressman Henry B. González becoming chairperson of the House Banking Committee?

Henry B. González's parents were among the scores of middle-class Mexicans who were forced to flee their homeland during the Mexican Revolution. They settled in San Antonio, Texas, where the future congressman and respected leader of the Mexican American community was born in 1916. Several decades later González would earn the honor of chairing the powerful House Banking Committee.

A TIME OF TROUBLES: MEXICAN AMERICA IN THE 1920s, 1930s, AND 1940s

When did the United States begin policing the border with Mexico?

In 1924, U.S. immigration laws were put in place that established quotas for people entering the country from different parts of the world. Northern Europeans were favored; southern Europeans could gain entry in limited numbers. Almost all Asians were excluded. However, no quotas were stipulated for immigrants from the Western Hemisphere—thus Mexico, our nearest neighbor to the south, became America's largest supplier of cheap labor.

For over a century, going north, *"al norte,"* had been a logical step for Mexicans seeking a better life, and they entered the United States with no questions asked. Countless Mexican farmhands, shepherds, cowboys, and miners in search of better and more highly paid work had crossed the border unimpeded. So too had political refugees fleeing the many upheavals during Mexico's formative years as a sovereign nation, especially after the Mexican Revolution of 1910. Then in 1924, the same year immigration quotas were established, the United States required Mexicans to provide proof of identity and other documentation to gain legal entry. Many Mexicans entered legally, but others saw the paperwork as an impediment and began dodging the border patrol. The term "illegal immigrant" entered the American vocabulary.

Why do Mexican Americans say the country was built on their backs?

The Mexican workers who fled the Mexican Revolution were accustomed to poor wages and appalling living conditions and were grateful just to have a job—even one with low pay. They were willing to plant and harvest crops from sunup to sundown without a break, and as a result the commercial farms throughout the Southwest and California flourished. By the 1920s, Mexicans and Mexican Americans had emerged as the single most important source of agricultural labor in California, and are so to this day, replacing the Chinese and the Japanese who had worked the fields at the turn of the century.

The early 1920s saw the expansion of the Southern Pacific Railroad, and Mexicans and Mexican Americans went to work on the tracks. A 1929 government report shows that as many as 70 to 90 percent of all workers on the Southwestern railroads were of Mexican origin. The Baltimore and Ohio Railroads also heavily recruited Mexicans and Mexican Americans.

Manufacturing and other industries also benefited from the influx of cheap labor from Mexico. In the 1920s, Mexicans and Mexican Americans found employment in steel factories, meat-packing plants, utility companies, construction, trucking, and dozens of other industries in the Midwest. They also worked in agriculture in that part of the country, such as in the sugar-beet fields of Michigan. As a result, Chicago's Mexican and Mexican American populations swelled from four thousand to twenty thousand between 1920 and 1930. The Mexican Americans met with much discrimination in their new home in the Midwest, especially from other ethnic groups such as Italian Americans and Polish Americans, who by the 1920s considered themselves real Americans and the Mexicans foreigners. As they contributed to the nation's prosperity, Mexican American families endured physical hardship. They often lived in substandard housing on the wrong side of the tracks, that is, in overcrowded ghettos known as *barrios* and *colonias*.

What's a barrio, and what's a colonia?

A *barrio* is a Latino neighborhood in a city or town. Many Mexican American *barrios* bear the name of the region of Mexico that the inhabitants came from. Since they first formed, *barrios*, like other immigrant ghettos, have provided their dwellers with a semblance of the old country. Many Mexican Americans eventually left the *barrios* and acculturated to mainstream American society. This holds true for all Latinos. In recent years, new generations of Latinos have chosen to return to the *barrios* where their parents or grandparents once lived to reclaim part of their heritage.

Colonias (Spanish for "colonies") are little towns or communities in rural areas that over time have provided a resting stop for Mexican newcomers to the United States in search of work. The *colonias* are homes away from home, where new immigrants have explored possible employment, or simply paused for a warm meal and a friendly chat on their way to "somewhere." *Colonias,* primarily in unincorporated rural areas all along the Mexico–U.S. border, are among the poorest communities in the nation. Most of the residents are impoverished Mexican Americans—not illegal immigrants, as is the widespread opinion. Texas has over 1,500 *colonias*.

Chicano go home? Why were Mexicans and Mexican Americans repatriated?

As the 1920s came to a close, the Great Depression was looming over the United States. Between 1930 and 1933, the number of unemployed Americans skyrocketed from four million to over thirteen million. Wages dropped from thirty-five cents an hour to fifteen cents an hour. Stockbrokers and financiers were leaping out of windows in New York City and college graduates were selling apples in the streets.

Mexican nationals and Mexican Americans, like most Americans, found themselves out of work as the railroads, automobile manufacturing plants, meat-packing plants, and steel mills in America came to a screeching halt. All across the country, they were fired from their jobs. In New Mexico, cattle ranchers laid off Mexican American ranchhands indefinitely, and many New Mexican Hispanos lost their land because they could not afford to pay the taxes or the assessments of the Middle Rio Grande Conservancy Project.

Thousands of Mexican Americans joined other Americans in roaming the country in search of whatever work they could get. Anglo immigrants from the Dust Bowl and other regions headed west, where they competed for the few jobs that had been traditionally filled by Mexicans and Mexican Americans. For instance, by 1937 over half the cotton pickers in Arizona came from out of state. The Mexican Americans, who were at the bottom of the opportunity ladder, had nowhere to turn. In Texas alone the number of jobless Mexican Americans hit 400,000 during the Great Depression.

Recognizing that Mexican Americans were particularly bad off, **President Franklin D. Roosevelt**'s New Deal administration established a number of agencies and projects aimed at ameliorating their situation. The Federal Emergency Relief Administration, among other agencies, provided temporary work and assistance to Mexican American workers. And the Works Progress Administration, created in 1935, put Mexican Americans to work as carpenters, masons, and unskilled laborers building bridges, libraries, and other municipal structures. In the midst of great anguish, this was a moment of pride for Mexican Americans, who were publicly recognized for their long tradition as master builders—a tradition harking back to the heyday of the Maya and Aztec.

In spite of the efforts of **Franklin Roosevelt** and **Eleanor Roosevelt** on behalf of Mexican Americans during the 1930s, a repatriation movement, which demanded that Mexicans and Mexican Americans be sent to Mexico, gathered enormous support during the Depression days. Many Anglos considered both Mexicans and Mexican Americans to be foreigners or itinerant laborers, who had no right to take the few existing jobs from "real" Americans at a time of such extreme economic duress.

In complete disregard for the civil rights of Mexican Americans, local government agencies began rounding up anyone who looked Mexican and sending them "home." Frequently they targeted undocumented immigrants, but they also sent first-generation Mexican Americans to Mexico, as well as Mexican Americans whose families had lived in the United States for centuries. Many Americans of Mexican descent could not bear the idea of being deported and fled to Mexico before they could be loaded onto the Southern Pacific or other railroads and dumped over the border in towns along the Tijuana and Brownsville lines.

All told, during the 1930s, approximately half a million people of Mexican descent, illegal immigrants included, were deported. About 132,000 of the deportees were from Texas, which had the largest Mexican American community. California was second in the number of deportees, followed by Indiana, Illinois, and Michigan. Mexican Americans in New

Mexico suffered the least; only ten percent of repatriates came from the state. This can be attributed to the fact that New Mexico was less industrialized than other states and thus less affected by the Depression. It also has to do with the fact that Mexican Americans in New Mexico were more integrated into mainstream Anglo society.

Faced with so many deportees, a distraught Mexican president, **Lázaro Cárdenas,** set up resettlement camps in the states of Guerrero, Michoacán, Oaxaca, and Chiapas, as well as a small colony in Matamoros, in the state of Tamaulipas. In the end, however, the Mexican economy could not absorb this influx, and few deportees became fully integrated into Mexican society. This situation served only to increase the outrage and disillusionment of Mexican American deportees, who felt that the United States, their own country, had brutally betrayed them.

During World War II, when the United States needed workers, repatriation efforts were reversed and Mexican Americans found their way back to their old towns in California and the Southwest. The bitter experience of being sent "home" when they were no longer needed and sent for again when cheap labor was in demand intensified the mistrust many Mexican American families had felt toward the Anglos for countless generations.

However, this great injustice, which many have compared to the internment of Japanese Americans in concentration camps during World War II, also led numerous politicians to take a fresh look at the Mexican American "question," and to seek ways to improve working and living conditions in the United States for minorities. The sad repatriation experience also stirred the desire in many Mexican Americans to empower themselves and their communities. Some entered the mainstream political arena. Although Spanish-language newspapers had existed in the Southwest as far back as the nineteenth century, publications with a political bent, as well as radio stations, cropped up in Mexican American communities. Since then, Spanish-language media have multiplied a hundredfold; in fact, today several Spanish television networks operate coast to coast.

What was the Bracero Program?

Bracero comes from *brazo*, the Spanish word for "arm." So a *bracero* is literally someone who works with his arms: a hired hand. Although there are plenty of female hired hands, the generic (masculine), *bracero*, is used when referring to *braceros* of both genders. *Bracera* connotes a particular woman laborer.

The Bracero Program—in effect from August 1942 until December 1947, and then from December 1948 to December 1964—brought thousands of Mexican nationals to the United States as temporary workers. The U.S. government initiated the first Bracero Program in the forties when American workers had gone off to fight in World War II and the nation desperately needed farm and industrial laborers to replace them. During that period, only about 250,000 *braceros* were hired to work seasonally in the United States, as the crops required. A contract usually lasted one year. Some *braceros* found themselves coming back year after year to work in the same region and even for the same employer.

The second Bracero Program was much more ambitious. From 1948 until the beginning of the Vietnam War, more than 4.5 million Mexican nationals came to toil in the United States. Most went to work in agriculture; *braceros* accounted for 25 percent of all farm workers in the United States during this period, and their work greatly benefited the states of Texas, California, Arizona, Arkansas, New Mexico, Colorado, and Michigan. Thousands also drove trucks that delivered crops and manufactured goods to American marketplaces, or worked on the Southern Pacific Railroad, despite opposition by U.S. labor.

Before the Bracero Programs, Mexicans had worked under deplorable conditions and were often paid little or nothing at all, like indentured servants. When ironing out the details of the Bracero Program, the Mexican government stipulated that the United States had to ensure that the itinerant Mexican workers would receive no less than the minimum wage, that their health and well-being would be protected, that labor practices would be fair, and that the workers would have the right to take legal action against American employers refusing to comply with the above stipulations. The labor shortage during World War II, coupled with the hue and cry over the illegal deportation of Mexican Americans during the Depression, prompted the U.S. government to agree to abide by mutual treaties that ensured basic rights for the Mexican workers.

Even with the laws on the books, many prejudiced American employers treated the *braceros* poorly. Mexican workers complained of bad food (their provisions often consisted exclusively of such things as tripe, chitterlings, pig's feet, chicken necks, and leftovers from earlier meals); excessive wage deductions, which left them with very little money to support themselves or send to their families back in Mexico; physical mistreatment; miserable housing that often amounted to nothing more than enlarged chicken coops; rampant prejudice; and exposure to deadly pesticides. Conditions for Mexican workers, *braceros* or not, were so bad in Texas, that the Mexican government at one point barred its citizens from working in that state.

Why did Texas pass a law declaring that all Mexicans were white?

In response to protests on the part of the Mexican government about the subhuman treatment of Mexicans and Mexican Americans in Texas, the Texas legislature passed the Caucasian Race Resolution in 1944, which declared all people of Mexican descent white and endorsed equal rights in public places of business and leisure for all Caucasians. In a strictly segregated society, this seemed like the only way the Texas legislature could grant Mexicans and Mexican Americans some rights. But the Mexican government considered the efforts of Texas insufficient, and Texas, like all other states, was forced to comply with the guarantees stipulated in the Bracero Program before Mexico again allowed its citizens to work north of the border.

After various human rights organizations, including the National Catholic Welfare Council, Americans for Democratic Action, the National Council of Churches of Christ in America, the National Farmers Union, and the AFL-CIO, alerted Congress about the mistreatment of *braceros*, the U.S. government also took action to right the wrongs and discourage further injustice. Secretary of Labor **Arthur Goldberg** established a minimum wage law that stipulated that *braceros* were to receive at least a dollar an hour in pay.

What brought an end to the Bracero Program?

In November 1946, with World War II over, the U.S. government informed Mexico that it wished to terminate the Bracero Program. However, most farm bosses in the United States had come to rely on the *braceros*, and they lobbied to keep the program alive. In 1947 the House of Representatives introduced a law that kept the Bracero Program in place for seventeen more years. In 1956 the postwar Bracero Program reached its peak when 445,000 Mexican *braceros* were processed.

However, increased mechanization in agriculture coupled with organized labor's growing opposition to the hiring of Mexican aliens, led to the final dissolution of the Bracero Program in 1964. Even after the program was officially terminated, *braceros* continued to work American farms for several more years; labor contracts were negotiated by *braceros* and their employers without government intervention. In those years the *braceros* were joined by other legal immigrants, *mojados* (wetbacks), day trippers, and other commuters.

What was the Sleepy Lagoon Case?

An incident that occurred in 1942 is just one of the countless encounters with prejudice that Mexicans and Mexican Americans have withstood in the United States over the centuries.

On August 2, 1942, a twenty-one-year-old Mexican American by the name of **José Díaz** was found beaten to death, presumably by Mexican American youths, near the Sleepy Lagoon reservoir on the outskirts of Los Angeles. In response, newspapers, such as the Hearst-owned *Los Angeles Examiner*, ran a series of sensationalist articles on the dangers posed by Mexican American gangs. The public became hysterical, and to calm fears the police rounded up over six hundred Mexican American youths it said were somehow connected to the Sleepy Lagoon case. Twenty-four of the Mexican Americans were indicted for murder. The three-month trial, one of the largest mass trials in American history, was a mockery of justice. First of all, the youths were made to sit in a "prisoners' box" apart from their lawyers. Not a single witness provided evidence that suggested that any of the defendants could possibly have been at the crime scene. Furthermore, the youths were vilified in the courtroom; one expert from the sheriff's department testified that "this Mexican element feels a desire to kill or at least draw blood." The press was also hostile toward the defendants, referring to them as "Sleepy Lagooners," and then simply as "goons."

Despite the weak case against them, seventeen of the youths were convicted on charges ranging from first-degree murder to assault with a deadly weapon. Two years later an appeals court overturned all the convictions and condemned the judge for his extreme prejudice. Still, the youths had spent two precious years of life in prison for a crime the court found they did not commit.

What were the Zoot Suit Riots?

The Sleepy Lagoon case fanned the flames of ethnic hatred in Los Angeles, and led to another racially motivated incident that left a wake of devastation in the Mexican American community. During the 1940s, Mexican American teenagers, who called themselves *pachucos*, commonly dressed in long jackets and wide pants and sported extremely long watch chains, outfits resembling the zoot suits worn by young men in Harlem. To Anglos, zoot suits were clothes that only hoodlums wore. Newspapers and magazines in Los Angeles ran stories about the sharp rise in crime in the city, and openly placed the blame on Mexican Americans, whom they dubbed "zoot suiters." Hatred toward people of Mexican descent boiled over when on June 3, 1943, eleven sailors on leave in Los Angeles walked into a *barrio* and became involved in a brawl with a group of Mexican Americans. Although the Mexican Americans had not instigated the brawl, news of the incident outraged Anglos in L.A. as well as the sailors' comrades onboard ship.

The next day two hundred sailors hired a fleet of taxis and circled the *barrios* of Los Angeles. Each time they came upon a young man who looked Mexican, they beat him to a pulp. African Americans and Filipinos were sometimes mistaken for Mexicans or were beaten just because they were not Caucasian. By June 7, thousands of civilians had joined in the riots. The young Mexican Americans fought back, but they were often outnumbered and outmaneuvered. The police looked the other way and even arrested the victimized Mexican American youths.

Downtown Los Angeles was eventually declared off-limits to military personnel, but by then the riots had become widespread. Soon the rest of the country was riding the anti–Mexican American wave, which sparked attacks in Beaumont, Texas; Chicago; San Diego; Detroit; Evansville, Indiana; Philadelphia; and New York City.

A citizens' committee appointed by California governor **Earl Warren** (later a Supreme Court justice) and headed by Bishop **Joseph McGucken** of Los Angeles determined that racial prejudice was the cause of the riots and that the police and press had further fanned the flames of violence. In spite of this, the Los Angeles City Council actually debated a proposal that would make it illegal to wear zoot suits. Shortly after the Zoot Suit Riots, a Los Angeles Commission on Human Rights was established to study the "race question" and prescribe measures to prevent future outbreaks of hate crimes.

The Zoot Suit Riots are memorialized in a highly acclaimed play entitled *Zoot Suit* by **Luis Valdez,** the son of migrant workers and the creator of the *Teatro Campesino*, a theatrical group comprised of striking members of the United Farm Workers, a union that was headed by the Mexican American **César Estrada Chávez.** *Zoot Suit,* which premiered on Broadway in 1979, was made into a motion picture by the same name in 1981. Luis Valdez also wrote and directed the 1987 film *La Bamba*, a chronicle of the life of **Ritchie Valens,** the Mexican American music star who died tragically in a plane crash in 1959 just as his career was taking off.

The Sleepy Lagoon case and the Zoot Suit Riots triggered the first stirring of a Mexican American civil rights movement that would gather full steam in the 1960s and 1970s, under the leadership of César Chávez, known to millions simply as César.

Mojados: *Illegal or undocumented?*

The first wave of Mexican immigration, a result of the Mexican Revolution, was followed by a second that essentially continues to this day. It consists of millions of legal immigrants as well as *mojados* (wetbacks) and migrant workers who came to work in the United States and then never returned home to Mexico. The *mojados*, which literally means "the wet ones," earned this name because they often swim across the Rio Grande to American soil. Mexicans who illegally enter the

United States along the western stretch of the border, especially in California, that is lined with high wire fences are referred to as *alambristas*—the word *alambre* being Spanish for "wire."

Mojados have long endured prejudice and ridicule because of their undocumented or "illegal" status. "Undocumented" is the preferred legal term, since "illegal" suggests a criminal element which, if the situation is seen in its proper light, does not apply to these impoverished workers who cross the border in search of honest work and are the backbone of agriculture in California, the Southwest, and elsewhere.

In the decades when the Bracero Program was in effect, *mojados* streamed into the country, unsupervised and unprotected by U.S. laws. Texas, which did not welcome the first Bracero Program, was the greatest beneficiary of this source of cheap Mexican labor. When the first Bracero Program came to an end in 1947, *mojado* smuggling increased sharply, since American agribusiness depended on Mexican labor for the planting, harvesting, and distribution of crops. Although it is impossible to determine how many *mojados* entered the United States in the decade after the first Bracero Program, between 1947 and 1955 alone over 4.3 million undocumented workers were caught and returned to Mexico.

The numbers who eluded *la migra* (immigration authorities) in the 1940s and 1950s are estimated to be in the millions. Of those, many returned to Mexico by choice, but countless others stayed and became part of the growing Mexican American community. The arrival of *mojados* caused many Mexican Americans from the Southwest to venture to industrial cities in the Northeast and Midwest, where they would not have to compete with the newcomers for the low-paying jobs of the frontier states. During the 1960s Mexican Americans moved to the Midwest and Northeast in record numbers. In fact, for every *mojado* who entered the United States, one Mexican American moved north.

The *mojado* immigration continues in many guises to this

day. Some workers brave it alone and roam dusty towns of the Southwest and California until they find work, or meet up with a friend or relative who has secured a job for them. Others are smuggled in by people who profit in the millions in this human traffic. Some are even smuggled in against their will, a situation that has been likened to the African slave trade. For instance, in 1997 U.S. federal authorities uncovered a ring that over the course of four years had brought more than fifty deaf and speech-impaired Mexicans into the United States. The ring's bosses lured the Mexicans into servitude with promises of good-paying jobs and a nice lifestyle in the United States. Instead, the enslaved Mexicans were forced to peddle trinkets in airports and on the streets of Los Angeles, New York, Chicago, Boston, Philadelphia, Washington, and Baltimore. Beatings, electroshock, and threats of violence were used to subdue them.

What was "drying out the wetbacks"?

By hiring *mojados*, American agriculturalists avoided minimum wage laws, bonding and contract fees, and all the other legal and moral obligations stipulated by the Bracero Program. The dire need for workers during World War II prompted authorities to look the other way. But after the war was over, the U.S. Immigration Service decided to launch what is known as a "drying out" program. It consisted of handing out ID papers to *mojados* employed at farms in the United States, returning them across the Mexican border, and then bringing them north again as "legal" workers. At one point the Mexican and U.S. governments agreed that thousands of undocumented workers in the border regions would be given a blanket "drying-out" sanction and would be legalized en masse.

What was the El Paso Incident?

In the fall of 1948, as the cotton harvest in Texas drew near, the Mexican government demanded that Mexican workers crossing the border be paid a minimum wage of $3.00 per hundred pounds of cotton harvested. American farmers refused to pay more than $2.50 to Mexicans—although they were paying the going rate of $3.00 to all other workers. The Mexican government stood firm and forbade its nationals from going north, guarding the border with armed tanks.

In October, American farmers informed the Immigration Service that their crops would rot in the ground if Mexican workers did not start coming fast. *La migra* responded by simply opening the El Paso border to Mexican workers. In spite of the Mexican army's blockade of the border, Mexicans crossed into the United States by the thousands, braving their own government's bullets. As soon as the Mexicans stepped foot on American soil, agents representing the Texas growers loaded them onto trucks and delivered them to labor camps with the full approval of the U.S. Immigration Service.

The Mexican government voiced such loud protests that the workers were released from the labor camps and the United States extended an official apology to Mexico—but not until all the Texas cotton was harvested.

Who are the commuters?

Commuters, or "dailys," represent yet another kind of Mexican presence in the United States. Visitor permits, or "border crossing cards," are issued by U.S. authorities to Mexicans seeking to enter the United States on shopping or business trips, or for a brief vacation. Card holders are supposed to stay within twenty-five miles of the border and return to Mexico within seventy-two hours.

Many Mexican women use the visitor permits legally to work as domestics during the day in the United States (earning as little as $5.00 or $10.00 per day) and then return to Mexico at night. Others use the visitor permits for illegal extended or even permanent stays. If they are caught, they claim they are *mojados* and get returned to Mexico. The next day, they show up at the border crossings with their visitor permits and return to the United States—this time, if they're lucky, for good.

Some Mexicans with visitor permits manage to remain by buying a round-trip airline ticket to a destination far from the border as soon as they enter the United States. Once in Chicago, Detroit, or some other place, they join friends or relatives who may have found them a job. At that point they sell their return airline tickets, which provides enough money until the first paycheck. The new arrivals lose themselves in the crowd and join the vast underground American economy—but, of course, without legal recourse, and always under the threat of discovery and deportation.

The permanent arrivals, as well as commuters, migrant workers, and undocumented workers, support whole communities in Mexico with their *remesas*, or remittances. These *remesas* add up to more than $4 billion per year and are Mexico's second largest source of income from abroad, after sales of oil.

IDENTITY, ACTIVISM, AND *VIVA LA RAZA*

How have Mexican Americans served their country?

With bravery. Over 500,000 Americans of Mexican ancestry served proudly in World War II and the Korean War. In these wars, thirty-eight Mexican Americans received Congressional Medals of Honor, the highest percentage of any minority group. During the Korean and Vietnam wars, the number of Mexican Americans on the front lines was greatly disproportionate to their percentage in the general population. Thousands fought courageously and died defending their country, as detailed congressional records and the thousands of names carved on the Vietnam War Memorial testify.

World War II was a catalyst for self-awareness on the part of Mexican Americans. This was due in part to the fact that many enlisted Mexican Americans left the crowded *barrios* for the first time and were suddenly exposed to new ideas of fairness and equality and to more comfortable surroundings. They also learned new skills in the military that they could not have developed in rural America, which gave them the impetus to further their education. After the war, many took advantage of the GI Bill and enrolled in college. During and after the war, many Mexican Americans left the towns of the Southwest and went to work in urban centers that were predominantly white or multiethnic.

As Mexican Americans assimilated into mainstream society, they met with new forms of discrimination in employment, since they were competing with Anglos for better blue-collar and white-collar jobs. They were also discriminated against when it came to housing, jury selection, law enforcement, and public accommodations.

How did Mexican American activism get its start?

Before World War I, Mexican American watchdog groups existed at the local level. One such group was the *Alianza Hispano-Americana*, which was founded in Arizona in 1894 and was much like the Masonic Order. After the war, several larger Mexican American organizations formed with the League of United Latin American Citizens (LULAC) at the forefront. Organized in 1929, LULAC provided legal aid to Mexican Americans, fought for their right to vote wherever it was denied, and participated in other activities to ensure equal rights. Today LULAC boasts more than 110,000 members nationwide and continues to fight for justice for all Latinos.

In the late 1940s, the Community Service Organization (CSO) was formed. Together with other Mexican American

organizations, the CSO groomed Mexican Americans for public office. The CSO adopted the guiding principles of **Saul
Alinksy,** who later became **César Chávez**'s mentor and
friend. The organization emphasized mass political involvement and was instrumental in engineering voter registration
drives.

As a result of these fledgling political efforts, **Edward R.
Roybal,** a Mexican American from East Los Angeles, won
election to the city council in 1949. Realizing what political organization could do for Mexican Americans, **Eduardo
Quevedo,** Roybal, and **Bert Corona** founded the Mexican
American Political Association (MAPA) in 1959, which is devoted to getting Mexican Americans elected to political office.
Corona, a union organizer and political activist, dedicated
much of his life to improving conditions for Mexican American workers. Other groups, such as the American G.I. Forum,
which was formed by a Mexican American veteran, fought discrimination in the workplace and in public arenas.

On the heels of **John F. Kennedy**'s election to the presidency in 1960 (in which he garnered 85 percent of the
Mexican American vote), leaders from MAPA, LULAC, the
CSO, and Cuban American and Puerto Rican groups, met
in Phoenix with spokespersons from the Viva Kennedy Organization. This historic meeting led to the creation of the Political Association of Spanish Speaking Organizations (PASSO)
led by **Albert Peña,** commissioner of Bexar County, Texas.
At the onset, PASSO concentrated much of its effort in
Texas, where it managed to defeat the entrenched Anglo
machinery and elect an all–Mexican American city council
and mayor in the town of Crystal City—a stunning first for
Mexican Americans and a harbinger of things to come.

Who was César Chávez?

César Chávez was a migrant worker who rose from the agricultural valley of Yuma, Arizona, to form America's first suc-

cessful farm workers' union. **Robert F. Kennedy** once described the civil rights leader as "one of the heroic figures of our time."

Born in 1927, César Chávez spent his early years on his family's small farm near Yuma, Arizona. During the Great Depression his parents lost their land and the family moved to California to labor in the fields as migrant workers. César joined his parents, harvesting carrots, cotton, and grapes under the burning sun wherever they could find work. The family pulled up stakes so often that young César attended over thirty elementary schools, many segregated, and then dropped out in the seventh grade to harvest crops full time.

After serving in the U.S. Navy during World War II, César Chávez settled in Delano, California, with his wife **Helen Fabela.** It was here that he resolved to help his people out of the miserable working conditions they had accepted for generations. In 1952 Chávez joined the Community Service Organization (CSO), an agency devoted to helping poor people across the nation. At the time the CSO was organizing Mexican Americans into a coalition so that they would eventually be able to confront the rampant discrimination in society. Chávez's job was to register Mexican Americans in San Jose to vote, and to serve as their advocate before welfare boards, immigration authorities, and the police. In 1958 Mexican American **Dolores Huerta** became his principal assistant.

By the 1960s, César Chávez had turned his full attention to the plight of exploited Mexican American farm workers. In 1962 he formed a union, the Farm Workers Association (FWA), which was the forerunner of the National Farm Workers Association (NFWA). By 1965 Chávez had recruited 1,700 families and had persuaded two large California growers to raise the wages of migrant workers. A year later the NFWA merged with an organization of Filipino workers to form the United Farm Workers Organizing Committee (UFWOC).

The UFWOC went to work immediately picketing grape growers in Delano who paid unfair wages. This marked the beginning of *La Huelga* ("The Strike"), the strike against grape growers in the San Joaquin, Imperial, and Coachella valleys, which lasted five years and raised America's consciousness about the horrendous conditions Mexican American farm workers had endured for many decades. To gain support for his cause, which he called *La Causa*, César Chávez staged hunger strikes, peaceful marches, and sing-ins, in the spirit of the Indian leader **Mahatma Gandhi.** He also had himself and UFWOC members arrested in order to gain attention.

Although he was a rather meek and self-effacing person whose gifts lay not so much in public speaking as in leading, César Chávez was able to rouse the multitudes with his deeply felt convictions. He also captured the imagination of fair-minded people all across the nation: seventeen million Americans joined his boycott and refused to buy California table grapes for five straight years. Priests, nuns, rabbis, Protestant ministers, college students, unionists, writers, and influential politicians, including **Hubert Humphrey** and **Robert F. Kennedy,** lent their support, demanding long-overdue justice for Mexican and Mexican American farm workers.

In 1970, after losing millions of dollars to *La Huelga*, the California grape growers capitulated and agreed to grant rights to workers and raise their minimum wage. It was the first of many successful boycotts that César Chávez was to lead on behalf of grape pickers, lettuce pickers, and all the other disenfranchised groups so dear to his heart. Chávez believed in fairness and equality for all people. He also fought for civil rights for African Americans, women, and in later years, gays and lesbians.

La Causa had its share of setbacks after that first victory and membership in the UFWOC waned, but Mexican Americans never lost faith in César Chávez, their beloved leader, who they likened to Moses, bringing them across the desert into a land of possibilities, with greater justice for all. César Chávez's untimely death on April 23, 1993, at the age of sixty-six, elicited eulogies and expressions of bereavement from national and international leaders, and warranted an obituary on the front page of the *New York Times*, in which he was described as a third-generation farm boy from Arizona who had dared to dream.

What is the Chicano Movement?

The Chicano Movement emerged from the unrest caused by the Vietnam War and the African American civil rights movement in the 1960s, led by **Martin Luther King, Jr.** By forming one of the first unions to fight for the rights of Mexican Americans, **César Chávez** did much to propel the Chicano Movement, and in many ways he has remained the symbolic leader of *la raza*. But several other early Mexican American civil rights advocates and groups also contributed to the formation of the Chicano Movement.

Chicano student organizations, particularly in California, were actively involved in educating Mexican Americans about the injustices they had suffered as a people and in urging them to fight for their rights as American citizens. The student organizations held demonstrations, demanding that their language, culture, and contributions be recognized in all educational institutions from elementary schools to universities. In the 1960s and 1970s the United Mexican Students, *El Movimiento Estudiantil Chicano de Aztlán* (MECHA) and many others were the first groups to call for an awareness of "Mexicanism" and Latino heritage. The famous Brown Berets, patterned after the Black Berets, formed dozens of chapters throughout the Southwest. Their platform, while committed to nonviolence, vigorously emphasized the inclusion of Mexican American contributions in all school curricula, as well as a permanent place for Mexican American writers and artists in cultural and civic institutions.

One of the legends of the early Chicano Movement is **Reies López Tijerina,** an activist born in Texas, whose family land had been seized by Anglos. Convinced that the social problems Mexican Americans faced was connected to the loss of their ancestral lands, Tijerina organized a separatist movement called *Alianza Federal de Mercedes* (Federal Alliance of Land Grants) in 1963. The organization demanded that millions of acres in New Mexico, Colorado, Utah, California, and Texas be returned to the descendants of their original Mexican owners. The *Alianza* grew to around twenty thousand members and proposed turning part of the "reclaimed" land into a utopian Mexican American separatist community. In the mid-1960s many confrontations arose between Tijerina's activists and army and state troopers who sought to prevent them from "seizing" the lands to which they laid claim.

On July 4, 1966, Tijerina led a sixty-two-mile march from Albuquerque to Santa Fe, New Mexico, where he presented New Mexico governor **Jack Campbell** with a petition requesting that legislation be passed that would allow for an investigation of Mexican land grants. Tijerina announced that he represented six thousand Mexican Americans who were direct heirs to lands that had unlawfully been seized from their forbears. Tijerina's efforts were unsuccessful and he resigned as leader of the *Alianza* in 1970, but his speeches and demonstrations served to focus attention on Mexican American grievances and the fight for equal rights. Tijerina's exploits eventually got him into trouble; in the 1970s he spent time behind bars for attempting to take over part of the Kit Carson National Forest. Chicano activist **Rodolfo "Corky" Gonzáles** founded *La Cruzada para La Justicia* (the Crusade for Justice), in Denver in 1966, which sought to address social ills in Mexican American communities. Gonzáles's vision, like Tijerina's, was separatist in nature. Among his goals was to persuade the United Nations to hold a plebiscite in the Southwest to determine independence for *la raza* and the creation of a separate Mexican American state.

Toward that aim, Gonzáles created *El Plan Espiritual de Aztlán*, the Spiritual Plan of Aztlán. Aztlán is the name Mexican Americans have given to their ancestral lands in the Southwest. It is a mythical homeland where the Aztec, a nomadic tribe, are said to have lived before journeying southward in 1325 and founding Tenochtitlán, the capital of the Aztec empire, on the site of present-day Mexico City. The Spiritual Plan of Aztlán, which was voted on in 1969 by two thousand representatives from one hundred Chicano organizations, called for a revival of Mexican American values and the creation of a political party based on self-determination. While a separate Mexican American state was never created under the plan, it served to reinforce Mexican American identity and self-respect, and to inspire Mexican American youth.

Corky Gonzáles is also well known for the 1964 epic poem he penned, *"Yo soy Joaquín,"* ("I Am Joaquín"—referring to **Joaquín Murieta**). In the poem Gonzáles explores the plight of Mexican Americans, and admonishes Chicano youth to aim high and seize their rightful place in American society. *"Yo soy Joaquín"* continues to inspire millions of young Mexican Americans and other Latino youths and is taught in many Latino history and literature courses in the United States today.

José Ángel Gutiérrez, another Chicano leader, established the political party *La Raza Unida* (Mexican Americans United) in 1970, which sought to end discrimination against Chicanos by helping them gain access to mainstream politics and financial institutions. Gutiérrez also advocated bilingual and bicultural education, which he saw as a means of preserving Mexican American identity.

César Chávez, Reies López Tijerina, Corky Gonzáles, José Ángel Gutiérrez, and other leaders of the Chicano Movement were instrumental in righting many of the wrongs the Mexican American community had withstood for centuries. With their efforts, Mexican American workers won the right to fair pay and humane treatment. Medical services, utilities, and sewage and water systems were introduced in impoverished Mexican American communities, doors to educational institutions were opened to Mexican Americans (and eventually Chicano studies programs were put in place), and works by Mexicans and Mexican Americans made it into libraries. These leaders also were instrumental in the election of hundreds of Mexican Americans to political office, school boards, and civic organizations, who continue to effect positive change.

MEXICAN AMERICAN WOMEN: REVOLUTIONARIES, THINKERS, HEALERS, AND MOTHERS

What exactly is machismo?

The word "machismo" has the same root as "macho," which is Spanish for "male gender." But, of course, machismo is much more than that—it connotes strength, bravery, power, and importance, all the qualities viewed as ideal in a patriarchal culture. The phrase "macho man," coined by the Village People in their hit song "Macho, Macho Man," refers to a tough hombre (another word Americans borrowed from Spanish, meaning, of course, "man") who struts his stuff and gets no guff.

With machismo in place, it is no wonder that historical accounts of Mexican Americans and all Latinos, until recent times, give short shrift to women's contributions. In this respect, Mexican American history is no different from Anglo history as it is described in books—men are almost always the protagonists.

Is there such a thing as macha?

There is one aspect of machismo that has eluded Anglos, but that is very much a part of the Mexican American, and to a lesser extent Latino, outlook on the world. This is that a woman can also be very macho (muy macha). In fact, mariachis on both sides of the border sing dozens of popular songs about how macha their women are. This does not mean that they are masculine or imitate men, but rather that they are brave, strong, and resolute, and probably drink tequila straight and eat jalapeño chiles whole—all macho virtues, but not necessarily limited to the male gender. Thus Mexicans and Mexican Americans often refer to a gutsy woman as *muy macha*, without challenging her womanliness in the least. If anything, being *muy macha* adds to it. After all, if a society holds certain qualities in high esteem, doesn't it figure that these qualities enhance the individual?

Still, institutionalized machismo has relegated Mexican American women and other Latinas to secondary status. Mexican American women have only recently strived to claim the respect they deserve. In her book entitled *To Split a Human: Mitos, Machos y la Mujer* (1985), feminist scholar **Carmen Tafolla** bemoans the fact that the "Chicana may . . . find herself curiously placed on a borderland between two forces. In one camp, her struggle against sexism is trivialized. In the other, her struggle against racism is ignored."

What's a curandera?

A *curandera* is a Mexican or Mexican American, usually a woman, who practices the ancient art of spiritual or herbal "folk" healing that is rooted in the Americas. Many *curanderas* combine their faith in the Virgin of Guadalupe with knowledge of herbology and a reverence for the ancient Maya and Aztec gods. Throughout California and the Southwest, thousands of cases have been documented of *curanderas* healing children and adults of every illness known to humanity—from whooping cough to cancer. *Curanderas* are so highly esteemed among Mexican Americans that they are often on the staff at medical clinics and are also consulted in psychiatric cases. Some *curanderas* have gained enormous recognition and give packed lectures and workshops on the art of *curanderismo*.

What's a partera?

A *partera* is a midwife—and much more. In economically deprived Mexican American communities where, increasingly, children are born into households headed by single women, *parteras* not only deliver babies at home, they serve as *curanderas*, help keep families running while mothers recover, and even baby-sit. Delivering a child at home is still preferred by many rural and urban Mexican Americans, especially in the Southwest, not only for financial reasons, but for the comfort derived from having someone they know well and trust in charge of the birth.

So who are the notable women in Mexican and Chicano history?

Even when their voices were silenced, the influence of Mexican and Mexican American women was profoundly felt throughout history.

Chicano feminists include **Sor Juana Inés de la Cruz** in their pantheon of heroines. Sor Juana, a Mexican nun and a mystic poet who lived in the seventeenth century, was the first known woman in Mexico to protest the violence perpetrated against women by men. She expressed her opinions on the matter in her classic essay *Contra las injusticias de hombre al hablar de la mujer* ("Against the Injustices of Men in Talking About Women"). Sor Juana dared challenge patriarchy and still remained a beloved saint for men as well as women—who regarded her as *muy macha*.

Another daring woman was **Francisca de Hozas** who accompanied **Francisco Vásquez de Coronado** during his early expeditions. She often knew the best way to go, though Coronado took her directions reluctantly. Other women explorers who accompanied Coronado on his dangerous forays into the Southwest were **María Maldonado** and **Señora Caballero**.

During Mexico's struggle for independence, women performed extraordinary acts of heroism. **Manuela Medina,** who was nicknamed *"La Capitana,"* led an entire company of rebels and won several crucial battles. **Doña Josefa Ortiz de Dominguez,** called *"La Corregidora,"* or "the Chief," also fought valiantly and distinguished herself with her flawless marksmanship. **Gertrudis Bocanegra** organized revolutionary armies and took part in the *Grito de Dolores* in 1810. She was later taken prisoner and executed by Spanish loyalists.

During the frontier days, hundreds of Mexican American women struggled bravely for their rights and sometimes paid with their lives. In 1863, **Doña Chepita Rodríguez,** who had fled to Texas with her father after **General Santa Anna** rose to power in 1835, fought off the advances of two Anglos who stormed into her cabin. She was accused of murdering one of the Anglos when his body was found a little while later. She has gone down in history as one of only three women hanged in Texas. In California, **Josefa Segovia** was lynched for stabbing a drunk Anglo miner who tore down the door of her cabin on July 4, 1851, and called her a whore when she asked him to pay for the damage.

The women warriors of the Mexican Revolution of 1910, and the countless other women who stayed behind the front lines cleaning equipment, preparing meals, and nursing the wounded, came to be known as *"Las Adelitas"* ("Little Adeles"). The original **Adela** was **Pancho Villa**'s lover and she often rode with him astride his horse, blasting away at the *hacendados* with a shotgun fired one-handed. *Las Adelitas* became a symbol of feminist empowerment for the Chicano Movement after the 1970s.

Mexican American heroines of the twentieth century include **Ema Tenayuca,** who in the 1930s organized the first successful strike of pecan shellers in San Antonio, Texas, and lit the flame of possibility that would later burn in **César Chávez**'s heart. During the mass deportation of Mexican Americans in the 1930s, **Josefina Sierro** organized an underground railroad in the tradition of **Harriet Tubman,** bringing hundreds of American citizens of Mexican descent back home to the United States. She also singlehandedly negotiated with **Vice President Henry Wallace** to make Los Angeles out of bounds to military personnel during the Zoot Suit Riots—an act that helped bring an end to the violence. (One aspect of the Zoot Suit Riots that is often ignored is that the attacks were not only racially motivated, but also sexually charged. The sailors and Anglo civilians who went looking for Mexican Americans to beat up also raped dozens of Mexican American women. This ignited the macho spirit of the Mexican American men, who did not want gringos near their women.)

Among the leaders of the Chicano labor movement of the 1960s and 1970s were **Marcela Lucero Trujillo,** an activist in **Corky Gonzáles**'s Crusade for Justice; **Virginia Musquiz,** who was instrumental in organizing *La Raza Unida* party; and **Dolores Huerta,** who aided César Chávez in organizing Mexican American farm workers into the United Farm Workers Organizing Committee (UFWOC). Huerta played a critical role in the union's success in *La Huelga*, the strike against grape growers in California. In 1988, she was brutally attacked by police officers in front of a hotel in San Francisco where **President George Bush** was attending a campaign dinner party. She was conducting a peaceful demonstration in response to the president's remarks that he would not support the UFWOC boycott of table grapes.

CULTURAL HERITAGE : A MOVABLE FIESTA

Who are some of the great Mexican American writers of today?

In the Southwest, where hundreds of ethnic jokes aimed at Mexican Americans make the rounds, there is one that goes: "Why is there no Mexican literature? Answer: Because spray paint went on the market not that long ago!" This double-edged joke insinuates that Mexican American mural artists paint nothing but graffiti and that Mexican Americans have created no body of literature, and thus no culture. This, of course, could not be further from the truth. In fact, Mexican Americans and other Latinos are among the most dynamic writers on the contemporary literary scene.

There are far too many Mexican American writers to count, but here are the most prominent, with just a few of their works cited. Among women writers are **Estela Portillo Trambley,** *Rain of Scorpions* (1975); **Patricia Preciado Martín,** *Images and Conversations: Mexican Americans Recall a Southwestern Past* (1983); **Sandra Cisneros,** *The House on Mango Street* (1984) and *Woman Hollering Creek and Other Stories* (1991); **Denise Chávez,** *The Last of the Menu Girls* (1986) and *Face of an Angel* (1993); **Ana Castillo,** *The Mixquiahuala Letters* (1986) and *Loverboys* (1996); **Cherríe Moraga,** who writes on feminist and lesbian themes and coedited *This Bridge Called My Back: Writings by Radical Women of Color* (1981) with **Gloria Anzaldúa,** editor of several anthologies; **Alma Villanueva,** *Bloodroot* (1977); **Helen María Viramontes,** *The Moths and Other Stories* (1985); **Montserrat Fontes,** *First Confession* (1991) and *Dreams of the Centaur* (1996); and **Demetria Martínez,** *Mother Tongue* (1994).

Among the men are: **John Rechy,** *City of Night* (1963); **Rodolfo "Corky" Gonzáles,** *"Yo soy Joaquín/I Am Joaquín"* (1964); **José Antonio Villareal,** *Pocho* (1970); **Tomás Rivera,** *And the Earth Did Not Devour Him* (1971); **Rolando Hinojosa,** *Estampas del valle y otras obras/Sketches of the Valley and Other Works* (1973); **Rudolfo Anaya,** *Bless Me, Ultima* (1972); **Oscar "Zeta" Acosta,** *The Autobiography of a Brown Buffalo* (1972); **Gary Soto,** *The Tale of Sunlight* (1978) and *Black Hair* (1985); activist **Rodolfo "Rudy" Acuña,** *Occupied America: A History of Chicanos* (1981); **Richard Rodriguez,** *Hunger of Memory: The Education of Richard Rodriguez* (1981) and *Days of Obligation: An Argument with My Mexican Father* (1993); and **Victor Villaseñor,** *Macho!* (1971) and *Rain of Gold* (1991).

Chicano mural painting: When is art on a wall not graffiti?

Chicano mural painting has its roots in ancient Mexico, when the early Olmecs adorned walls with paintings. The Mexican mural tradition underwent a renaissance in the 1920s with internationally acclaimed artists like **José Clemente Orozco, David Alfaro Siqueiros,** and **Diego Rivera,** also known as the Big Three, leading the way. In the 1920s and 1930s, the U.S. government commissioned these Mexican mural masters to create public murals in America that promoted the agenda of the Works Progress Administration and the New Deal, namely social reform to benefit the working class and end poverty.

Through their work in the United States, Orozco, Siqueiros, and Rivera laid the foundation for the emergence of the Chicano mural tradition in the 1960s and 1970s as an expression of the Chicano Movement. Hundreds of young Mexican Americans took to the streets of cities in California, the Southwest, and the Midwest to celebrate their cultural heritage and transform the bleak urban landscape of the *barrios* and working-class neighborhoods with large murals.

One of the founders of the mural movement in Los Angeles is **Judy Baca,** who launched the first mural program in Los Angeles in 1974, which created over 250 public murals during its ten years in operation. Judy Baca's most renowned work is *The Great Wall of Los Angeles*, a half-mile long mural that chronicles the history of Los Angeles. It took the efforts of 40 artists and nearly 450 young people from different ethnic backgrounds to complete the project. In 1988, Baca developed another mural program called the Great Walls Unlimited at the request of L.A. mayor **Tom Bradley.** Since its inception, the program has created over 70 murals in nearly every ethnic neighborhood in the city.

Other Los Angeles muralists painting politically motivated work in the 1970s were members of the group called Los Four: **Frank Romero, Carlos Almarez, Gilbert Sánchez Luján,** and **Beto de la Rocha.** An artist by the name of **Gronk** and others, under the guidance of **Charles Félix,** painted the Estradas Courts murals, the most extensive project in East Los Angeles. The murals, with their larger than life images of Aztec gods, figures from the Spanish conquest, and Our

Lady of Guadalupe, serve to remind Chicanos of their noble origins.

Chicano Park in San Diego contains some of the finest muralist art in the tradition of the 1920s and 1930s. It all started when some residents from the surrounding *barrio* were evicted from their dwellings in the late 1960s to make way for the Coronado Bridge. As compensation, the community earned the right to build a park and a Chicano cultural center in the area under the bridge. What had been a jungle of ugly concrete pillars metamorphosed into a park adorned with murals depicting the history and struggle of Mexican Americans. Murals at the freeway entrances portray **César Chávez** addressing Mexican Americans and the struggles of Mexican workers and peasants from the past, such as **Zapata**'s guerillas. These murals which Chicanos call "living museums," represent the artistic expression and cultural and social aspirations of a people whose voices are just now beginning to be heard.

How many holidays do Mexican Americans celebrate?

There are too many to count because many towns and cities with a sizable Mexican American population have their own special holidays celebrating patron saints (*santos*), which combine Spanish, Aztec, Maya, Pueblo, and other native cultural and religious elements. Fiestas in honor of patron saints usually commence in the main Catholic church or cathedral, where a special service is held. Then the people take the town *santo* to the main plaza and place it in a shrine or bower for all to see. They worship the saint by dancing around it, playing hypnotic drum music, and singing religious chants. At the end of the day the *santo* is returned to the church.

An important holiday observed by many Mexican Americans, particularly in California and the Southwest, is *El Día de los Muertos* (the Day of the Dead) which falls on

November 1, lasting until the next day. During the Day of the Dead festivities, Mexican Americans do not mourn the deceased family members and friends who are thought to pay a visit. Instead they interact with their souls in the belief that but a fragile boundary separates the living and dead. Many Mexican Americans set up *ofrendas*, or miniature altars, in their homes which they bedeck with candles, incense, favorite foods and objects of the deceased, flowers (especially yellow marigolds, the traditional flower of the dead), loaves of bread of the dead (commonly in the shape of skulls and crossbones), and little colorfully decorated candy skulls. The celebrants often go to the cemetery to tidy the graves and hold a picnic for the dead souls who are said to regain their appetite on this holiday.

Another important Mexican American celebration is the feast of Our Lady of Guadalupe, the patron saint of Mexico, who is honored on December 12. The holiday memorializes the appearance of the Virgin Mary to a converted native named **Juan Diego** in Mexico in 1521. The Virgin miraculously emblazoned her image on Juan Diego's poncho, and this miracle led to the conversion of masses of people in Mexico. When **Father Hidalgo** spoke her name as he rallied Mexicans to fight for independence with his *Grito de Dolores*, Our Lady of Guadalupe was transformed into an emblem of Mexican nationalism. Catholics have embraced the saint as their own. Many maintain that she is not the Virgin Mary at all, and they forgo the Festival of the Immaculate Conception of the Virgin Mary for the Feast of Our Lady of Guadalupe.

During the Christmas season, many Mexican Americans observe *Las Posadas*, the nine days before Christmas when mass is held at each sunrise and celebrants recreate Mary and Joseph's journey to Bethlehem and their search for shelter at an inn (*una posada*). *Las Posadas* culminates with *Misa de Gallo*, Midnight mass on Christmas Eve. On Christmas Day, most Mexican Americans stay at home and partake of traditional Mexican fare, but children do not get their presents until

January 6, *El Día de los Reyes Magos* (Three Kings' Day) which heralds the arrival of the Magi to Bethlehem bearing gifts for the baby Jesus.

In Santa Fe, New Mexico, the Burning of Zozobra (Old Man Gloom) is a major celebration. Old Man Gloom, a forty-foot marionette, taller than most buildings in the town, is burned on the main square. After "Gloom" has been consumed by fire, the townspeople dance in the streets, shouting *"Viva la fiesta!"* The next day, the town holds a pet parade, in which children can show off real or imaginary animal friends. The parade is so much fun that adults are known to borrow a child for the day so that they can march, too.

Why do Mexican Americans celebrate Cinco de Mayo?

Cinco de Mayo (the Fifth of May) commemorates Mexican independence from Napoleonic domination. On this day in 1862 the Mexicans defeated the French at the city of Puebla. Mexican independence from Spanish rule is celebrated on September 16. Both holidays are observed in Mexico, but in the United States *Cinco de Mayo* is considered the official independence day and is the biggest secular celebration of the year. Mexican Americans hold fiestas and parades to celebrate their cultural heritage in the hundreds of towns with large Mexican American communities. You might say that *Cinco de Mayo* is as important to Mexican Americans as St. Patrick's Day is to Irish Americans—and just as on St. Patrick's Day everyone is Irish, so it is on *Cinco de Mayo*, when even Anglos can turn Mexican overnight and join in the revelry.

What's a charreada?

The *charreada* is Mexico's national sport and a very popular one among Mexican Americans. *Charros* are Mexican cowboys and *charreadas* are rodeos. Only they tend to be slightly more dangerous than the regular Western ones. Skilled horsemen (and women) perform steps such as *el paso de la muerte* ("the pass of death"), in which the *charro* shimmies off the saddle and leaps onto the back of a speeding wild horse that has just been whipped into a frenzy by three other *charros*. *Charros* also perform intricate rope tricks while standing atop a moving horse, rope cows, bust steer, and do just about everything else imaginable on and off a bronco. The American rodeo is descended from the Mexican *charreada*. Incidentally, "rodeo" is a Spanish word meaning "a gathering place for cattle."

What are mariachis?

Mariachis, a hallmark of Mexican America, are strolling bands of musicians dressed in traditional Spanish costumes adorned with sequins, mirrors, glass, and other shiny materials, and sporting large-brimmed, richly decorated sombreros. The musicians, also called mariachis, play traditional romantic songs on the guitar and the violin and serenade the crowd in restaurants, at fiestas, and at weddings and other celebrations. Since 1979, when the first International Mariachi Conference took place in San Antonio, Texas, mariachi music has evolved into a symbol of Mexican culture in the United States. In recent years, the popularity of mariachi has skyrocketed as Mexican American youths explore their musical heritage. Women are just breaking into the male-dominated profession. The most famous of all the female mariachis is **Nydia Rojas,** a teen singing sensation who has even performed for **President Clinton.**

What's a piñata party?

Piñata parties are held on children's birthdays and other special occasions. The piñata (from *piño*, meaning pine tree) is a hollow clay or papier-mâché sculpture of a donkey, star, or other such shape, that is decorated with brightly colored paper and sequins. The piñata is filled with toys and candies and then hung from the ceiling. Once the party gets going, the children break the piñata by whacking it with long sticks, releasing the surprises hidden inside. The best part is scrambling for the goodies strewn on the floor.

Did Montezuma II eat tacos?

Montezuma II and the Aztec people savored versions of some of the same delicious dishes served today in the thousands of Mexican restaurants and *taquerías* (taco places) all across America. Among the many foods **Cortés** and his men discovered on Montezuma's lavish table were tomatoes, avocados, chiles, corn, coconuts, papayas, tamales, tortillas, turkey, duck, pork, and much to the disgust of the Spanish, little hairless dogs. Traditional Mexican cuisine, like Mexican culture, is a blend of native, Spanish, and to some extent African ingredients and methods. However, the ingredients prized by the native peoples who were living in Mexico and the American Southwest when the conquistadors made landfall are still at the heart of Mexican cooking to this day.

Are tacos, burritos, gorditas, and fajitas the Mexican national dishes?

No way. All of the above are generally regarded as *antojitos* ("little whims") or hors d'oeuvres—or to put it in more contemporary terms, fast food. Unfortunately very few Mexican restaurants in America serve anything but *antojitos*, and outside of cities and towns with a large Mexican American population the food is usually quite Americanized. For instance, in a really authentic *taquería* in America the fillings for tacos and burritos include a vast array of meats, including marinated pork, grilled beef, tongue, stewed pork brains, and braised head meat that are sliced to order into small pieces and folded into warm corn or flour tortillas. Diners then dress their order with an assortment of salsas, such as tomatillo salsa or tomato-cilantro salsa (*salsa fresca*).

In recent times, more and more restaurants serving authentic Mexican dinner fare have opened up, especially in southern California. In these establishments, some of which specialize in regional Mexican cooking, diners can sample everything from *Cabrito al horno*, roasted baby goat, to *Pollo pibil*, a Yucatecán dish of chicken baked in banana leaves, to *Pescado a la Veracruzana*, fish cooked in a sauce of tomatoes, capers, and green olives. Many also serve the national dish of Mexico: *Mole poblano,* pieces of chicken smothered in a scrumptious sauce made from chiles, nuts, seeds, onions, garlic, tomatoes, bread, cinnamon, cloves, coriander, and the secret ingredient: unsweetened chocolate.

Is chocolate really Mexican?

The Aztec were the first to husk, roast, and grind cocoa beans, *cacao*. They mixed the ground cocoa beans with spices for an unsweetened drink called *xocolatl*, meaning "bitter water." **Montezuma II** believed *xocolatl* was an aphrodisiac, and he supposedly drank fifty cups of the elixir each day. Europeans took cocoa beans back to the Old World, where they created their own hot chocolate by omitting the spices in the Aztec recipe and adding sugar. Europeans eventually developed the expertise to make all sorts of confections out of cocoa that nowadays have a worldwide following. For that reason, many people think of Belgium and Switzerland—not Mexico—when they hear the word chocolate.

Back in Mexico, Montezuma's elixir evolved, but never lost its spice. Nowadays Mexicans and Mexican Americans make the drink with steamed milk, sugar, vanilla extract, and lots of cinnamon.

CHILES

There are many varieties of chiles, used fresh or dried, in Mexican American kitchens. Immature chiles, which are usually green and rarely dried, are sold fresh and canned, either whole or diced. Most green chiles turn orange-red, red, or crimson when ripe. Ripe chiles are used fresh or are dried, and then left whole or pulverized. Chiles are hot thanks to a substance known as capsaicin that is concentrated in the ribs and seeds which are always removed for cooking. Contrary to popular belief, mature chiles are no hotter than immature ones.

FRESH CHILES
1. **Anaheim**   This mildly hot pale to bright green chile is also known as the **California chile pepper,** the **long green chile,** *chile verde,* and *chile verde del norte,* and is available year round in some parts of the country. Ripe red Anaheims have a sweet note. Dried red Anaheims are sold whole or ground.

2. **Güero**   This is the generic name for any pale yellow chile used in Mexican cooking that is three to five inches in length and one and a half to two inches in diameter.

3. **Habanero**   The habanero, meaning "from Havana" (although chiles play no part in mild Cuban cooking!) is the hottest of all chiles. It's thirty times hotter than a jalapeño.

4. **Jalapeño**   The medium-hot green jalapeño is the chile that has received the widest recognition in the United States. Red jalapeños have a sweet flavor, but are not as easy to obtain. Smoked, dried red jalapeños are called **chipotle chiles.**

5. **New Mexico**   Medium-hot New Mexico chiles, which are green when immature and red when mature, are grown

exclusively in New Mexico. They are one of the few chiles that are dried when still green. Dried red New Mexico chiles are used whole or ground.

6. **Pequín**   This very hot chile has a sweet, smoky flavor.

7. **Poblano**   Mildly hot poblano chiles are green-black when immature and turn red when ripe; they are sometimes mistakenly called **ancho** or **pasilla chiles.** The confusion stems from the fact that, when dried, poblanos change name. Dried red poblanos that are dark brown are known as **mulato chiles,** while those that are brick red are called ancho chiles.

8. **Serrano**   This chile, which measures one to two inches in length and one-half inch in diameter, is the hottest one commonly available in American supermarkets. It is green when immature and red when ripe.

9. **Tabasco**   This extremely hot chile is used almost exclusively in the manufacture of Tabasco Brand Pepper Sauce.

10. **Tepín**   This very hot chile the size of a cranberry grows wild in parts of the Southwest.

CHILES AVAILABLE MAINLY DRIED

1. **Cascabel**   This medium-hot chile gets its name from the rattling noise it makes when shaken (*cascabel* is Spanish for "rattle"). It is used most often ground.

2. **Cayenne**   These bright red chiles are very hot and are usually used ground.

3. **Chile de árbol**   These chiles are bright red when dried and are used whole or ground. (On rare occasions they may be found fresh in markets.)

4. **Guajillo**   This mild to medium-hot reddish-brown chile is used whole or ground.

How is New Southwestern Cuisine different from traditional Mexican cooking of the Southwest?

If you have ever tried a Curried Chicken Tortilla with Coconut Rice, Cucumber Raita, and Spicy Peanut Sauce (a creation of the Arizona Cafe in New York), you know the difference. This cooking style involves blending ingredients from the world's pantry (Asian and French elements dominate) with Mexican staples such as tortillas and chiles to create ingenius, tasty, and oftentimes whimsical dishes. New Southwestern Cuisine has been all the rage among foodies in the 1990s.

What are pulque, mescal, and tequila?

Pulque, the fermented sap of the maguey cactus, is a thick, sweet liquor. It has ancient roots; the Aztec commonly used it as a ceremonial drink. Mescal is a liquor derived from a relative of the maguey cactus and has a bitter-almond flavor. Mescal was originally made in Tequila, in the Mexican state of Jalisco, and so tequila is a kind of mescal. It closely resembles the cactus "juice" the native peoples drank many centuries ago. Tequila is often used as a chaser to cool down food spiced with hot chiles. Water is not recommended for cooling your lips; it gives you a little relief, but then your mouth feels hotter, as it spreads the hot oil from the chiles. In recent years, tequila has beaten pulque as the official Mexican alcoholic beverage.

CUATRO

Puerto Ricans

What is Puerto Rico?

EARLY HISTORY

Why do Puerto Ricans call their island Borinquen?

How did San Juan come to be called Puerto Rico, and Puerto Rico San Juan?

Why did Ponce de León bring African slaves to Puerto Rico?

What do Puerto Ricans mean when they say "negro"?

How did Sir Francis Drake get his comeuppance in Puerto Rico?

Who was Marshall Alejandro O'Reilly?

A GROWING NATIONAL IDENTITY

How did Puerto Ricans feel about Spanish rule?

What's a machete?

What's a jibaro?

Who was Luis Muñoz Rivera, and why is he called the George Washington of Puerto Rico?

Was Puerto Rico really free for only a week?

What was the Monroe Doctrine?

What was the Spanish-American War all about, and why is it called the first media-staged war?

Who were Teddy Roosevelt's Rough Riders, and how did they help him win the U.S. presidency?

What was the Roosevelt Corollary?

Who was Eugenio María de Hostos, and why is a school in New York City named after him?

How did Puerto Ricans feel about being a U.S. protectorate?

Who was the first elected Puerto Rican governor, and what did he do that was so important?

*How did Puerto Rico become a commonwealth . . .
and what's a commonwealth, anyway?*

*Why did the Independentistas try to assassinate
President Truman?*

*Why isn't Puerto Rican migration considered
immigration, and how did it get started?*

Commonwealth vs. statehood: What's the big deal?

*How many Puerto Ricans are there, and where do
they live?*

How are mainland Puerto Ricans doing?

PUERTO RICAN CULTURAL LIFE

What's a santo?

What's a botánica?

What's compadrazco?

What's a pahry?

So what do mainland Puerto Ricans do at a pahry?

*What is Puerto Rican cooking like, and what's the
Puerto Rican national dish?*

What is Puerto Rico?

Quick, name a place that's improperly called a country; whose residents are American citizens but are barred from voting in U.S. elections unless they happen to live on the mainland; whose capital city is nearly a hundred years older than Jamestown; and whose people are fiercely proud of their land, heritage, and Afro-Spanish traditions.

If you answered "Puerto Rico," you're familiar with some of the many contradictions that characterize the history and political status of this earthly paradise, which lies 1,000 miles southeast of Miami and measures about 100 miles long and 35 miles wide.

EARLY HISTORY

Why do Puerto Ricans call their island Borinquen?

Borinquen, which means "the land of the brave lord," is the name the Taino, the indigenous inhabitants of the island, gave Puerto Rico. Taino, by the way, was not what they called themselves before the Spanish conquest. **Christopher Columbus** christened this group of Arawak Indians Taino, meaning "peace," because it was the first word they uttered when they laid eyes on the conquistador.

The Taino were peaceful people indeed. They fished, hunted, and gathered berries, pineapples, and other fruits in their land of plenty. They slept in *hamacas*, a word that entered the English language as "hammock." So too did *huracán* ("hurricane"), the god of ferocious winds whom the Taino understood no one would ever tame.

Incidentally, "Boricua" from Borinquen, is what Puerto Ricans call each other, especially on the U.S. mainland, to reinforce ties and reaffirm ancient roots.

How did San Juan come to be called Puerto Rico, and Puerto Rico San Juan?

It all began on September 23, 1493, when **Christopher Columbus,** back in the New World on his second voyage, came upon several Taino Indians on the island of Guadaloupe who had been taken as slaves by the barbarous Carib people. They were from Borinquen, and begged Columbus to take them back to their island. He granted them their wish.

Columbus was impressed with the wealth of Borinquen, with its lush vegetation and more than two hundred species of birds. He immediately took possession of the island in the name of **Queen Isabella** and **King Ferdinand** of Spain. He called the isle San Juan Bautista, after **John the Baptist** and Isabella and Ferdinand's son, **Juan.** At first, the island of San Juan Bautista was ignored for the most part by the Spanish, who had bigger fish to fry in Mexico and Peru. As for Columbus, he was more interested in Hispaniola and did not settle Puerto Rico.

Fifteen years later, in 1508, the Spanish nobleman **Juan Ponce de León** was sent with a crew of fifty to explore the island and find out whether it harbored any gold. There was very little to speak of, as the Spanish found out later, but the minute Ponce de León glimpsed the bay at San Juan, he exclaimed, *"Ay que puerto rico!"* ("Oh what a rich port!"); from that moment on, the island was known as Puerto Rico, and the port where Ponce de León anchored as San Juan (short for San Juan Bautista). San Juan, of course, was designated the capital of Puerto Rico, and remains so to this day. Ponce de León was appointed the first governor of Puerto Rico. The island's second largest city and the hometown of thousands of mainland Puerto Ricans still bears his name—Ponce.

Why did Ponce de León bring African slaves to Puerto Rico?

The Taino welcomed the Spanish conquistadors with open arms, believing them to be gods. However, they soon regretted having been so friendly. The Spanish began their quest for gold by enslaving the native people and taking their lands. In exchange for mining the small deposits of placer gold found on the island and tending the fields to feed the conquistadors, the Taino were given lessons in Catholicism and Spanish history and culture. Hundreds of Taino died of exhaustion, malnutrition, and mistreatment. Still others perished because they had no defenses against the European diseases the Spanish soldiers brought with them. In desperation, the Taino rebelled in 1511 after their pleas for better working conditions went unanswered. **Ponce de León** responded by having 6,000 Taino shot on the spot. Those who survived the slaughter took to the mountains or rowed away to other islands.

Ponce de León was in a predicament. He needed laborers badly to keep Puerto Rico running smoothly. His solution was to ask **King Ferdinand** for permission to bring African slaves to the island. In 1513 the first shipload of Africans arrived. With them also came smallpox, which took thousands of Taino lives. By 1515, fewer than four thousand Taino remained in Puerto Rico—compared to the thirty or forty thousand **Columbus** had found.

Having given up on gold, Ponce de León decided to transform the island into an agricultural paradise. In 1515 he introduced sugarcane, and the Spanish government funded the building of sugar mills by the dozens. The African slaves and the few remaining Taino were put to work cultivating and harvesting the crop by hand from dawn till dusk under the hot tropical sun. The Africans proved sturdiest of all, and their population increased, while the Spanish and native populations dwindled. By 1531, the Spanish numbered 426 in Puerto Rico and the Africans 2,264.

Before long, land was parceled out to Spaniards who wished to settle in Puerto Rico. Each settler who agreed to farm the land (or, more accurately put, to oversee the slaves who farmed the land) and to stay more than five years, was granted between 200 and 1,400 acres. Soon coffee and spices were cultivated in addition to sugarcane, as these luxury items were in great demand back in Europe. By the seventeenth century tobacco and ginger emerged as the principal crops. With the wealth amassed on the backs of the Taino and African slaves, Puerto Rico thrived. Spain looked anew at its colony in the Caribbean and decided that indeed it was a "rich port," a good place to settle, farm, and grow wealthy.

African slavery persisted in Puerto Rico until **King Amadeo** of Spain abolished it in 1873. By then, the Africans, who believed that their ancient Yoruban deities had followed them to Puerto Rico, had grown deep roots in the fertile tropical soil of the island and felt quite at home there.

Intermarriage and interbreeding were common among the three ethnic groups—the Taino, Africans, and Spanish—which is why Puerto Rico is so racially diverse today. Puerto Rican art, music, philosophy, literature, religion, and cuisine all reflect the rich legacy of these three peoples.

What do Puerto Ricans mean when they say "negro"?

The word *negro* is Spanish for "black." Black color. Black race. Black sky. But in Puerto Rico, where people's complexions range from black to fair, there are many words that refer to skin color.

A dark-skinned or black person who is Puerto Rican is usually referred to as *de color*, meaning "of color." However, an African American in the United States with the same skin color is called *moreno*, or brown. A dark-skinned person is never called negro or *negrito*; this is strictly a term of endearment and can be used when addressing anyone, even the blond and blue-eyed. A person with light brown skin is called *trigueño* ("brunette" or "swarthy")—and this describes the majority of Puerto Ricans. *Blanco* ("white") is used for light-skinned persons. *Indio* refers to someone with native features.

How did Sir Francis Drake get his comeuppance in Puerto Rico?

In 1588, the year the Spanish Armada was defeated thanks to the maritime skills of English navigator **Sir Francis Drake,** the Spanish colonies in the Caribbean were in danger of falling into the hands of the English. It seems the Spanish had found little gold in Puerto Rico, but they realized that San Juan was the perfect stopover for galleons laden with treasure that were heading from Mexico and Peru to Spain. However, the galleons anchored in San Juan Bay were sitting ducks for raiders, pirates, and privateers who wanted the loot.

Sir Francis Drake was a pro at raiding Spanish caches in the New World, be they mule trains loaded with tons of silver or ships bearing treasure. In the last of his marauding expeditions, Drake set sail for Puerto Rico in 1595 with 27 ships and 4,500 troops. By then the Spanish had cottoned on to Drake's antics, and by the time his fleet sighted Puerto Rico, 1,500 Spanish sailors had joined the 300 stationed on the island. The Spanish purposely sank two of their ships to block Drake's entrance into San Juan Bay. When Sir Francis Drake and his men finally reached San Juan on November 22, 1595, they were met by an unceasing artillery blast. The English fleet quickly withdrew out to sea and then circled the island searching for a point of entry. But the Spanish were too well fortified to be penetrated. Sir Francis Drake admitted defeat, and as fate would have it, shortly thereafter died of dysentery.

However, another Englishman by the name of **George Clifford,** third earl of Cumberland, managed to wrest control of San Juan from the Spanish for five months in 1598. It seems a smallpox epidemic had stricken the Spanish soldiers on the island and they did not have the strength to keep the English at bay. The peoples of Puerto Rico did all they could to make life miserable for the conquerors, who soon succumbed to smallpox as well. The Dutch invaded in 1625 and even burned San Juan, but the Spanish fended off the attackers. Eventually they erected three fortresses around San Juan which served as adequate protection from future attacks by the English and Dutch.

IMPORTANT DATES

November 22, 1595 — Sir Francis Drake, the English buccaneer and explorer, sails into San Juan Bay.

December 10, 1898 — By the Treaty of Paris, ending the Spanish-American War, Puerto Rico is ceded to the United States.

March 2, 1917 — President Woodrow Wilson signs the Jones Act, granting all Puerto Ricans U.S. citizenship.

July 25, 1952 — The Commonwealth of Puerto Rico is proclaimed.

November 14, 1993 — The people of Puerto Rico elect to retain commonwealth status.

Who was Marshall Alejandro O'Reilly?

By the mid-1700s, illegal commerce was thriving in Puerto Rico as Puerto Ricans traded with European buccaneers and privateers behind Spain's back. What's more, the islanders were only farming five percent of the land. As a result, trade between Spain and Puerto Rico came to a virtual standstill. Spain was vexed because Spanish taxes were supporting the island and yet the Spanish were getting little in return. In 1765, the Spanish king sent **Marshall Alejandro O'Reilly,** a brilliant soldier and civic planner, to Puerto Rico to overhaul the system of government, enhance profitability, and improve the colony's defenses.

Alejandro O'Reilly came up with a plan called the O'Reilly Report, considered one of the most important documents Spain issued to its colonies, as for the first time the colonists' needs, not just the interests of the Spanish crown, were recognized. O'Reilly devised a way of legalizing trade between the colonies and other European nations that was beneficial to Spain. He also laid the groundwork for a system of land distribution whereby new Spanish settlers were given agricultural acres for free if they were willing to farm them. Thanks to Marshall Alejandro O'Reilly, new schools were opened and new towns were constructed. Houses built in the Spanish style, with thick stone walls that kept the interiors cool, sprang up from coast to coast. Spain's new interest in Puerto Rico led to the enhancement of the island's cultural life. **José Campeche,** who is considered the first great Puerto Rican painter, did his work during this progressive era.

A GROWING NATIONAL IDENTITY

How did Puerto Ricans feel about Spanish rule?

By the nineteenth century, many citizens of Puerto Rico were convinced that it was time to leave "home" (Spain) and start a household of their own. By then a cultural and national identity, distinct from Spain, had arisen in Puerto Rico. In striving for autonomy, Puerto Ricans demanded educational reform, the formation of labor unions, and less taxation and more representation. They also insisted that Puerto Ricans, not

Spaniards, be appointed to local government posts, which had been strictly off limits to all *criollos*.

Navy lieutenant **Ramón Power** was among the first Puerto Ricans to raise a voice of dissension. In 1810 he went to Spain to plead Puerto Rico's case before the Spanish Cortes. He argued that as part of the Spanish empire, Puerto Rico should have the same rights granted to Spain's provinces. Power succeeded in securing both a more liberal constitution for Puerto Rico and the right to Spanish citizenship. His provisions for greater self-rule, including the distribution of land to natives and freedom from taxation for those willing to work the land, were contained in the Ley Power (the Power Act), and later in the *Real Cédula de Gracias* issued by **Ferdinand VII** in 1815.

Spanish leniency did not last long. When **José María Quiñones,** another father of Puerto Rican independence, requested that Puerto Rico be granted complete autonomy, Spain responded by sending despotic military governors to the island, who demanded greater allegiance to the mother country and higher taxes from the Puerto Ricans. From 1837 to 1864 the governors denied the islanders a voice in their own affairs and persecuted many Puerto Rican leaders, sending some into exile.

One such leader was a physician and patriot named **Ramón Emeterio Betances,** who in the late 1860s was expelled from Puerto Rico by the island's governor for his revolutionary ideas. Betances went to live in the United States, and on several other Caribbean islands, where he planned an armed revolt for independence. He wanted an end to slavery, which in spite of being officially abolished was in full bloom. He also demanded freedom of speech and freedom of religion for the people of the island. In September 1868, thousands of Betances supporters marched into the small town of Lares, in western Puerto Rico, wielding firearms and machetes. They set up a provisional government and declared the island the Republic of Puerto Rico. This revolt, which the Spanish easily squelched, became known as *El Grito de Lares*

("The Cry of Lares") and is celebrated as a national holiday by Puerto Ricans both on the island and the mainland.

What's a machete?

A machete is the traditional sword used by *jíbaros* to cut cane. But a machete is more than just a long, sharp knife—it's the symbol of Caribbean farmers, much as the hammer and sickle was the symbol of the Bolsheviks. In recent times, a group calling itself the *macheteros* (machete wielders) has advocated Puerto Rican independence from the United States.

What's a jíbaro?

A *jíbaro* is a Puerto Rican farm worker, who is usually an expert at hacking cane and wielding a machete. The *jíbaro* is revered as the backbone of the early Puerto Rican agricultural economy. He is also mocked and vilified. Nowadays in urban centers on the mainland, the word *jíbaro* is often used to mean "hick."

Who was Luis Muñoz Rivera, and why is he called the George Washington of Puerto Rico?

In 1870 the first political parties were formed in Puerto Rico. In 1887 **Román Baldorioty de Castro** organized liberals advocating reform under the banner of the Autonomist Party. After Baldorioty died in 1889, **Luis Muñoz Rivera** took control of the party. He proposed that the Autonomist Party and other splinter parties form a coalition with the Spanish Fusionist Party, which he believed would soon gain power in Spain. He envisioned that once the Spanish Fusionist Party controlled Spain, a deal for Puerto Rican independence could be worked out.

Was Puerto Rico really free for only a week?

As it turned out, **Luis Muñoz Rivera** was correct in his assumption. In 1898, the controlling Spanish Fusionist Party granted Puerto Ricans the same privileges as all Spanish citizens, as well as the right to elect a Puerto Rican governor general to head a provisional assembly which would have full control over local taxes, budgets, and education, and elect representatives to the Spanish Parliament. Luis Muñoz Rivera won the election for governor general, becoming the first independent governor of Puerto Rico—a giant step toward full independence for the island. The autonomous parliament of Puerto Rico assembled for the first time on July 17, 1898. On July 25, the United States invaded the island.

What was the Monroe Doctrine?

When **James Monroe** was elected president of the United States in 1817, at the age of 58, he had a long and distinguished political career behind him that included service as secretary of state, governor of Virginia, and most notably, as an engineer of the Louisiana Purchase. Under Monroe, U.S. industry prospered and Manifest Destiny reared its head well beyond the nation's borders.

In 1823 President Monroe's secretary of state, **John Quincy Adams,** delivered a speech before Congress in which he declared that the United States would not tolerate European expansion in the Americas. The policy grew out of concern that England was flexing too much muscle in the hemisphere (having seized territory by nibbling off Belize and the Mosquito Coast of Nicaragua) and that France, under **Napoleon III,** had designs on Mexico and intended to turn it into a client state by imposing a Hapsburg prince on a briefly restored Mexican throne. The Monroe Doctrine clearly sent a message to the empires of Europe to cease and desist.

However, the Monroe Doctrine did not promise that the

United States would do the same—that is, refrain from interfering in colonies and nations in the Americas that were not its own. In fact, while the Monroe Doctrine appeared to be a simple exercise in isolationism and good-neighbor policy toward the fledgling new republics to the south, such as Mexico, it actually paved the way for the free ride U.S. imperialism took throughout the Western Hemisphere for many decades to come. Puerto Rico was one of the stops along the way.

What was the Spanish-American War all about, and why is it called the first media-staged war?

On the record, the reason for the Spanish-American War of 1898 was to help liberate Cuba from Spanish domination. By then Cuba and Puerto Rico were the only Spanish colonies left in the Western Hemisphere. The war began when the USS *Maine*, which was docked in Havana harbor to keep an eye on the Spanish in case they went too far with the Cubans, was blown up. The word was that Spanish soldiers had blown the *Maine* to smithereens.

In fact, Cuban freedom fighters (*libertadores*) **José Martí, Antonio Maceo y Grojales,** and many others had already made great strides toward liberating their country by the time the United States stepped in. It has been widely speculated that the *Maine* might actually have been blown up by American soldiers in search of a reason to go to war. A victory over Spain and "necessary" intervention in Cuba and Puerto Rico would ensure the expansion and protection of U.S. foreign markets in lush lands rich in sugar, coffee, tobacco, and minerals.

At first, **President William McKinley** was reluctant to enter a war against Spain, but overwhelmingly imperialistic sentiment had overtaken the nation. **Henry Cabot Lodge,** the powerful senator from Massachusetts, and **Theodore Roosevelt,** who was then assistant secretary of the navy, both lobbied intensely for U.S. involvement in the Caribbean. Roosevelt supposedly told a friend, "I should welcome almost any war, for I think the country needs one."

There was also another powerful faction that seemed to want war: the press—specifically, newspaper barons **William Randolph Hearst** and **Joseph Pulitzer**, both of whom had learned from the American Civil War that wars sell papers. The Hearst and Pulitzer papers began running stories (many of them true) about the atrocities the Spanish were committing against the Cubans and urging the president to step in.

At one point, William Randolph Hearst is said to have dispatched artist **Frederic Remington** to Cuba to send back pictures of the horrendous war. When Remington couldn't find anything really bloody to paint, Hearst was furious. "You furnish the pictures," he told the artist, "and I'll furnish the war!"

Who were Teddy Roosevelt's Rough Riders, and how did they help him win the U.S. presidency?

On April 25, 1898, the United States declared war on Spain, with lieutenant colonel **Teddy Roosevelt** and his Rough Riders in the vanguard. Roosevelt and his men of the First Regiment of United States Cavalry Volunteers were called Rough Riders because many among them were actually ranchers and cowboys. Roosevelt was declared a hero when he led a daring charge up Kettle Hill (incorrectly called San Juan Hill) in eastern Cuba, in the province of Santiago de Cuba on July 1, 1898, a battle heavily publicized in the American press.

The same day, **General Nelson Appleton Miles** led 16,000 American troops into the town of Guanica in southwestern Puerto Rico. It was no contest. Spain, a dwindling empire on its last legs, soon surrendered. The Spanish-American War lasted only a few months, and most of it was actually fought at the bargaining table. Yet there were over 5,000 American casualties in what secretary of state **John Hay** had described as a "splendid little war," though only 379 were battle casualties. The rest of the deaths were caused by yellow fever, malaria, and other tropical diseases that plagued the American troops.

With the Treaty of Paris, signed on December 10, 1898, the United States found itself in possession of Cuba, Puerto Rico, Wake Island, Guam, and the Philippines; in other words, Spain's remaining colonies. You might say Spain was forced to throw in everything but the kitchen sink, and the United States wound up with a lot of land on its hands.

Puerto Rico, which had savored relative freedom for seven days after Spain had voluntarily granted the island many autonomous rights, suddenly found itself a U.S. protectorate. Most Puerto Ricans believed the American presence would be transitory and was simply a formal way of capping 405 years of Spanish domination. However, it turned out to be the beginning of a tumultuous marriage—called by many different names over the years—that prevails to this day. Elsewhere, Cuba remained a U.S. protectorate until 1902, when it declared itself a free and independent nation. The Philippines won independence in 1946. Guam and Wake Island remain under direct U.S. control.

Teddy Roosevelt garnered great popularity from his victory and was elected governor of New York in 1898. In 1900 **President McKinley** won reelection with Roosevelt as his vice president. Before the regular session of the Senate opened, McKinley was assassinated and Roosevelt became president of the United States on September 14, 1901. Three years later, he was still popular and was elected to the presidency in his own right by a resounding majority.

What was the Roosevelt Corollary?

In 1904 **President Teddy Roosevelt** issued the Roosevelt Corollary, which served as an amendment to the Monroe Doctrine and went one step further—some say, one step too far. The corollary gave the United States the right to act as "an international police power" wherever "chronic wrongdoing, or an impotence which results in a general loosening of the ties of civilized society" requires intervention "by some civilized nation."

To many Latin Americans, the Roosevelt Corollary packed a wallop. It not only allowed the United States to intervene unilaterally in the affairs of any country in the hemisphere, but it elevated Manifest Destiny to new heights by stating that the United States was "civilized" and the rest of the nations in the hemisphere were not. This belief in American supremacy led to U.S. intervention in various Caribbean and Central American nations, which even involved the overthrow of governments deemed harmful to American investments and the installation of puppet rulers who would follow the policies outlined by Washington.

Although Roosevelt characterized his foreign policy with the adage "speak softly and carry a big stick," he seldom spoke softly—and he didn't need to. United States imperialism had reached its zenith.

Who was Eugenio María de Hostos, and why is a school in New York City named after him?

Eugenio María de Hostos was a Puerto Rican journalist, philosopher, writer, and freedom fighter. He was born near Mayagüez, Puerto Rico, in 1839, educated in Spain, and then became a lawyer. Hostos believed that Puerto Rico should be autonomous, and when the island was under the control of Spain, he had lobbied the Spanish government incessantly for independence, until he was forced into exile for his "liberal" opinions. During Cuba's struggle for independence from Spain, Hostos joined forces with the Cubans and fought alongside **José Martí,** Cuba's "George Washington."

In 1869 Hostos moved to New York, where he published a famous newspaper, *La America Ilustrada*. He organized the League of Patriots in New York City to aid in the transition from a U.S. military government to a civil government in Puerto Rico. Hostos maintained that Puerto Ricans should have the right to decide, by means of a plebiscite, whether they wanted to be independent, or annexed by the United States.

However, when U.S. ambassadors met with Spanish delegates to negotiate the end of the Spanish-American War and the fate of Spain's colonies, the few Puerto Rican officials whom Hostos had convinced the United States to invite to the table had no say in the final outcome. With the Treaty of Paris, Puerto Rico became a U.S. protectorate with fewer rights to self-government than it had enjoyed in recent years under Spain.

Eugenio María de Hostos continued his fight from the Dominican Republic, where he went to live in 1875. He published the newspaper *Las Tres Antillas*, which advocated autonomy for all three Spanish-speaking Caribbean islands: Cuba, Puerto Rico, and the Dominican Republic. Hostos favored an Antilles Confederacy, in which all three would be united as a kind of commonwealth. Aside from his political and journalistic career, Hostos was a dedicated teacher. He believed that only through education could an oppressed people rise and take charge of their lives. In 1879 Eugenio María de Hostos founded the first normal school in the Dominican Republic, where he inherited the title *"El Maestro"* ("the teacher" or "the master"). Later he moved to Chile, where he was named president of the Chilean Athenaeum, headed two schools, and taught constitutional law at the Universidad Chilena in Santiago de Chile, where he fought for the admission of women.

A prolific writer, Hostos penned fifty volumes in the course of his lifetime, including the 1863 political novel, *La Peregrinación de Bayoán (The Pilgrimage of Bayoan)* and the 1887 political treatise, *Lecciones de derecho constitucional (Lessons on Constitutional Rights)*. Eugenio María de Hostos died in the Dominican Republic in 1903, one year after Cuba gained its independence. He never saw his dreams for an independent

Puerto Rico realized. Hostos Community College in the Bronx, New York, is named in his honor and holds fast to the philosophy of "progress through education," which he so vigorously defended.

How did Puerto Ricans feel about being a U.S. protectorate?

Puerto Rico's transition to a U.S. protectorate was difficult for most islanders. The language barrier, which necessitated the use of interpreters and translators so that Puerto Rican leaders and American military authorities could communicate, created tensions and misunderstanding. The cultural barrier, which led Americans to question even the most minute details of Puerto Rican criminal and civil laws—and, in many cases, overturn them—went even deeper.

In 1900, almost two years after officially taking over, the United States declared Puerto Rico a U.S. territory under the Foraker Act. According to this piece of legislation, Puerto Ricans were neither American citizens nor citizens of an independent nation. A civil administration replaced the transitional military government and allowed for the election of Puerto Ricans to a house of delegates, where they could implement laws related to internal affairs. However, the U.S. president was responsible for appointing a governor to head the house of delegates—and that governor, who would have the final say, was to be an American, not a Puerto Rican. The Foraker Act also put an extra economic squeeze on Puerto Rico by imposing a heavy tariff on products coming from the island. This was done to protect American sugar and tobacco interests from Puerto Rican competition.

Puerto Ricans were not terribly satisfied with the Foraker Act and their political status. **Luis Muñoz Rivera,** who had emerged as the leading Puerto Rican statesman and represented the island in Congress from 1910 to 1916, wrote to **President McKinley** that the Foraker Act was "unworthy of the United States which imposes it and of Puerto Ricans who have to endure it."

Discontent over the state of affairs on the island led to the formation of the Puerto Rican Unionist Party. The party's platform repudiated U.S. domination and supported any of three options: statehood, nationhood, or semi-independence under American protection. However, the Supreme Court ruled that Congress had the perfect right to set up the territories just as it had done—and thus the Foraker Act was upheld. With its underlying philosophy of "tutelage," a buzzword of that era, the Foraker Act remained in effect until World War I.

"Tutelage" implied that it was the United States' duty to instruct Puerto Ricans in how to behave like a progressive, civilized nation. The idea of tutelage carried with it the seeds of economic development and Americanization, and was rooted in the philosophy expounded by writer and clergyman **Josiah Strong** in his best-selling book of 1885, *Our Country*. In the book Strong argues that the United States is the torchbearer of Anglo-Saxon virtue, and is therefore destined to "move down upon Mexico, down upon Central and South America, out upon the islands of the sea, over upon Africa and beyond." And he asks rhetorically, "Can anyone doubt that the result of this competition of the races will be the survival of the fittest?"

Puerto Ricans remained noncitizens of the world as dictated by the Foraker Act until the rising threat of World War I, as well as unremitting pressure from the islanders, led **President Woodrow Wilson** to sign the Jones Act on March 2, 1917. With one sweep of the pen, the president granted U.S. citizenship to all Puerto Ricans, unless they signed a document explicitly refusing it. Refusing citizenship meant giving up many civil rights, and there were few refusals. A non–Puerto Rican governor appointed by the U.S. president would continue to rule over all the internal affairs of the island and its new American citizens.

Puerto Ricans instantly inherited all the obligations of citizenship and became eligible for the draft. During World

War I, almost 20,000 Puerto Ricans served in the U.S. armed forces. Thousands died on the front lines. The Puerto Rican people also donated hundreds of thousands of dollars to the war effort and bought more than $10 million in war bonds.

During the 1920s and 1930s, Puerto Ricans continued to ask for greater autonomy in local affairs. **Theodore Roosevelt, Jr.** (Teddy's son), served as governor of the island from 1929 to 1932. He launched several economic and cultural programs that were favorable to Puerto Ricans and also envisioned greater self-government for the people.

In the late 1930s, after the sugar market collapsed and workers were teetering on the edge of starvation, Puerto Rico's plea for greater autonomy turned violent. A group of Puerto Rican nationalists, led by *Independentista* fighter **Albizu Campos,** demanded Puerto Rican independence in the streets of Ponce, unleashing a revolt that left 19 dead and more than a hundred wounded. In the aftermath of this "unexpected" episode, two bills were introduced to Congress proposing that Puerto Rico be granted independence. Both failed on the grounds that social and economic conditions on the island needed to be improved before independence could be seriously considered.

Who was the first elected Puerto Rican governor, and what did he do that was so important?

In 1946, the United States appointed **Jesús T. Piñero,** a former resident commissioner, the first native Puerto Rican governor of the island. One year later, though, Congress passed the Elective Governors Act, giving Puerto Ricans the right to choose their governor and granting the governor full authority to appoint all officials, except the auditor and members of the Supreme Court.

In 1949, **Luis Muñoz Marín,** the son of the early patriot **Luis Muñoz Rivera** and leader of the majority Popular Democratic Party, became the first native son elected governor by the people of Puerto Rico. Muñoz Marín had first been exposed to American politics while a teenager because his father's tenure as a Puerto Rican representative to Congress brought the family to Washington, D.C. He went on to study law and became a respected lawyer and a well-known man about Washington. Muñoz Marín contributed to such magazines as *The New Republic* and *The Nation*, and was the editor of the Latin American cultural journal *La Revista de las Indias*. A lover of verse, he translated several books of poetry into Spanish, including the works of **Walt Whitman.**

In 1916, Luis Muñoz Marín returned to Puerto Rico to edit the paper his father had started, *La Democracia*. He was elected to the Puerto Rican Senate in 1932, the same year **Franklin Delano Roosevelt** took office. Among Muñoz Marín's many friends and supporters was **Eleanor Roosevelt.** After surveying the rural areas of Puerto Rico in 1933, the First Lady voiced grave concern over the poor state of Puerto Rican farming and the island economy, and lobbied for change. At her bidding, President Roosevelt denounced the "hopeless drive to remodel Puerto Ricans so that they should become similar in language, habits, and thoughts to continental Americans."

As governor, duly elected by the people, and a member of the newly formed Popular Democratic Party (PPD), Muñoz Marín would see to it that Washington, now with **Harry S. Truman** in the White House, supported him in his efforts to revitalize the Puerto Rican economy. He adopted a program based on economic reform and expansion that before long would bring industry to the island and raise the per capita income. Slowly, a new era was dawning.

How did Puerto Rico become a commonwealth . . . and what's a commonwealth, anyway?

As the economic situation improved in Puerto Rico, **Luis Muñoz Marín** turned his attention to questions of political status. Earlier in his career, he had rejected the notion of establishing a "Commonwealth state," known as the Irish Solution, as it is patterned after Ireland's relationship with Great Britain. He felt that commonwealth status would amount to nothing more than freedom "on a very long chain." But now that Puerto Rico's economy was on the mend, severing ties with the United States would mean giving up no-tariff status and other perquisites that had created a building boom and a strong tourist economy and were keeping the island industry percolating.

Statehood was another option, and although Muñoz Marín might have opposed it in principle, he was a very practical person. He reasoned that it would take the United States too long to accept his Latin island as another state. He said: "If we seek statehood, we die waiting for Congress." So his PPD Party decided to adopt what was termed the "intermediate solution"—commonwealth status.

Luis Muñoz Marín was so popular in Washington that when he spoke politicians listened. In 1950, the U.S. Congress passed Public Law 600, calling for an election in Puerto Rico in which the people would determine whether commonwealth status, what Muñoz Marín called the "free associated state," *estado libre asociado*, would be adopted. Muñoz Marín had created the term "free associated state" to please all three dominant political philosophies. To those who favored independence, the word "free" looked promising. To those who wanted some association or dependence, the word "associated" sounded good. And, finally, for those who advocated U.S. statehood, the word "state" struck a chord.

As far as Luis Muñoz Marín was concerned, commonwealth status granted Puerto Rico a significant amount of independence, and it ensured that the island would continue to enjoy the economic and social privileges that ties with the United States provided. Legally, the arrangement had a lot of holes, since it was a unilateral agreement that Congress could abrogate any time it pleased.

The people of Puerto Rico followed their governor's lead

and voted for commonwealth status, which was proclaimed on July 25, 1952. Luis Muñoz Marín was elected governor of Puerto Rico three more times, and would probably have died in office if he had not opted to retire in 1964. Under his leadership, Puerto Rico gained political respect and flew its own flag for the first time. With the passage of the Puerto Rican Federal Relations Act of 1950, the island was granted the right to draft and enact its own constitution, whose provisions could not overstep the limitations placed on a U.S. territory. The constitution was ratified March 3, 1952, approved by the U.S. Congress July 3, and became effective on July 25, exactly 54 years to the day the United States seized control of Guanica during the Spanish-American War.

Why did the Independentistas *try to assassinate* President Truman?

The *Independentista* Party, a proindependence movement, which called for nothing short of complete independence and whose members refused to participate in the commonwealth elections of 1950, felt ignored by **Luis Muñoz Marín** and the commonwealth partisans. On March 1, 1954, three Puerto Rican members of the movement attempted to assassinate **President Harry Truman.** The three terrorists, **Rafael Candel Miranda, Andrés Cordero,** and **Lolita Lebrón,** fired at the president from the galley of the U.S. House of Representatives. President Truman emerged from the attack unscathed, but several congressmen were wounded. The terrorists were sent to prison, and until their release in 1979 they worked for Puerto Rican independence from behind bars. Terrorists who called themselves the *Macheteros* (the Machete Wielders) took up the dark cause. Among other antics, several *Macheteros* robbed an armored-car company in West Hartford, Connecticut, in 1983, and drove away with $1.7 million to finance their organization.

Why isn't Puerto Rican migration considered immigration, and how did it get started?

Ever since Puerto Rico was declared a U.S. protectorate, islanders have been coming to the U.S. mainland, but the first significant migration took place after World War II. The reasons were many, but it all boiled down to one factor: economics. During World War II, 100,000 Puerto Ricans served in the armed forces. Military life exposed many islanders to mainland prosperity, fueling their desire to move north. In addition, Puerto Rico's population doubled in size to two million during the first quarter of the century, and continued to grow at a rapid rate due to improvements in medical services. With so many more people on the island, the standard of living did not rise substantially and the unemployment rate soared. By contrast, jobs on the mainland were plentiful, especially in the booming Garment District in New York City (where Puerto Rican women were considered excellent workers), as well as in the service industries, which hired unskilled and semiskilled workers.

Puerto Ricans in search of jobs and better living conditions migrated to the mainland in a steady stream from the post-war era until the 1960s. Since then, Puerto Rican islanders have settled on the mainland in spurts, depending on the number of jobs available. Most Puerto Ricans who decide to make a go of it in the continental United States tend to settle in urban areas. Some also travel to the U.S. mainland as contract farm workers under the auspices of the Office of the Commonwealth of Puerto Rico, which was established in 1948. These workers come on a seasonal basis to harvest potatoes on Long Island, fruits and vegetables in New Jersey, tobacco in Connecticut, and sugar beets in Michigan. Since they are U.S. citizens, and not foreigners, these laborers—and all Puerto Ricans, for that matter—can travel freely back and forth between the island and the continental United

States. In other words, their movement constitutes migration, not immigration.

Over the years Puerto Ricans have introduced their spiritual practices, literature, art, music, and cuisine to many different cities across the U.S. mainland, particularly New York, where Spanish Harlem, which Puerto Ricans call *El Barrio*, is alive with island traditions.

Commonwealth vs. statehood: What's the big deal?

The question of Puerto Rico's status has been hanging in the balance for over a century. Back in 1964, the United States–Puerto Rico Commission on the Status of Puerto Rico decided that both commonwealth status and statehood were viable options for Puerto Rico, and that Puerto Ricans must determine which way they wanted to go. However, the commission, chaired by **James A. Rowe, Jr.,** did point out that statehood might impose undue economic hardships on the island.

Right after the commission's report became public, **Luis Muñoz Marín,** who favored commonwealth status, and **Luis Ferré,** who headed the opposition party (PNP) and supported statehood, went back to the polls to try to resolve the issue. In the end, 61 percent of the people voted for commonwealth status, while 39 percent chose statehood. Four years later, in 1968, Luis Ferré was elected governor of the island. While his election might have appeared to signal a desire for statehood on the part of Puerto Ricans, the island remained polarized on the question, and no action was taken to bring the matter before Congress for quite some time.

In 1978 **President Jimmy Carter** called for another referendum on the issue; he was apparently concerned that the United Nations was going to officially accuse the United States of colonialism in Puerto Rico. The referendum never took place. **President George Bush** took up the issue in his first speech before Congress in 1989 and declared that he favored statehood. No progress was made to resolve the question of statehood until November 1992, when Puerto Ricans elected **Pedro Roselló** governor. Roselló, a strong advocate of statehood, announced soon after that a plebiscite to decide the status of Puerto Rico would be held. The three choices on the ballot were commonwealth status, statehood, or independence. On November 14, 1993, the people of Puerto Rico went to the polls in unprecedented numbers. Forty-eight percent voted to retain commonwealth status, forty-six percent favored statehood, and only four percent chose independence. It was a very close vote—but one that affirmed Puerto Rico's ambiguous relationship with the United States. A poll of mainland Puerto Ricans conducted by the Latino National Political Survey produced less ambiguous results: sixty-eight percent favored commonwealth status, twenty-seven percent statehood, and four percent independence.

If Puerto Rico ever does become a state, many significant changes affecting the island would occur overnight. For one, Puerto Rico's population exceeds that of twenty-six states, which means that the island would send two senators to the Senate and seven representatives to the House. These congresspersons would represent a state in which 70 percent of the 3.6 million (mostly Democratic) residents speak only Spanish.

However, as a state Puerto Rico would lose many essential economic breaks. For instance, Section 936 of the Internal Revenue Code exempts mainland companies operating in U.S. possessions from most federal taxation on profits. If Puerto Rico ever becomes a state, the law will no longer apply, and American companies will most likely flee to Mexico and other Latin American nations, leaving more than 160,000 workers on the island without jobs. And, of course, all the small ancillary businesses that assist the hundreds of U.S. companies operating in Puerto Rico would be enormously affected as well. In 1990 the U.S. Congressional Budget Office calculated that statehood would raise Puerto Rico's unemployment rate to 30 percent. Puerto Ricans would also have to pay federal income tax, from which they are now exempt, which would cause even more economic hardship. A recession with far more devastating effects than a hurricane would be almost guaranteed to hit the island.

Either way, the issue of statehood is a big deal. As a state, Puerto Rico would emerge as the most powerful Latino political voice in the nation. America would move one step closer to *hermandad*—brotherhood and sisterhood—with all the Spanish-speaking countries in the hemisphere. And so, despite the outcome of the 1993 vote, the dream of statehood is still alive and well in the minds of millions of Puerto Ricans. In fact, in early 1998 the House decided by a margin of only 209–208 to permit Puerto Ricans to vote on the issue at the end of 1998. House Republican leaders pushed for a vote as part of a campaign to bring into the fold Latino voters who feel alienated from the GOP thanks to the passage of Proposition 187 in California in 1994 and the 1996 bill to declare English the official language of the United States which got through the House but was never taken up by the Senate.

How many Puerto Ricans are there, and where do they live?

According to the 1990 U.S. census, there are approximately 2,652,000 mainland Puerto Ricans. About 900,000 mainlanders live in New York City, the center of Puerto Rican culture in the continental United States. A significant number of Puerto Ricans also reside in New Jersey (320,000), Florida (247,000), Massachusetts (151,000), Pennsylvania (149,000), Connecticut (147,000), and Illinois (146,000).

How are mainland Puerto Ricans doing?

One third of all mainland Puerto Ricans live in poverty. Despite the brilliant leaders and accomplished scientists, artists, and entrepreneurs in the Puerto Rican community, as well as the seeming advantages of U.S. citizenship, Puerto Ricans are a socially and economically disadvantaged group. Drugs, crime, and a lack of education are all too common among the Puerto Ricans of *El Barrio* in New York City and else-where. In explaining this phenomenon, some social observers have pointed out that Puerto Ricans, because they are mostly of mixed African and Spanish descent, have been victims of the same kind of institutionalized discrimination that African Americans have suffered. In addition, they say that the language barrier and a feeling of being neither here nor there—straddling two cultures and two languages—have only helped alienate Puerto Ricans further.

Others, such as **Linda Chavez,** author of *Out of the Barrio: Toward a New Politics of Hispanic Assimilation* (1991) and director of the Center for the New American Community, whose agenda it is to oppose multiculturalism which supposedly threatens the dissolution of society, have pointed a finger at the breakdown of the Puerto Rican family unit. A majority of Puerto Rican households are headed by poor, single women. Still others argue that the reason Puerto Ricans are economically disadvantaged is that manufacturing jobs, particularly in New York City's Garment District, fell on bad times in the 1960s and 1970s, and Puerto Ricans are still suffering from that loss.

However, it is also important to point out that large numbers of Puerto Ricans hold career-track white-collar positions and that in 1993, 50 percent had professional, managerial, technical, and administrative support jobs. In that same year just over 53 percent of mainlanders age 25 or older had finished high school. However, when the second generation of Puerto Rican mainlanders is considered separately, their educational level approaches the national average, and their occupational status is advancing at a steady pace. Also, whereas New York City is still the home of an economically underprivileged class of Puerto Ricans, in other regions of the nation, Puerto Ricans do much better.

PUERTO RICAN CULTURAL LIFE

What's a santo?

For Spanish-speaking Caribbean Americans, a *santo* is a saint in the Roman Catholic tradition who also has a counterpart among West African deities. For example, the Catholic St. Barbara is the equivalent of the Yoruban god Chango; the Virgin of Regla is also the Yoruban goddess Yemaya, and so on. This practice of worshipping saints and Yoruban deities is called *Santería*, and it is just one example of the kind of syncretism that took place when the Spanish and Africans came in contact in the Caribbean. The center of *Santería* was in Cuba, and the religion has many followers in Miami and other cities with a significant Cuban American community. There are many Puerto Rican followers of *Santería* both on the island and the mainland.

What's a botánica?

A *botánica* is a store that sells herbs and "natural" medicines—and there are many in every Puerto Rican neighborhood in America. But a *botánica* is also a shop that carries religious items for followers of *Santería*: everything from candles and bead necklaces to religious medals and statues. Most *botánicas* are owned by a *santera*, or priestess (there are a few priests, but the majority are women), who gives consultations to followers of the religion.

LATINO HEARTTHROBS OF ALL TIME

1. Irene Cara — Dancer and singer who recorded the hits "Fame" and "Flashdance (What a Feeling)," and won an Oscar for writing the latter.

2. Mariah Carey — Pop superstar of Venezuelan, Irish, and African descent who in 1991 won two Grammy Awards, one for Best Pop Female Vocalist and one for Best New Artist with her first album *Mariah Carey*.

3. Julie Carmen — Actress who won accolades for her performance in the 1988 film *The Milagro Beanfield War*.

4. Vikki Carr — Mexican American entertainer who by 1994 had recorded fifty best-selling albums, seventeen of which went gold. Her 1966 song, "It Must Be Him," catapulted the singer to fame.

5. Charo — Known as the "Latin bombshell," this singer has been entertaining Americans for decades with her songs and guitar playing.

6. Chayanne — This singer was one of *People* magazine's Fifty Most Beautiful People for 1993.

7. Plácido Domingo — Born in Madrid, Domingo is one of the world's greatest lyric-dramatic tenors.

8. Gloria Estefan — This Cuban American singing sensation has millions of fans the world over.

9. Emilio Estevez   One of Martin Sheen's sons, this highly acclaimed actor and director is a top box-office draw.

10. Andy García   This Cuban American actor has starred in such films as *The Godfather III* and *The Untouchables*.

11. Cristina Gonzalez   Dancer with the Alvin Ailey Repertory Ensemble.

12. Rita Hayworth   Called the "Great American Love Goddess," she performed with the likes of Gary Cooper and Glenn Ford.

13. Julio Iglesias   Born in Madrid, this romantic crooner has won the hearts of both Spanish- and English-speaking fans around the globe.

14. Ricardo Montalbán   This Mexican American actor starred in the TV series *Fantasy Island*, and countless other TV shows, commercials, and films.

15. Ramón Novarro   This Mexican American heartthrob was cast as a "Latin Lover" in silent films and talkies.

16. Rosie Pérez   Actress and choreographer of Puerto Rican descent; she played Tina in Spike Lee's film *Do the Right Thing*.

17. Chita Rivera   This Puerto Rican stage actress and dancer won a Tony in 1984 for her performance in *The Rink*, and in 1993 for

	the Broadway hit *Kiss of the Spider Woman*.
18. César Romero	From the 1930s to the 1960s, this popular Cuban American actor played leading men and villains, including the Joker in the TV show *Batman*.
19. Linda Ronstadt	Everyone thought this renowned singer with Mexican roots was an Anglo until she recorded an album in Spanish.
20. Jon Secada	This Cuban American pop idol got his start in Gloria Estefan's band.
21. Charlie Sheen	One of Martin Sheen's sons and the highest-paid Latino in Hollywood.
22. Ritchie Valens	This 1950s singer of Mexican ancestry was the first to marry Latin rhythms and rock. The film *La Bamba* recounts his rise to fame and his tragic death in a plane crash.
23. Raquel Welch	This model, actress, and dancer with Bolivian roots was a sex symbol of the seventies and a serious performer of the eighties.

What's compadrazco?

Compadrazco, Spanish for "coparenting," is a critical feature of the Puerto Rican social and extended family structure. It may also be found among other Latino groups. It's a system in which friends select each other to act as second parents, *madrinas* and *padrinos* (godmothers and godfathers), to their children. Often, the *madrina* is the one who buys the wedding ring for her godchild. Close friends often refer to each other as *compadre* and *comadre* as a way of reinforcing ties.

What's a pahry?

A *pahry* is a fiesta—a "party." Which is not to say that Puerto Ricans don't use the word "fiesta" when they celebrate—it's just that *pahry* belongs to the ever-expanding "Spanglish" vocabulary.

So what do mainland Puerto Ricans do at a pahry?

At salsa parties the bongos keep pace with the maracas and the maracas chase the blues away.

Often Puerto Ricans celebrate at home or at social clubs, but they also take their partying out into the street. The biggest street party of all is the Puerto Rican Day Parade in New York City each June, when *comparsas* (carnival dancing groups) and marching bands follow the floats, which are followed by politicians looking for votes. In recent years, the Puerto Rican Day Parade has attracted larger crowds along Fifth Avenue than the Saint Patrick's Day Parade. In 1997, an estimated two million people lined the parade route on Puerto Rican Day.

The *Fiesta del Apostol Santiago* or *Fiestas Padronales de Santiago Apostal* (St. James' Day), also brings out the dancers in New York City's *El Barrio* and other Puerto Rican neighborhoods. Both men and women wear traditional island costumes that look quite African and dance down the middle of the street to fast carnival rhythms, singing *bombas*—African couplets accompanied by drum music.

What is Puerto Rican cooking like, and what's the Puerto Rican national dish?

Mainland Puerto Ricans (and islanders, too) love typical American fare such as spaghetti, but they also have a rich tropical cuisine all their own. Among the best-known Puerto Rican culinary delights are *pasteles* (a kind of *tamal* made with plantains and tubers such as *yuca* and *yautía*, not corn, and stuffed with meat), *lechón asado* (roast suckling pig), and *arroz con gandules* (rice and pigeon peas). *Asopao,* a fragrant chicken and rice stew, could perhaps be called the national dish of Puerto Rico, since a pot of it is often found simmering on the stove in many a Puerto Rican household.

Spanish, African, and Taino elements are clearly visible in Puerto Rican cuisine. Puerto Rican cooks use *achiote* seeds (annatto), which was an essential Taino ingredient, to impart an orange color and a subtle flavor to the oil in which foods are sautéed. Many dishes such as paella and *caldo gallego* (a rich bean soup) are straight from the Spanish kitchen, but with a tropical twist. Others, such as *mofongo*, "meatballs" made with crushed fried plantains, pork cracklings, and garlic, are clearly of African origin.

Two critical ingredients in Puerto Rican cooking cannot go without mention. One, called *adobo*, is a seasoning composed of lemon juice, garlic, pepper, and oregano that is rubbed into meat, poultry, and fish. The other is *sofrito*, a marinade or sauce made of tomatoes, onion, garlic, fresh chiles, cilantro, and *recao* (an herb found in Puerto Rican and Asian markets), that is the foundation for countless dishes, including *asopao*. Many Puerto Rican cooks keep a batch of *sofrito* tucked away in the refrigerator or freezer, since so many dishes call for it.

CINCO

Cuban Americans

BEFORE THE *CUBA LIBRE* WAS INVENTED

What was Cuba like before Fidel Castro?

Did the Siboney and Taino invent Cuban cigars?

What did the Spanish want with Cuba, and why was it so important?

How did Havana come to be swapped for Florida?

What part did the English play when it came to African slavery in Cuba?

Does that mean the Africans didn't mind being taken to Cuba?

Why did it take Cubans so long to gain their independence from Spain, and how was slavery a key factor?

How was Cuba almost annexed to the United States in the 1840s?

What was the Grito de Yara, and why did Cuban landowners change their minds and join the rest of the folks?

How did U.S. business interests profit from Cuba's Ten Years' War?

Who was José Martí?

Who wrote the song "Guantanamera"?

What role did José Martí play in Cuba's second bid for independence?

So why did the United States fight the Spanish-American War?

Is it true that the Cuban revolutionaries would have won the war without American intervention?

If lust for Cuba was the reason the United States went to war with Spain, how come Cuba got its independence by 1902?

What's a Cuba libre?

What was the Platt Amendment, and why did it open a bucket of worms that helped fuel the 1959 Revolution led by Fidel Castro?

What's Guantánamo Bay?

Who was Fulgencio Batista?

If Cuba was doing so well, how come a revolution was waiting in the wings?

Who is Fidel Castro, and what happened to his idealistic revolution that sent Cubans fleeing to Miami by the thousands?

What's a gusano?

Who was Che Guevara?

What has Fidel done for Cuba?

What happened at the Bay of Pigs, and why did Cuban Americans blame President Kennedy?

What caused the Cuban Missile Crisis?

How many Cubans fled Cuba in the 1960s and 1970s, and how did they fare?

What was the Cuban Adjustment Act?

Who were the Marielitos, and why did so many people hate them?

What was the 1994 Rafter Refugee Crisis, and why was the Cuban Adjustment Act suddenly repealed?

What happened to the Brothers to the Rescue?

What will happen to Cuba after Castro falls?

HAVANA, U.S.A.: THE LAND OF THE FIESTA, BUT NOT THE SIESTA

What's Little Havana, and why isn't it so Havana anymore?

Why is Miami called the "capital of Latin America"?

How do Cuban Americans feel about Castro and the trade embargo against Cuba?

Since Cuba is only ninety miles from Florida, do Cuban Americans visit?

What's a YUCA?

Are all Cuban Americans rich?

What's Santería?

What's a fiesta de quince?

What foods do Cuban Americans like?

BEFORE THE *CUBA LIBRE* WAS INVENTED

What was Cuba like before Fidel Castro?

In 1492, when **Christopher Columbus** first made landfall on Cuba, the largest and westernmost island of the Antillean archipelago, this is what he wrote in his journals: "[I have] never seen anything so beautiful . . . [everything I saw] was so lovely that my eyes could not weary of beholding such beauty, nor could I weary of the songs of the birds large and small. . . . Flocks of parrots darken the sun. There are trees of a thousand species, each has its particular fruit, and all of marvelous flavor."

The Taino and Siboney, two tribes in the Arawak federation, inhabited the island and lived by fishing, hunting, and farming. They grew corn, sweet potatoes, *yuca* (a tuber that is still very popular among Cubans and Cuban Americans), tomatoes, pineapples, and other fruits. The people were also skilled at many crafts, including woodwork, ceramics, and textile production. Out of wild cotton and palm fibers they made hammocks, fishing lines, and many other useful tools. Columbus observed in one of his letters that the women seemed to work more than the men, but he was unsure whether they were allowed to own property.

Although the exact number of Taino and Siboney inhabiting Cuba when Columbus arrived is not known (some sources estimate 100,000), it is certain that within a few decades after Columbus stepped foot on Cuba, their population was nearly decimated by European diseases and the hard labor imposed on them by the Spaniards. As a result of interbreeding with the Spanish, pure-blooded Arawak eventually disappeared entirely from the island. Another Arawak tribe, known as the Mayari, also inhabited Cuba before the Spanish *conquista*, but, as with the Siboney and Taino, few traces of them remain.

Did the Siboney and Taino invent Cuban cigars?

You could say so, since they cultivated tobacco extensively and taught **Columbus** and other conquistadors how to roll and smoke cigars. The word "tobacco" comes from the Taino *tabaco*. Curiously, the process of rolling these popular leaves has not changed much over the centuries.

What did the Spanish want with Cuba, and why was it so important?

At first, as was their custom, the Spanish prospected for gold. **Diego Velázquez,** a rich landowner from Hispaniola (an island that is now the Dominican Republic and Haiti) who had won many battles against the native peoples, was sent to Cuba by the Spanish crown in 1511 to secure the island and establish settlements for the purpose of mining gold. Between 1512 and 1515, Velázquez founded Baracoa, Bayamo, Trinidad, Sancti Spiritus, Havana, Puerto Principe, and Santiago de Cuba. Gold was discovered in the central highland ranges of the Sierra Maestra in the western part of the island (the same mountain range from which **Fidel Castro** would launch his 1959 revolution), but the amount was not significant. Cuba's wealth really lay in its strategic location and rich soil.

Cuba is flanked by the Gulf of Mexico and the Caribbean Sea, and lies at the crossroads of three main maritime routes: the Straits of Florida to the north, the Windward Passage to the east, and the Yucatán Channel to the west. For this reason, the island was the perfect pitstop for Spanish conquistadors exploring other corners of the Americas. However, this easy access to maritime routes also made Cuba vulnerable to foreign aggression—namely English, Dutch, and French pirates and privateers stalking Spanish galleons en route from Mexico and Peru, their holds filled with gold and other goodies.

Thus, from the early days of the Spanish conquest, Spain

valued Cuba for its location. When African slaves were brought to the island by the thousands to work in the fields, and Cuba prospered from its agricultural pursuits, Spain saw this as a handsome side benefit.

How did Havana come to be swapped for Florida?

Spain became involved in the Seven Years War (1756–63), which was essentially waged between France and England. After the fiasco the English dubbed the defeat of the Spanish Armada, the Spanish were not about to take Britain's side in the war and came to the aid of the French. As a result, the English targeted Spain's New World colonies. In 1762, Britain decided that Cuba, where sugar, coffee, and tobacco grew in abundance and the trade winds were always in the mariner's favor, would make a nice little colony. They struck Havana harbor and seized control of the city.

Some good things came out of the English occupation for the *criollos* of Cuba, who until then had been forced to trade almost exclusively with Spain, or else deal in the black market with other European powers. Trade taxes were abolished. With the English in charge, the island was thrown wide open to commerce with merchants and traders from England and the American colonies. All at once Cuba, which had been regarded merely as a stopping place for Spaniards, saw that it had great prospects for a thriving economy. But the English occupation was short-lived, lasting only ten months, since the Spanish could not bear to lose their Caribbean jewel. In 1763 the Spanish swapped the English Florida (which was practically unfit for habitation) for Cuba.

What part did the English play when it came to African slavery in Cuba?

The Spanish had not opposed African slavery (in fact, they were among the first to engage in the slave trade), they just never saw a great demand for it in Cuba. The English, however, realized that an effective way to tap Cuba's potential in agriculture was to import slaves. During the brief English occupation, African slaves were a highly coveted commodity. Encouraged by the English, slave traders from all over the world descended on Cuba for a share of the newly opened market. In the ten months of English rule in Cuba, over ten thousand African slaves were introduced—many more than would ordinarily have entered Cuba under Spain over a period of ten years or more.

Thanks to the influx of African slaves, sugarcane, tobacco, coffee, and other crops flourished in Cuba. The English favored the cultivation of sugarcane and thus it became the main crop of the island. Cuba's reliance on a single-crop economy, which has been both the joy and the bane of the island's existence to this day, had begun. In 1779 Cubans were given authorization to conduct free trade with North America and were granted exemptions from startup taxes for new sugar mills. As a result, sugar plantations sprouted all over the island and more slaves were brought over to keep up with the demand from international markets. Cuba was transformed overnight; that transformation brought growth. By the end of the eighteenth century, Havana ranked as one of the largest cities in the New World.

The African slaves in Cuba were treated better than in other Spanish colonies. The number of "free colored" people in Cuba was higher than elsewhere for two reasons. First, white Spanish slaveowners customarily freed their many illegitimate children. Second, slaves in Cuba had the right to purchase their freedom or their children's freedom from their owners, an arrangement called *coartación*. They had to give their owner a down payment and then a fixed sum in installments. The *coartación* was possible because the Spanish looked upon the Africans not as a people they were born to possess but merely as a commodity, a source of cheap labor. The Spanish were not obsessed with issues of race. To a Spaniard, if you looked white, you were white, even if one of your parents or grandparents was a person of color. The Anglo concept of the "octoroon" was virtually inconceivable to the Spanish. This is not to say that racial prejudice was absent in Cuba and other Spanish New World colonies—just that the rules of the game were different.

Does that mean the Africans didn't mind being taken to Cuba?

The Africans longed for their homelands in Western Africa (as many of their soulful ballads remind us); they longed for freedom, and of course, they very much minded being exploited. And exploited they were, especially in remote areas of Cuba, where slaveowners paid less heed to the laws of *coartación*. As a result, there were thousands of *cimarrones*, or runaway slaves, and numerous slave uprisings occurred in Cuba in the 1700s and 1800s. In 1727, three hundred slaves rebelled on one Havana plantation alone. Four years later, another slave revolt closed down the copper mines of Santiago de Cuba.

These uprisings gave way to a more organized movement for emancipation. In 1811, a free African Cuban carpenter named **José Antonio Aponte** organized a large rebellion in Havana, demanding that all the slaves be set free. Aponte's cause was supported by some whites, as well as free Africans and slaves. During this time, many intellectuals in Cuba awakened to the injustices of slavery. Aponte's rebellion, as well as hundreds of others throughout the island—in Matanzas, Holguín, Puerto Principe, Manzanillo, and almost every village and hamlet in Cuba—resulted not only in a new social awareness but in a terrible backlash by *criollo* and Spanish-born slaveowners. In retaliation for their insurrection, African Cubans were tortured and slaughtered. Some were flogged to death "to set an example." An uprising in Matanzas province in the early 1800s, involving more than three hundred slaves from fifteen sugar plantations, ended when a local squadron of Spanish lancers attacked and dispersed hundreds of brave fighters, killing many in the process.

However, the slaves' struggle was not in vain. By the mid-1800s, an African Cuban was to emerge a leader in the fight for emancipation. His name was **Antonio Maceo,** and it is thanks to him and three other important revolutionaries, **Carlos Manuel de Céspedes, Máximo Gómez,** and **José Martí,** that Cuba won its independence from Spain.

Why did it take Cubans so long to gain their independence from Spain, and how was slavery a key factor?

Whereas the rest of Latin America (except Puerto Rico) had gained its independence from Spain by the middle of the nineteenth century, Cuba remained a Spanish colony until the Spanish-American War of 1898. There are many reasons for this delay in fulfilling the dreams of generations of Cuban *criollos* who had envisioned a nation separate from Spain since the middle of the eighteenth century.

What held Cuba back was the Cuban *criollo* elite, who owned the sugar and tobacco plantations. The elite sought reforms that would benefit them, while they disregarded the needs of the Cuban population at large. They wanted lower tariffs and freer trade with the rest of the world, but they feared that independence from Spain might be bad for business.

By 1817, England was putting pressure on Spain to abolish the slave trade in its colonies. In 1845, the Spanish enacted the Law of Abolition and Repression of the Slave Trade, which states that all slaves introduced to Cuba after 1820 were in illegal bondage and were entitled to their freedom. Although the law did little to diminish the supply of slaves to Cuba, it certainly made doing business and growing sugarcane a lot more expensive. For one, slave mortality, which previously had caused little concern to plantation owners, now presented a problem. Before, slaves could be replaced at the drop of a sombrero and for the cost of one, but since importing slaves was against the law, their price skyrocketed.

Between 1800 and 1820, the price of a male slave dropped from 300 to 60 pesos, but by the 1860s, a slave might go for as much as 1500 pesos. Ironically the slave trade grew during this time, and in fact, the majority of slaves entered Cuba after 1820. Between 1821 and 1831, more than 300 expeditions brought an estimated sixty thousand slaves to Cuba, and between 1830 and 1850 an average of ten thousand slaves arrived in Cuba annually. This open defiance of Spanish law constitutes an odd sort of insurrection by the *criollo* landed gentry, who decided it was best to be independent of Spain, but did not advocate freedom and the pursuit of happiness for all.

IMPORTANT DATES

1763	Spain hands Florida to the English in exchange for Cuba.
May 19, 1895	José Martí, who fought for Cuba's freedom, dies at the Battle of Dos Rios.
May 20, 1902	Cuba wins its independence and elects its first president, Tomás Estrada Palma.
January 1, 1959	Fulgencio Batista flees Cuba in the early dawn for safety in Spain.
October 22, 1962	President Kennedy announces that Russian atomic-missile sites are being built in Cuba, a threat to the region's security. He calls for a blockade of Cuba and demands the withdrawal of all offensive weapons.

How was Cuba almost annexed to the United States in the 1840s?

The Cuban *criollo* elite—i.e., the landowners, not the intellectuals—felt disaffected from Spain, a nation which charged Cubans high taxes and threatened to abolish slavery. It occurred to the Cuban elite that if the United States annexed Cuba they could preserve slavery and sell their sugar, tobacco, and coffee to North America duty-free. The elite saw the annexation of Texas, which was allowed to join the Union as a slave state, as the perfect example of the kind of setup they envisioned for Cuba.

Just as the *criollo* elite were considering the United States, the Americans were also intensely eyeing Cuba during the nineteenth century. The notion of Manifest Destiny had excited the imagination of Americans—and the island seemed like an ideal piece of real estate. In a speech delivered in 1823, **John Quincy Adams** voiced America's belief that the annexation of Cuba was something of a natural law: "There are laws political as of physical gravitation," said Adams, "and if an apple, severed by a tempest from its native tree, cannot choose but to fall to the ground, Cuba, forcibly disjoined from its own natural connection to Spain, and incapable of self-support, can gravitate only towards the North American Union, which, by the same law of nature, cannot cast her off from her bosom." An operative phrase in Adam's speech is "incapable of self-support." Over this idea alone wars have been fought.

Adams never managed to secure Cuba for the United States, but his ideas about the island were never forgotten and had a profound impact on future generations in Washington. As annexation fever grew among the *criollo* elite in the 1840s, the U.S. government bolstered its efforts to obtain Cuba. First, **President James Polk** offered Spain $100 million for the island in 1848, but the Spanish declined. Then in 1854 **President Franklin Pierce** upped the ante to $130 million, but again Spain turned down the offer. That same year, American ministers to Spain, England, and France met in Ostend, Belgium, and proclaimed loudly and publicly that the United States wished to buy Cuba. The Ostend Manifesto, as it came to be known, also contained a warning to the Spanish that if they did not acquiesce, then "by any law human and divine, we shall be justified in wresting it [Cuba] from Spain if we possess the power." Anyone with a little foresight could have predicted that, sooner or later, a Spanish-American War would be fought.

But the United States suddenly became involved in domestic affairs that pivoted on the issue of slavery. Within ten years, the nation was embroiled in the Civil War, which brought activity on the international front to a virtual halt. At the same time, Cuban *criollos* with justice on their minds were becoming more organized, inspired by Latin American leaders such as **Simon Bolívar** and **José Francisco de San Martín,** who were forging independent democratic republics in South America.

What was the Grito de Yara, and why did Cuban landowners change their minds and join the rest of the folks?

In May 1865, the Reformist Party, which was composed mainly of the *criollo* elite, directed a memorandum to the Spanish Parliament with four key demands: that Cubans be represented in the Parliament, the tariff system be completely reformed, *criollos* (Cuban-born Caucasians with Spanish blood) be given the same rights as *peninsulares* (those born in Spain), and that slavery be permanently abolished in Cuba with compensation.

Many factors led to the sudden about-face on the issue of slavery for the *criollo* elite. First, it was clear that slavery had to end sooner or later. Second, Cuban planters had turned their attention to other groups of laborers: Chinese contract workers. Between 1840 and 1870, about 125,000 Chinese men and women became indentured workers in Cuba. At the same time poor or displaced Spanish workers, primarily from the Canary Islands, Galicia, and Asturias, who were bearing the brunt of a crumbling economy at home, were pouring into Cuba. These white immigrants went to work at *ingenios* (sugar mills), *cafetales* (coffee plantations), and other places where Africans traditionally toiled.

With its economy in the throes of a depression caused by the loss of its New World colonies and mishaps at home, Spain tightened the screws on Cuba and, in the view of many patriots, hammered the first nail into its imperialist coffin on the island. Instead of letting the Cubans be, the Spanish augmented the authority of their military tribunals, denied Cubans any parliamentary voice, banned political meetings, raised taxes a whopping six percent, and imposed protectionist duties on all foreign products. In response to Spain's protectionist duties, the United States raised tariffs on Cuban goods by ten percent. Cuban producers were caught in the middle, squeezed from both sides, with ever-diminishing profits and foreign markets.

Within a couple of years, cattle barons from Camagüey, sugar landlords from Oriente, and members of the Cuban elite from all over the island convened in the town of Yara to plan a mass rebellion against Spain. Whites, African Cubans, small farmers, free men and slaves, and people of all classes joined in the rebellion by the thousands. The gathering on October 10, 1868, called *El Grito de Yara* (the Cry from Yara), proclaimed Cuban independence and the establishment of a provisional republic. The protesters decried unfair taxation and called for free trade with all nations, a freely elected representative government, and "universal manhood suffrage." As you might guess, women were excluded from voting (it was not until the 1930s that Cuban women got the right to vote), but in the context of the times, it was clearly a step toward greater equality.

This first cry for independence escalated into a bloody civil war against Spain that is known as the Ten Years' War.

The Spanish, seeing their prized colony slipping away—an island they had previously dubbed "Cuba most faithful" because it had remained loyal while Mexico, Venezuela, and other colonies were breaking their ties with Spain—took no prisoners. They destroyed the sugar mills, torched the land, and conducted mass executions. When the conflict ended in defeat for Cuba in 1878, the island was left in a state of utter desperation. Spain simply took up where it had left off and forbade the Cubans from having any say in government and imposed steep taxes.

How did U.S. business interests profit from Cuba's Ten Years' War?

Devastated by the war, many Cuban growers relinquished their ownership positions in the *ingenios* and *cafetales*. They traded their property titles for stock options in American corporations, which took over their land. In effect, Cuban growers became administrators of companies owned by American corporations. Some American corporations, such as the E. Atkins Company in Boston, foreclosed on estates they had loaned money to for agricultural operations, and subsequently acquired vast sugar properties and other holdings from insolvent Cuban landlords. By 1895 less than 20 percent of mill owners in Cuba were Cubans. Almost immediately 95 percent of all Cuban sugar exports found their way to the United States. The island had a single-crop economy with a single country to sell to. The stage was set for what would eventually become one of Cuba's greatest tragedies.

Who was José Martí?

José Martí y Pérez was Cuba's George Washington and Thomas Jefferson all rolled into one. Born in Havana to Spanish parents on January 28, 1853, Martí is remembered throughout the Spanish-speaking world not only as a brilliant political leader but also as a great poet. He was the founder of the *modernismo* literary style in Cuba—the precursor of the symbolist movement, which stressed simplicity and directness and broke away from the florid style of the nineteenth century. Among Martí's literary works are the books of poetry, *Isma-elillo* (1882) and *Versos sencillos* (*Plain Verse*, 1891), and a short story collection *La edad de oro* (*The Golden Age*, 1898).

José Martí answered the call to rebellion against the oppressive Spanish regime early in life. At the tender age of sixteen, he was arrested for sedition and sent into exile. He spent his first period of exile (1871–1878) in Spain, Mexico, and Guatemala, where he penned his famous poem "*La niña de Guatemala.*" The second time he was exiled from Cuba, Martí went to England and the United States, where he lived from 1880 until 1895. He resided in New York City on Water Street, near the Fulton Fish Market, for several years. There he wrote some extraordinary political prose that many years later became the blueprint of the unofficial constitution of anti-Castro Cuban Americans in Miami. His writings have also served **Fidel Castro** well in many of his political speeches and proclamations.

Who wrote the song "Guantanamera"?

"*Guantanamera/Guajira guantanamera . . .*" The song, made popular by the group the Weavers, is based on a traditional Cuban ballad (sung to a *guajira*—farm girl—from Guantánamo) and contains lines from a famous poem by **José Martí:** "*Yo soy un hombre sincero / de donde crece la palma / y antes de morirme quiero / cantar mis versos del alma.*" "I am an honest man / from the land where palm trees grow / and before I die I want / to sing the poems in my heart."

What role did José Martí play in Cuba's second bid for independence?

While in the United States, **José Martí** was instrumental in planning Cuba's second struggle for independence. He studied the Ten Years' War and another failed war, called the *Guerra Chiquita* (the Small War) and concluded that Cuba had failed in its efforts toward independence for lack of organization. He wrote in 1882: "The revolution is ... a detailed understanding based on advanced planning and great foresight." Martí also understood that independence was only a first step toward creating a thriving nation. In 1892 he proclaimed: "Our goal is not so much a mere political change as a good, sound, and just equitable social system without demagogic fawning or arrogance of authority. And let us never forget that the greater the suffering, the greater the right to justice, and the prejudices of men and social inequities cannot prevail over the equality which nature has created." Martí also addressed concerns about the control of wealth by a few, and put forth an advanced democratic philosophy when he wrote: "A country with a few rich men is not rich—only the country where everyone possesses a little wealth is rich. In political economy and good government, distribution is the source of prosperity."

Just after war broke out in Cuba in 1895, José Martí returned to the island with the intent of leading the fight for liberation. For Martí, as for the revolutionaries at his side, liberation meant freedom from oppression, racism, and all foreign dominance, whether by the empire across the Atlantic or the empire to the north. He believed that "to change masters is not to be free." José Martí would not live to see the outcome of Cuba's quest for freedom. He died at the Battle of Dos Rios on May 19, 1895, about three years before the United States got involved in the war.

So why did the United States fight the Spanish-American War?

The United States had been itching to gain control of Cuba for most of the nineteenth century. When the Cuban *criollos* proved mighty and it became evident that Cuba would soon not only be free from Spanish domination but become a sovereign nation, the U.S. government decided that unusual measures were needed. The United States found the perfect excuse to get involved when, on February 15, 1898, the American battleship *Maine* was blown up in Havana harbor. In April 1898, **President William McKinley** issued a resolution to Congress to send troops to Cuba to subdue both the Spanish and the Cubans. "The forcible intervention of the United States," President McKinley told Congress, "involves . . . hostile constraint against both Spaniards and Cubans, the means to establish grounds upon which to neutralize the two competing claims of sovereignty and establish by superior force of arms a third." That "third," needless to say, was the United States of America, which clearly had no intention of merely helping the Cubans liberate themselves from Spain.

The Spanish-American War was declared and then won by the Americans in a matter of ten weeks. In the fallout, the United States acquired Puerto Rico, the Philippines, Guam, and the Wake Islands (see Chapter Cuatro). The United States also took control of Cuba, but only until 1902.

Is it true that the Cuban revolutionaries would have won the war without American intervention?

Yes. As 1898 dawned, the Cubans, who thanks to **José Martí** had mounted a carefully planned war of insurrection, were in complete control of the countryside, and they were already marching into several urban centers. The Spanish knew they were no match against the Cuban rebels and that it was just a matter of time before they would have to lay down their arms.

All the people of Cuba were behind the revolutionary efforts, and Spain could not possibly stem the tide of history. Cuban independence and Cuban rule were destiny manifest.

If lust for Cuba was the reason the United States went to war with Spain, how come Cuba got its independence by 1902?

The Cuban rebels had carefully studied **President McKinley**'s declaration of war, and having been forewarned by **José Martí** about America's desire to acquire Cuba, they mounted an unprecedented public relations campaign to ensure that the United States would agree to recognize *Cuba libre*—an independent Cuba. Many Americans, journalists and liberal politicians among them, supported Cuba's call for independence. President McKinley and others on Capitol Hill opposed Cuba's bid for sovereignty. Finally a compromise was reached between the hawkish president and the more liberal wing of government. The United States did not have to recognize Cuban independence outright as long as there was some sort of disclaimer. That disclaimer is Article IV of the American War Resolution, known as the Teller Amendment, which reads as follows: "[The United States] hereby disclaims any disposition of intention to exercise sovereignty, jurisdiction, or control over said island except for pacification thereof, and asserts its determination, when that is accomplished, to leave the government and control of the island to its people."

What's a Cuba libre?

Cuba libre means literally "Free Cuba," and is a phrase taken from the nineteenth-century Cuban revolutionary cry, *"Viva Cuba libre!"* A *Cuba libre* is a popular cocktail that is one part rum and two parts Coca-Cola. The implication is obvious: Cuba became free thanks to one part Cuban effort (rum, the Cuban national beverage) and two parts U.S. muscle

(Coca-Cola, the quintessential American soft drink). The irony of it did not escape Cubans. Until the death of **Roberto C. Goizueta** in 1997, a Cuban American who fled **Castro**'s regime and settled in the United States, where he served as the chief executive officer of the Coca-Cola Company, it looked as if the *Cuba libre* was mostly Cuban American. Incidentally, under the direction of Roberto Goizueta, the Coca-Cola Company grew by leaps and bounds, opening whole new markets, including the vast one of China.

What was the Platt Amendment, and why did it open a bucket of worms that helped fuel the 1959 Revolution led by Fidel Castro?

The Teller Amendment clearly stated that the United States wouldn't try to take over Cuba—but interpreted another way (the way the U.S. government interpreted it), it didn't mean that the United States should not "protect" Cuba from itself and help the island along. Thus, in 1900, the McKinley administration chose Cuban candidates whom it believed Cubans should elect to public office. But the Cuban people refused to elect those candidates. This uppity attitude enraged **President McKinley** and many members of Congress, who decided that Cubans were unwise and thus unable to rule themselves.

Finally, secretary of war **Elihu Root** put forth a proposal, later named the Platt Amendment, which advocated letting Cubans go their own way, as long as "in transferring the control of Cuba to the government established under the new constitution the United States reserves and retains the right of intervention for the preservation of Cuban independence and the maintenance of a stable government." The proposal also stipulated that "no government organized under the constitution shall be deemed to have authority to enter into any treaty or engagement with any foreign power which may tend to impair or interfere with the independence of Cuba." It stated, too, that the United States could "acquire and hold the title to land, and maintain naval stations at certain specified stations." Translation? The United States had the right to tell the Cuban people how to govern themselves, establish naval stations on the island, ultimately interfere in Cuba's foreign policy when it deemed necessary, and impose trade restrictions.

Despite the fact that the Platt Amendment was approved in June 1901, Cuba tried as best it could to go about its business. The Cuban people assembled their own government, and in 1902 elected their first president, **Tomás Estrada Palma.** But the United States was clearly in the picture. Shortly thereafter, the U.S. government installed a naval base at Guantánamo Bay and proceeded to keep a close watch over Cuban affairs. At the same time, American business interests invested heavily in sugar, coffee, tobacco, and other crops on the island. The Cuban economy flourished as never before. Cuba's place as the chief supplier of sugar to America was firmly established—but it was this one-crop economic system that later caused so much distress.

The idea that Cubans were not the masters of their fate, thanks to the Platt Amendment, remained a thorn in the side of Cuban patriots. That thorn caused a great deal of irritation on three separate occasions: in 1906, 1912, and 1917, when U.S. military forces invaded Cuba and took provisional charge of its government to protect American interests from internal political unrest and corruption. After those invasions, Cuban presidents and representatives ran on anti-Platt Amendment platforms, promising to have it repealed.

That would not happen until 1934, when Cuba's great democratic president, **Ramón Grau San Martín,** proclaimed the abrogation of the Platt Amendment on the day of his inauguration. The United States, however, did get to keep its lease of Guantánamo Bay. After **Fidel Castro** seized power in 1959, he reminded the Cuban people that they had been under U.S. imperialist domination ever since the day the Platt Amendment took effect. The Platt Amendment had become such a symbol of oppression in the minds of Cubans that the mere mention of it was enough to get governments elected and new dictators cheered into office.

What's Guantánamo Bay?

Guantánamo Bay is a large deep-water bay on the southeastern shore of Cuba. Covering thirty square miles, it is one of the best-protected bays in the world. The British were the first to establish a naval station there during their brief sojourn in Cuba. Then, in 1903, the U.S. government took control of Guantánamo Bay by a treaty that cannot be annulled unilaterally. The American military presence on what **Fidel Castro** and other Cubans consider Cuban territory has long been a source of disagreement between the two countries. American naval operations also serve to remind Castro's government just how close the United States is.

Who was Fulgencio Batista?

Fulgencio Batista y Zaldívar was the most powerful political figure in Cuba from 1933 to 1944. As an army sergeant, Batista participated in the 1933 ouster of **Gerardo Machado,** a much-hated dictator who ruled Cuba by graft, corruption, and nepotism (at one point during his regime, almost everyone in high office was related to him). That same year Batista orchestrated a coup that led to the overthrow of the provisional government of **Carlos Manuel de Céspedes** (a direct descendant of the great nineteenth-century revolutionary by the same name), which had been put in place by the United States. But Batista managed to gain the confidence of the U.S. ambassador to Cuba, who secured him the unconditional backing of the United States. From 1933 to 1940 Batista ruled Cuba from behind the scenes, then in 1940 he was elected president of Cuba. Of mixed Indian, African, and Spanish descent, Batista came from humble beginnings—a first for a Cuban president, as those who preceded him belonged to the ruling white elite. He served as president until 1944 when his term ended, and in keeping with the constitution he stepped out of office. **Ramón Grau San Martín** was elected to his post.

Batista retired to Florida in 1944, but in 1952 he returned to Cuba with the intent of ruling the island. This time he led a bloodless coup d'état and seized the reins of the government from the then-democratically elected president, **Carlos Prío Socarrás.** Cubans were angry over Batista's disregard for the democratic process, but he promised them free elections. He did hold presidential elections in 1954 and 1958, but he won handily through graft and ballot fixing. Over time, Batista grew from a corrupt Latin American-style dictator to a power-hungry, ruthless politico who stuffed his pockets and crushed dissent. As **Fidel Castro** and other opposition leaders decried his dictatorship, Batista intensified his efforts to create a police state, sending countless members of the opposition to jail or to their deaths.

When he could not do away with the opposition, Batista unashamedly bought their favors. After taking money for himself from the proceeds of the national lottery and other sources, Batista doled out the rest in exchange for political backing. In 1957, *Revista Carteles,* a weekly Cuban news magazine, disclosed that twenty members of the Batista government owned numbered Swiss bank accounts, each with deposits of over $1 million. Batista also gave $1.6 million to the Roman Catholic Church; $5 million to labor unions; and, unbelievably, $1 million a month to newspaper editors and reporters in exchange for their silence. It was no wonder that somewhere in the Sierra Maestra of Oriente Province, a revolution was brewing.

In spite of the undeniable corruption of Batista's dictatorship, on the surface Cuba's economy appeared to be thriving. The island enjoyed one of the highest per capita incomes in Latin America (second only to oil-rich Venezuela) and one of the region's highest standards of living. Havana was as sophisticated and cultured a city as any European capital. By 1957, there were more television sets in Cuba (one per twenty-five inhabitants) than in any other Latin American country. And Cuba was first in telephones, automobiles, and railroads. The island was held up as an example by many nations that aspired to such creature comforts and general well-being.

If Cuba was doing so well, how come a revolution was waiting in the wings?

In the 1950s, Cuba was a mass of contradictions. Yes, the economy was among the strongest in Latin America. But Cuba's economy was tied not to other Latin American countries but to the United States, which exerted enormous influence. The island subsisted almost exclusively on imports from the United States and paid American prices for them. In 1950, Cuba imported $515 million worth of goods from the United States. By 1958 that figure had risen to $777 million. During the same period, the island's per capita annual income was $374, compared to $2,000 in the United States.

To add insult to injury, in the mid-1950s, the price of sugar, the old reliable crop that made it possible for Cubans to survive, suddenly plummeted in markets around the world. **Fulgencio Batista** imposed no tariff protection and thereby discouraged the development of any other national industries since they would not be able to compete against American-made goods.

Then, too, a seemingly unbridgeable chasm yawned between the haves and the have-nots. Although Havana was one of the most expensive cities in the world, with the largest per capita number of Cadillacs, the vast majority of Cubans lived in poverty. Out of a population of almost six million, only 620,000 were considered middle-class, with another 200,000 civil servants and 200,000 service workers just slightly below the middle class. The rest of the population was made up of peasants and agricultural workers, large numbers of unemployed, and the very rich, who accounted for a very small percentage of Cubans.

The vast *latifundios*, or agricultural estates, were owned by a handful of wealthy Cubans, as well as American syndicates, who held 25 percent of all the land in production. The American syndicates often kept the land idle, awaiting a sudden demand for sugar in the world market before bothering to plant or harvest the crop. As a result, the 25 percent of the Cuban people who were employed as sugar workers could only find work an average of one hundred days a year. The daily wages of these workers severely declined during the 1950s, and so did social services. The sharp disparity in the standard of living between the rural and urban populations intensified. For instance, while 80 percent of city dwellers had electricity and running water, only 15 percent of rural folk could count on such amenities. In Havana, the ratio of doctors to patients was 1 to 227, while in Oriente Province (the westernmost rural province, where Castro comes from), it was a dismal 1 to 2,423. Illiteracy was on the rise, as fewer children attended school in the 1950s than had done so in the 1920s.

To make matters worse, most of Cuba's wealth was being siphoned out of the country, either by American companies that took their profits home, or by wealthy Cuban nationals, who, fearing a debacle in their very unstable society and a depression thanks to Cuba's single-crop economy, put their money to work elsewhere—primarily in American real estate, banks, and investment institutions. In the meantime, the Cuban middle class, one of the strongest in Latin America, saw its buying power dwindle and white-collar jobs diminish. Middle-class Cubans, as well as the rural poor, were unable to improve their lot, since they lacked the wherewithal to take their meager savings out of the country or to invest them in a safe vehicle, such as Cuban real estate, which in a matter of years had tripled in price as a result of inflation.

Compounding the social and economic disparities, and the dire consequences of an almost exclusive dependence on sugar, was a deep moral malaise that afflicted the people of this beautiful island. Casinos, controlled by American organized crime and sanctioned by Batista (who took a hefty cut of the profits) were a thriving industry. Illegal drugs were sold openly. Pornography clubs, as well as brothels, became attractive employers for thousands of Cuban women from rural areas who could find no other means of supporting their families. By the end of 1958, an estimated 11,500 women earned livings as prostitutes. In addition, hundreds of underage girls and some boys (as young as eight or nine) were kidnapped into prostitution. Newborn babies were abandoned at the doorsteps of local orphanages by the hundreds. Juvenile delinquency, hopelessness, and suicide had become the norm. The vast majority of the hardworking poor and middle class were caught in an unbearable vise.

While Cuba was falling apart, an idealistic political leader by the name of **Fidel Castro** was organizing an army of revolutionaries, demanding a clean sweep of government corruption and inefficiency, and promising to end American economic domination of Cuba and foreign exploitation of Cuban women and minors. In the cities and throughout the countryside, the people revolted; they gathered at mass demonstrations, planted bombs in movie theaters and other public places, and demanded that the dictator leave at once. Seeing his control slipping, Fulgencio Batista instituted a Gestapo-like police force that conducted witch hunts and executed people en masse.

The foreign press—particularly the American press—was well aware of the human rights violations of the Batista regime. Articles in foreign newspapers shed light on one significant fact: the weapons Batista used to carry out his atrocities were being furnished by none other than the United States of America. **President Dwight Eisenhower** found himself in a very serious dilemma. Although Batista's government protected the interests of American companies and investments on the island, and cooperated when it came to American military operations in Cuba, the U.S. government found Batista's totalitarian measures completely at odds with America's principles. And while ambassador **Earl T. Smith** warned Eisenhower that Castro was believed to be a communist (a word that made Americans shudder in those terrible Cold War years), the American president felt he could no longer justify the sale of arms to Fulgencio Batista.

Toward the end of 1958, the United States canceled the sale of tanks and other weapons to Batista's regime. In the dawn of January 1, 1959, the dictator, seeing the writing on the wall, fled Cuba for Spain, where he died a rich man in 1973. At about the same hour, Fidel Castro, **Che Guevara, Raul Castro, Camilo Cienfuegos,** and a host of other revolutionaries began their long descent from the Sierra Maestra toward the capital. They rode in open jeeps, sporting their trademark beards and khaki uniforms, greeting the droves of cheering, hopeful Cubans along the highways and byways who believed that, at last, democracy and fundamental ethical morality would be restored in their beloved country.

Who is Fidel Castro, and what happened to his idealistic revolution that sent Cubans fleeing to Miami by the thousands?

Fidel Castro Ruiz, better known as "Fidel" to friend and foe alike, was born in the province of Oriente on August 13, 1926. He attended Jesuit schools in Santiago de Cuba, Oriente's capital city, and in Havana. In 1950 Castro graduated from the University of Havana with a degree in law. His only marriage (to **Mirta Díaz-Balart**) ended in divorce. While his only son, **Fidel Castro Díaz-Balart,** born in 1949, has served as head of Cuba's atomic energy commission, Fidel's ex-wife and members of her family declared themselves loyal anti-Castro democrats and fled to the United States in the wake of the revolution. Fidel's nephew, **Lincoln Díaz-Balart,** has been a Republican congressman, representing Florida, since 1993.

Fidel Castro was a political animal from an early age. As a

member of the social democratic party *Partido Ortodoxo* in the 1940s and 1950s, he opposed **Batista**'s regime from the start. On July 26, 1953, Castro launched a daring attack on the Moncada army barracks in Santiago de Cuba with the intent of seizing arms for his guerillas and igniting a popular revolt. This assault against Batista's regime failed, and Castro was sentenced to fifteen years in prison, but his maneuver brought him instant recognition. From prison, he wrote his famous book, *La historia me absolvera* (*History Will Absolve Me*), which presents his antiimperialist, reformist, and nationalistic ideals. At the time, Castro did not reveal that he was a Marxist-Leninist, or propose outright a communist agenda.

In 1955, Batista's government granted Fidel Castro amnesty with the promise that he would leave Cuba for good. Castro went into exile in Mexico, where he founded the Twenty-sixth of July Movement (celebrated in Cuba today with as much fanfare as the Fourth of July in the United States) for the purpose of overthrowing the Batista dictatorship. In December 1956, Castro and eighty-one other rebels, including his brother **Raul Castro** and the Argentine revolutionary **Ernesto "Che" Guevara,** traveled by boat to Cuba. Only twelve rebels, including the Castro brothers and Che Guevara, survived a botched landfall, and they immediately set up military headquarters in the westernmost part of the Sierra Maestra in Oriente Province.

From there, Fidel Castro and his followers organized a revolution against the Cuban government, recruiting thousands of disaffected peasants in the interior of Cuba and exciting the imagination of millions of Cubans of all social and economic classes, who viewed Castro as a New World messiah with the vision to restore Cuba to sanity, law and order, and prosperity. By 1957 Castro had the backing of foreign countries, thanks to an interview he gave the *New York Times* that painted a portrait of him as a courageous romantic figure. By 1958, many of Cuba's opposition groups had lent Castro their support. That year Castro and his guerilla forces took over numerous cities, and Batista knew his days were numbered.

When Fidel Castro seized control of Cuba in 1959, his revolutionary regime welcomed many middle-of-the-road politicians and citizens, who saw him as a democratic reformer who would simply clean up the corruption in Cuba's government and get on with the island's constitutional democracy. In a matter of months, however, Castro began implementing socialist reforms, which included the confiscation of land and industries that were privately owned. As early as 1961, he publicly declared, "I have been a Marxist-Leninist all along, and will remain one until I die." Castro proceeded to fully align himself with the Soviet Union both economically and politically, in effect handing the island over to Soviet Prime Minister **Nikita Khrushchev.**

At home Castro put Cuban Communist Party members or sympathizers in charge of the media, the schools and universities, and every other important institution. Like all communist leaders, he could not tolerate or afford dissent, and he set up organizations to monitor the Cuban people. For instance, every district had a Committee for the Defense of the Revolution, which made an inventory of each resident's personal property and recorded his or her activities. In those days it was hard to know who you could trust—neighbors and even friends betrayed each other. Those who strayed from communist doctrine were dealt with harshly. Thousands upon thousands of Cuban nationals who opposed communism were executed or incarcerated in concentration camps. Castro's puritanical regime also sent gay men and lesbians, no matter their political bent, to a concentration camp known as *Guanahacabibes*. Writers, filmmakers, singers, composers, and artists were put on notice: Let your art reflect communist ideology or else.

As early as 1959, Cuba's political elite, mainly Batista supporters, *Batistianos,* who knew Castro wanted them dead, fled the island. Then hundreds of thousands of Cubans who had believed Castro to be a true democratic leader woke up to the realization that they had exchanged one dictator for another, and that their island had become a perilous beachhead for the Soviet Union, where any minute a nuclear war between the superpowers could explode in their midst. By 1960, a large wave of Cuban immigration to the United States was unleashed. Upper-class, middle-class, and lower-middle-class Cubans began fleeing the island for the United States, in particular Miami, where the American government welcomed them as political refugees.

What's a gusano?

Gusano, Spanish for "worm," is what Castro Cubans call Cuban exiles, or Cuban Americans. Many Latinos also call Cuban Americans *gusanos*—sometimes in jest and sometimes not. Another name Latinos have for Cuban Americans (particularly those who came in the 1960s) is *los tenía*—literally, "the I-used-to-have people," because they often speak about all they used to have back in the old country.

Who was Che Guevara?

Ernesto "Che" Guevara was born in Argentina in 1928. His nickname, "Che," means "Hey, buddy!" and is a word Argentines use to call each other. Although he was trained as a physician, Che Guevara was first and foremost a student of Marxist-Leninist ideology and a revolutionary. In Argentina, where he was a member of the Communist Party, he led revolts against **President Juan Perón** (**Evita**'s husband) in 1952, and in 1953 he went to Guatemala, where he joined the leftist regime of **Jacobo Arbenz Guzmán.** After Arbenz was overthrown in 1954, Che Guevara joined **Fidel Castro** in Mexico to help plan the communist revolution in Cuba. When Castro's rebels invaded Cuba in 1956, Guevara performed superbly and became one of Castro's most trusted comrades. Although Che Guevara held many important posts in the Castro government, such as minister of industry (1961–1965), his efforts to turn Latin America into a communist playground took precedence. In 1965 he went on a secret mission to Bolivia to train a guerilla force. Two years later, Guevara was captured by Bolivian government troops near Santa Cruz and executed.

Che Guevara is remembered for his goatee and his black Argentine beret, as well as for his guerilla training manuals and Marxist-Leninist revolutionary books, *Guerrilla Warfare* and *Guerrilla Warfare: A Method*. His life story was made into a play and a Hollywood movie in the 1970s.

What has Fidel done for Cuba?

Aside from aligning the country with the Soviet bloc and assisting Marxist-Leninist revolutions around the world (most notably in Angola, where hundreds of Cuban soldiers died), **Fidel Castro**'s greatest claim to fame is undoubtedly the successful consolidation of a communist regime within ninety miles of American shores.

During his reign of over thirty-five years, Castro has invested much effort into education, and as a result Cuba enjoys the highest literacy rate in Latin America. He has stressed technology and science (like most communist countries, including the former Soviet Union). One of his early revolutionary aims was to transform Cuba's economy from one based on a single crop to one that was technology- and service-oriented. In reality, Castro has not succeeded any more than his predecessors in bringing Cuba out of its single-crop economic nightmare. He simply found another buyer for Cuban sugar. Whereas previous Cuban governments sold sugar to the United States, Castro sold it to the former Soviet Union—at least until that country collapsed in 1989, sending the Cuban economy into an even steeper decline.

Castro's government also initially placed great emphasis on cradle-to-grave social services, what were called "achievements of the revolution." As a result Cuban nationals have access to doctors, nurses, hospitals, and other social welfare benefits that had been denied them during the Batista years. However, Cuba is in such desperate economic straits that medical supplies, including basic medicines, are scarce and Cubans suffer needlessly. Furthermore, many of the illnesses from which Cubans suffer are the direct result of poor nutrition and a lack of preventive care for which only the Castro regime is to blame.

What happened at the Bay of Pigs, and why did Cuban Americans blame President Kennedy?

The mass exodus of Cubans from the island that began in 1959, as well as **Fidel Castro**'s ceaseless tirades against the United States, put the U.S. government on notice. When Castro signed a long-term agreement with the Soviet Union and completely nationalized all American-owned property on the island, in effect declaring an ideological war against his nearest and most powerful neighbor, the U.S. government had had enough. On January 3, 1961, **President Dwight Eisenhower** broke off diplomatic relations with Cuba. Then **Allen Dulles,** who had served as CIA director under Eisenhower (and then under **President John F. Kennedy**), developed a plan to invade Cuba and oust Castro with the aid of Cuban refugees in Miami.

Dulles convinced the newly elected Kennedy to allow the CIA to train a brigade of Cuban exiles whose mission would be to invade Cuba with the intent of igniting a carefully orchestrated popular revolt with the help of anti-Castro agents strategically positioned on the island. Another facet of the plan, which was not revealed to the public until a Senate investigation of President Kennedy's assassination brought it to light years later, was the CIA's plot to assassinate Fidel Castro with the help of the Mafia, namely **Sam Giancana** and **John Roselli**'s hit men. Giancana was murdered before he could tell the Senate the inside story, and Roselli testified, but his decomposed body was found floating in an oil drum in Florida shortly thereafter.

U.S. Brigade 2506—the Cuban *Brigada*—initially received President Kennedy's full backing, but the Cuban invasion was ill conceived from the start. First of all, the 1,400 middle-class Cuban exiles in the brigade, most of whom had never held a rifle, were poorly trained and underequipped. They were also kept in the dark as to what their next move would be once they reached Cuba. Secondly, the U.S. government apparently had vast quantities of misinformation in its files regarding the topography of the island and the military installations around the designated landing site, *bahía de Cochinos* (the Bay of Pigs) in western Cuba. Cuban exiles who knew the territory well warned U.S. intelligence that dangerous coral reefs at the proposed landing site would jeopardize the mission, but the CIA did not heed their warning. The CIA also failed to notice that Fidel Castro had recently built himself a beach house very near the Bay of Pigs, and thus the whole area was heavily guarded. If that were not bad enough, the so-called "secret" mission was leaked to the press—and no doubt Castro's soldiers and loyal militia, who were fully prepared to greet the Cuban Brigade with armored tanks and heavy ammunition when it reached Cuba's shores on April 17, 1961.

In planning the invasion, the CIA assured the *Brigada* that the United States would provide full air cover during the entire operation, and that should the exiles be captured the U.S. military would come to their aid. The exiles had insisted that the government agree to these terms since they knew they did not stand a chance on their own. At the last minute, once the invasion was underway, President Kennedy changed his mind and ordered all U.S. support withdrawn from the *Brigada*. Some have speculated that the president was suddenly overcome by fear that a direct confrontation with a Soviet bloc country would precipitate the next world war. Whatever President Kennedy's reasons, his decision cost 114 Cuban exiles their lives at the Bay of Pigs. Another 1,189 were taken prisoner as proof positive to the world of the United States' invasion. Attorney general **Robert F. Kennedy** later gave Cuba food as ransom to secure the release of the exiles.

The refugees' families in Miami also handed Castro hard cash for the release of the young invaders. Some Cuban refugees wired their entire life savings to Fidel in exchange for their sons.

In later years, once their U.S. citizenship papers were in order, the overwhelming majority of Cuban Americans of the first wave registered Republican. Their preference for the Republican Party was founded on the belief that the Republicans were more effective in combating communism and dictatorships in Cuba and around the globe. They were unwilling to forget the "Kennedy betrayal." Older generations of Cuban Americans in Miami even call a person who is weak-spined and probably leftist a *kennedito* ("little Kennedy"). Anti-Kennedy sentiment ran so strong in the Cuban American community in the early 1960s that after President Kennedy was assassinated in 1963, some pointed the finger at Cuban Americans as possible conspirators. **Oliver Stone** deals with the possible Cuban American role in the Kennedy assassination in his film *JFK*. Unfortunately, the director paints a stereotypical picture of Cuban Americans as a devious, power-hungry bunch capable of such a heinous act.

What caused the Cuban Missile Crisis?

Soviet prime minister **Nikita Khrushchev** interpreted the United States' failure at the Bay of Pigs as a sign that he was dealing with a weak U.S. president. He decided to seize the day and establish a nuclear beachhead at **President Kennedy**'s doorstep. At **Castro**'s behest, Khrushchev swiftly ordered the assembly of launching sites for medium-range nuclear missiles in Cuba. The aim was to protect the island from the possibility of future U.S. invasions and to guarantee the Soviet Union a more favorable balance of power as a Soviet presence in the Caribbean would offset the U.S. military bases in Turkey.

Once aerial photographs by U.S. military intelligence uncovered the frightening time bomb at America's threshold, the Pentagon advised President Kennedy to launch a full-scale surprise attack on Cuba that would bring an end to Castro's regime. Instead, Kennedy decided to issue a public ultimatum to the USSR on October 22, 1962. He declared a naval blockade on Cuba and demanded the immediate withdrawal of all offensive missiles. The world held its breath for two long weeks as both countries stood on the brink of nuclear warfare. Finally, Khrushchev gave in to Kennedy's demands in exchange for reassurances that the United States would refrain from attempting to overthrow Castro's government. The Cuban Missile Crisis brought to a close a very long chapter in history for most Cuban Americans. Although many still hoped against hope that they would return to their beloved homeland, the vast majority awoke to the realization that the United States was truly home and that Castro's downfall might take quite a number of years. Given the political climate in those days, it was hard for many Americans to fathom that a communist regime would be allowed to exist only ninety miles from American shores, but as Bob Dylan's popular ballad proclaimed, the times they were a-changing. And President Kennedy had another war to wage just then—this time in a country called Vietnam.

How many Cubans fled Cuba in the 1960s and 1970s, and how did they fare?

In the early days of the mass exodus from Cuba, Cubans were free to board any of the Pan American flights departing the island for Miami. **Fidel Castro** saw this as a surefire method of purging the country of enemies of the state. Those Cubans who left after the spring of 1961 had to hand over all their life savings and possessions to the Cuban government, except for five dollars and one outfit of clothing. Despite the losses, about two thousand Cubans fled Cuba each week. Then, during the summer of 1961, in the aftermath of the Bay of Pigs invasion, Castro made emigration a kind of roulette: he punished some for merely applying to leave, while granting permission to others. After **President Kennedy** imposed a naval blockade of Cuba, all flights to Miami were canceled, and emigration was outlawed. This ban on emigration lasted until 1965. Still, in those days about 30,000 Cubans managed to escape Cuba by sailing or floating across the Florida Straits, or flying first to Mexico or Spain and then on to the United States.

In 1965, when Castro opened the floodgates of emigration once again, flotillas of Cuban exiles headed to Cuba to pick up their relatives. The U.S. government also organized an airlift of Cubans and 3,700 entered the country each month. In 1973 Castro again slammed the doors shut on emigration. For the next seven years, until 1980, virtually the only way to leave Cuba was to steal away on a makeshift raft and sail across the treacherous, shark-infested Florida Straits to Miami and freedom. Many Cubans who attempted the journey died in rough seas along the way, or succumbed to exposure or attacks by sharks.

Those Cubans who came to the United States during the 1960s and 1970s—the first large wave of Cuban refugees—wasted no time in rebuilding their lives in Miami, though a minority settled in New Jersey, New York, and Washington, D.C. Many initially received aid in the form of temporary shelter, meals, medical care, and $100 a month from the Cuban Refugee Emergency Center in Miami, but they swiftly gained a footing in their new country. Within a year, some Cuban refugees who had come penniless to American shores owned businesses or held white-collar jobs. Their education and skills, and their fervent desire to succeed, as well as the fact that the great majority were Caucasian and did not experience overt racial prejudice, enabled the refugees to quickly establish a thriving Cuban American enclave in Miami. By 1970 Cuban exiles controlled the service sector in Miami. In the decades to come they would transform the city from a retirement beach town built on a swamp to what international bankers, politicians, and businesspeople call the "Capital of Latin America."

What was the Cuban Adjustment Act?

In 1966 Congress passed the Cuban Adjustment Act, which gave all Cubans seeking asylum in the United States the special status of political refugees. The Cubans faced none of the restrictions governing immigration, such as presenting proof of persecution at home. This legislation virtually guaranteed permanent resettlement in the United States to all who escaped Cuba, whether they simply overstayed their tourist visas, or reached Florida's shores with no documentation at all. While the Cuban Adjustment Act was in place, over half a million Cubans settled in the United States.

Who were the Marielitos, and why did so many people hate them?

In the spring of 1980, twelve Cubans, with no legal way of leaving Cuba, crashed through the gates of the Peruvian Embassy in Havana, demanding political asylum. A few days later, **Fidel Castro** dropped his seven-year ban on emigration and announced that all Cubans wishing to leave the island should report to the port of Mariel, where Americans could pick them up by boat. Eleven thousand Cubans showed up, unleashing a second wave of Cuban immigration. Castro then flung open his prisons, and from April 21, 1980, until September 26, 1980, he allowed Cuban Americans from Miami to load over 125,000 Cubans onto shrimp boats and other vessels, dubbed the "Freedom Flotilla." The Cuban refugees, known as Marielitos because they departed from the port of Mariel, were boatlifted to Key West. **President Jimmy Carter** gave the okay to take in the refugees, and they were airlifted to regions of the country where they could find housing and employment.

There was only one problem with the whole operation: while the vast majority of Marielitos had been legitimate political prisoners in Cuba, whose only crime was to oppose the communist regime, hundreds were common criminals with long felony records, "mentally defective," or clinically insane. When it became clear that some of the refugees were part of a dastardly ruse played on an amiable President Carter by Castro to get rid of his Cuban undesirables, Americans were up in arms. All hell broke loose later, when dozens of Marielitos, who had been cleared by U.S. authorities, began committing crimes around the country. Cuban Americans in Miami, who had rushed to the aid of the new arrivals with the full weight of their highly organized private charitable organizations, were horrified. They feared that this wave of Cubans would tarnish the stellar image they had worked so hard to build. Many criticized President Carter's decision to let the Marielitos enter the United States in the first place.

. The U.S. government responded by initially detaining 22,000 of the original 125,000 arrivals, but most were found to have committed only political crimes in Cuba and were set free. In the end, only some 3,700 Mariel Cubans were deemed "excludable aliens" by the Immigration and Naturalization Service. Excludable aliens, unlike illegal aliens, are not considered persons under the Constitution, and therefore have no rights. However, the immigration authorities in Key West believed they could not very well return the excludables to Cuba, so they simply shipped them to two penal institutions, one a regular prison in Oakdale, Louisiana, and the other a maximum-security prison in Atlanta that had once housed **Al Capone.** These excludables remained behind bars, with no right to legal counsel, for seven years, until 1987, when a sudden change in U.S.-Cuba relations brought the whole matter to a head.

In November 1987, the United States and Cuba reached an agreement that attempted to place controls on the flow of Cubans into the United States. The agreement established a quota of 20,000 Cuban immigrants each year as long as Castro followed through on his promise to take back 2,500 Cubans with criminal records in American prisons. In the immigration process, the United States gave priority to former Cuban political prisoners and their relatives. Those who saw no way out of Cuba or could not bear to wait were forced to take to the seas in small boats.

CLASSIC FILMS ABOUT LATINOS

1. *West Side Story* (1961)

2. *Zoot Suit* (1982)

3. *El Norte* (1983)

4. *Scarface* (1983)

5. *Crossover Dreams* (1985)

6. *La Bamba* (1987)

7. *Stand and Deliver* (1988)

8. *The Milagro Beanfield War* (1988)

9. *American Me* (1992)

10. *El Mariachi* (1992)

11. *A Million to Juan* (1994)

12. *I Like It Like That* (1994)

13. *Mi Familia* (1995)

14. *Star Maps* (1997)

What was the 1994 Rafter Refugee Crisis, and why was the Cuban Adjustment Act suddenly repealed?

The Cuban Adjustment Act, which was passed in 1966, granted all Cubans seeking asylum in the United States the special status of political refugees, not immigrants. In 1994, a crisis broke out when 40,000 Cuban boat people headed en masse to Florida's shores. Fearful that **Castro** would unleash a mass emigration from the island and that Florida would be inundated, **President Bill Clinton,** after consulting with Cuban American **Jorge Mas Canosa,** who was one of the most powerful lobbyists in America at that time, refused the Cuban rafters permission to enter the United States. Instead, they were interned along with Haitian boat people at the American military base in Guantánamo Bay and at the base in Krome, Florida. Clinton also severed all flight service between Miami and Cuba for family members, made it unlawful for U.S. residents to send cash remittances to relatives in Cuba, and expanded Radio Martí—a kind of Voice of America station whose broadcasts are aimed at Cuba. (Some critics say that Clinton acted so swiftly and decisively because his brother-in-law **Hugh Rodham** is married to **María Victoria Arias,** who shares Mas Canosa's sentiments about Cuba.) Some in the Cuban exile community were up in arms over the way the Cuban rafters were treated, and ultimately the Clinton administration allowed the Cubans at Guantánamo Bay to enter the United States.

Then in 1995, the Clinton administration repealed the Cuban Adjustment Act, thereby terminating Cuban Americans' special treatment as refugees which they had enjoyed for decades. The United States vowed to send back all Cubans fleeing the island, even those who actually made it across the Florida Straits to freedom. As a result, the number of Cubans fleeing the communist island slowed to a trickle.

What happened to the Brothers to the Rescue?

Ever since the Cuban Missile Crisis ended in disaster, the U.S. government has refrained from lending official military backing to Cuban American schemes to oust **Fidel Castro** from power. However, to this day the United States continues to condemn Castro's dictatorship and has not lifted the trade embargo against Cuba which **President Kennedy** ordered. The U.S. government has also looked the other way whenever Cuban American exile groups in South Florida plan and execute attacks against the island.

One such group is Brothers to the Rescue, which was organized for the purpose of finding and saving Cubans fleeing the island on makeshift rafts who were in danger. On these search-and-rescue missions, pilots from Brothers to the Rescue have penetrated Cuban airspace from time to time. In February 1996, a Cuban MIG-29 shot down two unarmed aircraft operated by Brothers to the Rescue over international waters, killing four fliers. Fidel Castro, who personally gave the order for the attack, claimed that the fliers had violated Cuban airspace. The Cuban government defended its harsh actions by saying that earlier in the year the Brothers to the Rescue had twice dropped anti-Castro leaflets over Havana, forcing the Cuban government to issue a warning that in the future it would shoot down any aircraft violating its airspace. The Cuban American community expressed outrage over the incident, as summed up in the remarks of Cuban American representative **Ileana Ros-Lehtinen** (R-Florida), who was quoted as saying, "I think this is an act of aggression, of terrorism."

President Clinton condemned Castro for shooting down planes that posed no threat to Cuba's security and declared that the act was a clear violation of international law. The Clinton administration imposed sanctions to punish Cuba, such as severing charter flights (the only passenger air service in place) between the two countries, giving more financial backing to Radio Martí, and compensating each of the victims' families with $300,000 of frozen Cuban assets. The president also dropped his opposition to the Helms-Burton bill, which permits U.S. residents to sue foreign companies doing business in Cuba that use properties confiscated in the 1959 revolution.

What will happen to Cuba after Castro falls?

As required by the Helms-Burton Act, the White House issued a report in 1997 on American support for a Cuban transition to democracy. The report states that the U.S. government would organize an international donor drive to provide four to eight billion dollars to Cuba once **Castro** falls (or dies) *and* the island shows a commitment "to the establishment of a fully democratic, pluralistic society." The Clinton administration even pledged to relinquish the U.S. base at Guantánamo Bay or "to renegotiate the present agreement under mutually agreeable terms." In the report, the White House estimated that Cuban Americans would send about one billion dollars annually to relatives on the island in the event of Castro's fall, and that foreign investments would stream into Cuba. In the end, this program to facilitate democracy in Cuba would cost more than the Marshall Plan, which enabled Europe to recover from the devastation of World War II.

HAVANA, U.S.A.: THE LAND OF THE FIESTA, BUT NOT THE SIESTA

What's little Havana, and why isn't it so Havana anymore?

Little Havana, in downtown Miami, was the primary enclave of the first wave of Cuban exiles in the 1960s and 1970s and is still the capital of Cuban America. Eighth Street, officially called *Calle Ocho*, runs through the heart of Little Havana, and all along it are stands selling Cuban sandwiches, Cuban coffee and *batidos* (tropical fruit milk shakes) as well as *botánicas*, supermarkets, and every conceivable type of Cuban-style shop.

There are as many Cuban restaurants along *Calle Ocho* as you would find in four districts in Havana, Cuba. Centro Vasco, one of Miami's hundreds of popular Cuban Spanish restaurants, reflects the taste, mood, and politics of Cuban Americans. In the open courtyard are photographs of **José Martí** propped against a signed photo of **President Ronald Reagan,** who made it a point to stop by when campaigning in Miami years ago. The Cuban and American flags hang side by side, beating each other like flyswatters, aided by ubiquitous little electric fans. The music of **Gloria Estefan** and **Jon Secada** and Spanish guitars play so loudly you can hardly hear your companions speak, and the sumptuous food keeps coming till you forget there was ever such a thing as a *dieta* (diet).

Along the streets of Little Havana, which sport more signs in Spanish than in English (some even say "English Spoken Here"), fifty- and sixty-something men gather around small card tables, smoking cigars and playing dominoes. This game was brought to the Caribbean by Spanish colonists in the seventeenth century, and is probably the favorite island pastime for Cubans, as well as for Puerto Ricans and Dominicans. While the men scramble the dominoes, they talk politics, sip strong Cuban espresso from little paper cups, ponder when **Fidel Castro**'s regime will topple, and perhaps put down a bet on *la bolita*, an illegal lottery that no one cares to crack down on.

But that's the old Little Havana. It's still there, filled with melancholy warriors and plenty of Anglo tourists, who come down to savor the flavor and visit a "foreign country" without having to trouble with a passport. (Actually, Miami residents themselves joke that the reason they live in Miami is because it's so close to the United States.) But the more recent generations of Cuban Americans have left Little Havana for the elegant suburbs of Coral Gables, Hialeah, Coconut Grove, Key Biscayne, and even South Beach, the trendy Art Deco strip of heavenly beach that Jewish retirees from points north developed and made famous in the 1950s. Even as they have fanned out over Miami and joined the mainstream, Cuban Americans have remained faithful to their heritage, and Cuban flavors nowadays permeate all of Miami.

Little Havana, Cuban Americans say, is neither so little nor so entirely Havana anymore. Little Managua, a growing community of Nicaraguan immigrants, is gradually blending with the old Little Havana, and these days the newer Spanish-speaking arrivals serve the food and even run some of the stores that younger generations of Cuban Americans left behind. Residents with roots in Colombia, and other Central and South American countries, lured by the Spanish climate Cubans have created, can also be found strolling the streets of Little Havana and Greater Miami.

Why is Miami called the "capital of Latin America"?

Behind Little Havana, and miles from the comfortable suburbs where many of the more than half a million Cuban Americans make their homes, looms Miami's thriving commercial center with its tall glass buildings and hundreds of international banks. This is also part of the city that Cuban Americans are rightly credited with transforming. Since the 1960s Cuban Americans, many of whom are topnotch entrepreneurs and are well versed in both American and Latin ways, have served as liaisons between U.S. corporations and Latin American companies eager to trade with the United States. The natural synergism and desire for enterprise between Cuban Americans and their contacts to the south and north turned Miami— which had been an alligator-infested swamp (in the 1920s) and a retirees' colony (from the 1950s to the 1970s)—into the thriving "Capital of Latin America," as **Xavier Suarez,** one of Miami's Cuban American mayors, called the city.

Cuban Americans are not only at the helm of international trade and banking in this cosmopolitan city, they hold nearly every top administrative and elected post in Miami—and all throughout Dade County, for that matter. The mayor and city manager of Miami are Cuban Americans. The metro police chief is a Cuban American. And the presidents of Florida International University and Miami-Dade Community College are of Cuban descent.

How do Cuban Americans feel about Castro and the trade embargo against Cuba?

Most Cuban Americans have nothing good to say about **Fidel Castro,** the dictator who stole their country, forced them into exile, and caused them such suffering and pain. They call him *el tirano* ("the tyrant"), *el diablo* ("the devil"), *la bola de churre* ("the dust ball"), and other choice names. Driving down the streets of Miami one cannot help but notice bumper stickers with sayings such as "No Castro, No Problem." Even Cuban Americans who left Cuba at a young age, or who were born in the United States, share the older generations' fury over Castro, which is echoed in Miami's Spanish-language newspapers and radio programs, and in conversations in cafes and around the dinner table.

Cuban Americans as a group continue to support the trade embargo, even as American corporations, who have been eyeing Cuba, exert pressure on the U.S. government to lift it.

Since Cuba is only ninety miles from Florida, do Cuban Americans visit?

For most of the nearly four decades that Fidel Castro has governed Cuba, the island has been off-limits to Cuban Americans and permanent residents—and all American citizens, for that matter—in keeping with regulations issued in 1963 by the U.S. Treasury Department as part of the trade embargo against Cuba. According to these regulations, Americans are not expressly forbidden from traveling to Cuba but are required to obtain a special license and refrain from spending U.S. dollars on the island. The catch is that only a select few, namely Cuban Americans, government officials, journalists, educators, and researchers may apply for these licenses. Anyone caught violating these regulations could face fines up to $250,000 and a maximum of ten years in prison. Nonetheless, Cuban Americans—and American tourists—have visited Cuba over the years via third countries, such as Mexico, without these special licenses. The U.S. government has rarely pursued criminal prosecution; most of the civil actions initiated each year involve contraband.

For a short while in 1995 travel to Cuba was made easier. That year Washington revised the regulations regarding visits to Cuba by American citizens. Special licenses were no longer required, and Cuban Americans were granted permission to visit relatives in Cuba once a year in cases of "extreme humanitarian need." In 1995 over 100,000 Cuban Americans made the trip back to their roots. The relaxation on restrictions on visits to Cuba came to an abrupt end in early 1996 when Cubans, under direct orders from **Fidel Castro,** shot down a civilian aircraft flown by the Miami Cuban exile group Brothers to the Rescue.

Nowadays, to visit Cuba legally, a U.S. resident must either spend no money there or obtain a license from the U.S. Treasury Department which allows up to $100 in spending per diem. Just as before, only a select few may receive these licenses.

In January 1998, the Clinton White House made an exception to the U.S. travel ban so that American Catholics could go to Cuba for the visit of **Pope John Paul II.** Over a thousand Cuban Americans, in what was described as the largest mass return of Cuban exiles to the island in history, ventured to Cuba. Not all Cuban Americans were in favor of easing the embargo for the pope's visit. Many, such as Republican representative **Ileana Ros-Lehtinen,** would have preferred all Cuban Americans to stay home and watch the papal festivities on television. Those opposed to the pilgrimage feared that it would send a message of support to Castro and lend credibility to his repressive regime.

What's a YUCA?

Yuca (or cassava) is a fibrous tuber that the Arawak Indians cultivated. A fixture at the Cuban table, it is commonly served fried like french fries or boiled until tender and then bathed with *mojo*, olive oil flavored with garlic and citrus juice. A YUCA is a Cuban yuppie—a young, upwardly mobile Cuban American.

This thirty-something group, most of whom were either born in America or came at such an early age they only remember the island from their parents' photographs of palm trees and the Malecon wall in Havana, are a bilingual, bicultural, and economically successful lot. They speak both English and Spanish flawlessly (with no accent), and are likely to lapse into one or the other without realizing it. YUCAs are mostly Caucasian and considerably more liberal in their attitudes than their parents and grandparents. They prefer to listen to *La Cadena Azul* and *La Cubanísima* (two Miami Spanish-language music stations) than to Radio Martí. They tend to vote Democratic, and many are in favor of ending the economic blockade of Cuba and normalizing relations between the United States and the island as a way to promote democracy in Cuba. As a group they are eager to help the millions of people in Cuba who are in dire straits as a result of the collapse of the Soviet Union, but the majority have no desire to return to Cuba to live when **Castro** falls.

The generations that follow the YUCAs (those thirty and younger) have even fewer ties to Cuba, and most prefer to speak English and surf the Net rather than listen to their grandparents' tales of Fidel and his revolution.

Are all Cuban Americans Rich?

The very enterprising nature of these Latinos has led many to stereotype them as *los ricos*, "the rich kids." While about forty percent of the nation's wealthiest Latinos are Cuban American, when it comes to finances Cuban Americans mirror to a great extent the non-Latino whites in the general population. Their income about equals the national average.

What's Santería?

Santería is a New World religion that arose from the blending of the ancient Yoruban religions brought to the Caribbean by West African slaves and Roman Catholic beliefs introduced by the Spanish. The gods, or *santos*, of *Santería* are fused with the Catholic saints. So, for instance, the African god Babalu is also the Catholic St. Lazarus; and Yemaya, the African goddess of the waters, is the Catholic *Virgen de las Mercedes*. Practitioners of *Santería*, the "religion of the saints," not only worship a pantheon of deities, they also consult *santeros*, priests, who are usually women. The *santeros* dispense candles, beads, ointments, and other objects, as well as advice on how to solve any problem imaginable.

Early on in Cuba, *Santería* was practiced in secret to conceal it from the Spanish, who sought to do away with such "primitive" and "superstitious" practices. Despite the secrecy, *Santería* grew very popular in Cuba, and among its followers were not only slaves and their descendants but also Cubans with no African blood. In the 1950s, it was recorded in a government gazette that Cuban president **Carlos Prío Socarrás,** a white, democratically elected president, donated government money to both the Catholic Church and the *Santería* religion. Traditionally, *Santería* has served as more a religion of the poor, and because the faithful think it is misunderstood, they seldom discuss their beliefs with outsiders.

Today *Santería* is practiced in Miami, New York, and almost every city with a large Cuban, Puerto Rican, or Dominican community, but it is difficult to estimate how many followers there are. Mainstream America has not always looked kindly on *Santería*, partly because one of its rituals involves animal (not human) sacrifice for the purpose of honoring the gods. In June 1993, the Supreme Court ruled that a 1987 ban on animal sacrifice in Hialeah, Florida, violated the First Amendment right to religious expression for Afro-Cuban followers of *Santería*. Cuban Americans and other Latinos, even those who did not practice *Santería*, viewed this decision as a victory for ethnic understanding.

What's a fiesta de quince?

It is the equivalent of a "sweet sixteen" party, only it's for fifteen-year-olds. *Quinceañera* parties are very popular in Miami, and like debutante balls they are often held in large ballrooms or country clubs and end up costing Cuban American parents thousands of dollars and months of planning. Other Latino groups also celebrate girls' coming of age with *fiestas de quince*.

What foods do Cuban Americans like?

Cuban Americans tend to blend typical American fare with the flavors of the old country. Unlike other Latin American cuisines such as Mexican and Guatemalan, Cuban cooking is not spicy. Garlic, onions, and olive oil—not chiles—add flavor and aroma to Cuban dishes. The most popular Cuban main entrées are *lechón asado* (juicy, garlicky roast suckling pig), *picadillo* (a ground meat stew studded with green olives and raisins), and *ropa vieja* (a stew of shredded beef that translates literally as "old clothes"). These are usually served with copious amounts of *tostones* (fried green plantains), *plátanos maduros fritos* (fried ripe plantains), or *yuca con mojo* (*yuca* in garlic-flavored oil), and rice and black beans. Cuban Americans love to snack on Cuban sandwiches, which are stacked with slices of roast pork, ham, cheese, and pickles. Cuban sandwiches and other fast foods are sold at little stands and restaurants all over Miami and in other cities with a sizable Cuban American community.

SEIS

Dominican Americans

EARLY HISTORY

Is the Dominican Republic an island?

When did the Spanish colonize Hispaniola?

A TIME OF TROUBLES

Why did the United States intervene in the affairs of the Dominican Republic?

Who was Rafael Trujillo, and what were his passions?

Who were "the Butterflies"?

Why did the United States get involved in the Dominican Republic in the 1960s?

How did Joaquín Balaguer assume power a second time?

When did the Dominicans finally experience democratic elections?

LIFE IN DOMINICAN AMERICA

What brought Dominicans to American shores, and where have they settled?

Who are the retornados?

How have Dominican Americans fared?

Who are some famous Dominican Americans?

What is the favorite pastime of many Dominican Americans?

What kinds of foods do Dominican Americans like?

EARLY HISTORY

Is the Dominican Republic an island?

Sort of. The Dominican Republic actually shares the Caribbean island of Hispaniola with Haiti. The island nation occupies the eastern two thirds of Hispaniola and Haiti the western one third. To the west of Hispaniola lies Cuba, and 54 miles to the east is Puerto Rico.

When did the Spanish colonize Hispaniola?

Christopher Columbus made landfall on Hispaniola in 1492 and established the very first Spanish colony in the New World, which he named Española for Spain itself. The explorer was delighted when the Taino, the native peoples of Hispaniola, came to him bearing masks and amulets made of gold, for he supposed that the island harbored great riches. In fact, Columbus, or the Admiral, as the native peoples referred to him, was so taken with Hispaniola, that he made it his home. Dominicans have claimed Columbus as a virtual native son, and maintain that his remains lie in the cathedral of Santo Domingo, but the Spanish insist that the explorer's remains are in Seville.

The Spanish crown was also eager to settle Hispaniola and get to work mining gold, and so in 1496 Columbus's brother, **Bartolomeo,** founded Santo Domingo, the capital of the Dominican Republic. By 1543 the Spanish had mined all the gold in Hispaniola and turned their attention to Mexico and Peru, which held great promise.

The Spanish colonizers who came to Hispaniola gravitated to the eastern part of the island, where they established plantations. They neglected the western third of the island and in 1697 ceded it to the French, who christened it Saint-Domingue. The French colonists who settled in Saint-Domingue imported thousands of African slaves to work the land, as most of the native peoples had succumbed to overwork or disease.

In 1795 the Spanish relinquished the eastern two thirds of Hispaniola to France. Nine years later, in 1804, the African slaves in Hispaniola revolted against the French and declared the western region of the island an independent nation called Haiti. The Spanish colonists of Santo Domingo weren't happy with the way France handled their affairs either, and in 1808 they rebelled against the French and reestablished rule.

With the European nations out of the picture, the two halves of the island of Hispaniola duked it out. In 1822 the Haitians invaded and conquered Santo Domingo. They ruled over the island of Hispaniola until 1844, when the Spanish-speaking inhabitants of Santo Domingo, with **Juan Pablo Duarte** as their leader, rebelled against the Haitians. (Duarte is considered the greatest national hero of the Dominican Republic.) On February 27, 1844, the Spanish-speaking half of Hispaniola proclaimed its independence, establishing a separate nation called the Dominican Republic. From 1861 to 1865, the Dominican Republic submitted to Spanish rule once again, in an attempt to ward off the Haitians who had annexation on their mind.

A TIME OF TROUBLES

Why did the United States intervene in the affairs of the Dominican Republic?

Juan Pablo Duarte, the father of Dominican independence, envisioned a peaceful democracy for the Dominican Republic. Duarte, blinded by idealism, procrastinated in taking control of the nation, and did not survive the political free-for-all that followed independence. He soon found himself exiled to Venezuela, where he remained for twenty years. From 1865 to 1899, two political factions controlled the government of the Dominican Republic: the Reds, who were directed by **Buenaventura Báez,** and the Blues, who after 1878 were led by **General Ulises Heureaux.** The ruthless Heureaux eventually got a grip on the reins of power and imposed a dictatorship in the Dominican Republic—complete with bribery, assassinations, and secret police—that lasted from 1882 until his assassination in 1899.

Even with the dictator gone, Dominicans in power still could not establish economic stability on the island, which by now was dotted with sugar mills, or pay back the mounting foreign debt. By 1905 the Dominican Republic was bankrupt, and European countries threatened to intervene in the island's affairs. Instead **President Teddy Roosevelt** stepped in, in keeping with the Roosevelt Corollary of the Monroe Doctrine. In accordance with a treaty signed in 1905 with the Dominican Republic, the U.S. government exercised the right to claim partial control of the island to sort out claims by European governments and to protect American investments. Still the unrest continued. From 1906 to 1911 **Ramón Cáceres** served as president of the Dominican Republic and the nation experienced a period of modernization and reform.

After Cáceres was assassinated, the country was again visited by violence and fiscal chaos. In 1916 **President Woodrow Wilson** felt he had no other recourse than to invade the Dominican Republic (U.S. marines and all) to restore peace. The marines were not withdrawn until 1924, and their presence embittered many Dominicans. Still the island made many strides during the U.S. occupation. Foreign debts were wiped out, schools, sanitation facilities, and roads were built, and a new constitution was drafted and then approved in 1924.

Who was Rafael Trujillo, and what were his passions?

Ironically, the United States occupation forces also helped the Dominicans organize a new national guard, which was placed under the command of **Rafael Leonidas Trujillo Molina.** Trujillo used his domination of the military to steal the election in 1930, essentially overthrowing Dominican leader **Horacio Vásquez.** This marked the beginning of one of the longest, most violent dictatorships in history, lasting until Trujillo's assassination in 1961. It was also one of the richest dictatorships in history. In the 1950s, Rafael Trujillo, who was the son of a lower-middle-class postal clerk, ranked as one of the world's wealthiest people. By the time of his death, he had a net worth of $800 million. According to *Time* magazine, he invested $100 million of that wealth in the United States and Puerto Rico alone. Besides money, the dictator had a passion for erotic poetry, and it is said that his aides leafed through medical journals in search of information on the latest stimulants and enhancers of virility.

Trujillo, who patterned his uniforms after those of dictator **Heureaux,** also had a passion for control and cruelty. He controlled the press and the schools with an iron fist, and thus the minds of the Dominican people. He quelled dissent through genocidal massacres of the opposition and by keeping each and every citizen under close scrutiny and instilling fear in all. For instance, every Dominican had to carry not only a personal identity card at all times, but also a certificate of good conduct issued by the police. And by 1957 Trujillo had six spy operations in place which supplied him with an endless stream of information on "unreliables" and ordinary citizens. Dominicans soon learned that a neighbor or even a trusted friend might be a spy, and they became paranoid of each other, heeding the proverb *en bocas cerradas no entran moscas* (flies do not enter closed mouths).

For over thirty years, Dominicans endured Trujillo's reign of terror. During most of this time, the United States did not balk at the state of domestic affairs in the Dominican Republic, as Trujillo made sure he was always on the good side of the U.S. government. For instance, during World War II he was a ready supplier of coffee, tobacco, sugar, and cocoa, which were sorely needed in the United States, and when the Cold War raged, he was one of few Latin American leaders to loudly condemn communism.

By the mid-1950s the United States was well aware of the extent of the violence and repression in Trujillo's Dominican Republic. In 1956 Trujillo had ordered the kidnapping and murder of **Jesús de Galíndez,** a professor from Columbia University, who had published an account of the atrocities the dictator had committed. Many in Congress were up in arms, and they were doubly appalled when they learned that Trujillo had condemned to death the American pilot who had transported the kidnapped Galíndez to the Dominican Republic. The events of 1959 were the straw that broke the camel's back. On June 14, 1959, Dominican exiles staged an aborted invasion of the Dominican Republic. Those who were taken captive were tortured then murdered, as Trujillo had ordered. The Organization of American States (OAS) responded by imposing economic sanctions on the Dominican Republic. Trujillo's days were numbered.

As a result of the sanctions, the Dominican economy went into a nosedive. Dominicans could take no more. On the night of May 30, 1961, Rafael Trujillo was gunned down along Santo Domingo's waterfront. His dictatorship had ended as abruptly as it had started.

Who were "the Butterflies"?

Three sisters, **Patria, Minerva,** and **María Teresa Mirabal,** known by those around them as "the Butterflies," came from a prominent family and were actively involved in the anti-Trujillo underground. In 1960, the dictator, who was threatened by the sisters' activities, had them executed. In the years after Trujillo's assassination, the sisters emerged as popular heroines and emblems of feminist resistance. Their tragic story is poignantly told by Julia Alvarez in her 1995 historical novel *In the Time of the Butterflies.* The sisters' heroism and commitment to political activism has been kept alive by the next generation of Mirabals as two members of the family now serve as vice president and deputy foreign minister in the Dominican Republic.

Why did the United States get involved in the Dominican Republic in the 1960s?

After the assassination of **Rafael Trujillo,** the Dominican Republic experienced a power vacuum. **Joaquín Balaguer** formed a Council of State to oversee the Dominican Republic's transition from dictatorship to democracy, and as a result the OAS lifted its sanctions and support poured in from the United States. In December 1962, Dominicans held their first free elections in forty years and elected a "leftist" populist reformer, **Juan Bosch,** by a comfortable majority. The United States became perplexed when Bosch entertained establishing diplomatic ties with Castro's Cuba. Right-wing opposition to Bosch soon grew intense, and he was ousted by a military coup in September 1963. When his supporters, who called themselves Constitutionalists because they advocated a constitutional government, attempted to put Bosch back in power, civil war broke out in the Dominican Republic.

In 1965, **President Johnson,** under the pretext that the lives of Americans in the Dominican Republic were endangered and that the island would become a "second Cuba," once again sent in the marines (and airborne units) to restore peace. After much conflict, a new constitution was written and elections, supervised by the OAS, were held in June 1966. Juan Bosch and Joaquín Balaguer were the leading candidates, and the latter emerged the victor.

Joaquín Balaguer ruled the Dominican Republic with the same spirit of authoritarianism as Trujillo—though he was not a ruthless dictator—and enjoyed the backing of the military, the right, and the Church. The Dominican Republic was also experiencing an economic miracle thanks to a dramatic rise in the price of sugar on the world market. Balaguer used the revenues to build schools, hospitals, roads, dams, and bridges to the great pleasure of the Dominican people, who reelected him in 1970 and 1974.

With a decline in world demand for sugar, coffee, and

cocoa, the economic boom of the 1970s went bust and in the 1978 election, **Antonio Guzmán Fernández** of the opposition Dominican Revolutionary Party emerged the victor. Four years later he committed suicide upon learning that members of his family were embroiled in a scandal.

How did Joaquín Balaguer assume power a second time?

Salvador Jorge Blanco won the elections held in 1982, but he was no better at coping with the country's mounting debt or the plunge in the demand for sugar than his predecessors. When in 1984, Blanco raised the price of basic foodstuffs such as rice and beans, Dominicans rioted in the streets and the police and military were called in to restore order.

In 1986 the disillusioned people of the Dominican Republic voted **Joaquín Balaguer,** by then elderly and legally blind from glaucoma, back into office by the narrowest margin. Counting the ballots took weeks. A narrow margin and a long wait before votes are counted usually means one thing in Latin America: in a close election, extra votes can always be found. Joaquín Balaguer, who was reelected in 1990 and 1994, would run the country until 1996. He was victorious in the 1994 election by insinuating that his Afro-Dominican opponent was in cahoots with the Haitians. This ploy worked, as many Dominicans harbored concerns that an overpopulated Haiti would invade. During Balaguer's terms in office, economic conditions in the Dominican Republic did not improve. Hyperinflation, unemployment, a collapsing infrastructure, a shortage of hospitals and educational institutions, pollution, and emigration became the norm. In 1990, over half of the seven million people of the Dominican Republic lived in poverty.

Though he was ninety, blind, and partially deaf by the time he stepped down, Balaguer did not want to relinquish power, but was forced to because of a constitutional amendment. Just months after leaving office, Joaquín Bala-guer was accused of ordering the assassination of three politi-cal opponents and misappropriating at least $740 million in government funds.

When did the Dominicans finally experience democratic elections?

Not until 1996, when Dominicans democratically elected **Leonel Fernández,** a young, vigorous man, into office. It would be the first time in history that the entire island of His-paniola would have democratically minded leaders.

LIFE IN DOMINICAN AMERICA

What brought Dominicans to American shores, and where have they settled?

Before 1960, few Dominicans ventured to the United States. Dominican immigration rose to significant levels in the 1960s in response to the civil war in the Dominican Republic. The number of Dominicans leaving the Dominican Republic for the United States remained steady through the 1970s. Then in the 1980s, during the economic depression, immigration soared. In that decade alone, 250,000 Dominicans entered the United States legally, constituting the second largest na-tional group of immigrants from the Western Hemisphere, with Mexicans as the largest.

The 1990s have also seen the arrival of Dominican immi-grants in unprecedented numbers. According to a report re-leased in 1997 by New York City's planning department, between 1990 and 1994 the largest single group of immi-grants to come to the city was the Dominicans, who beat out over 150 other ethnic groups for the distinction.

Over half of the 506,000 Americans of Dominican descent counted in the 1990 census reside in New York and New Jersey. Washington Heights in Manhattan boasts by far the largest Dominican American community in the nation. Dominican Americans refer to it as Quisqueya Heights (after the native name for Hispaniola). Massachusetts and Florida are also home to a small number of Dominican Americans. Quite a number of Dominicans have also settled in Puerto Rico, where they have found jobs in the service sector. Some have moved on and established new lives in the continental United States.

In addition to Dominicans who enter the country through legal channels and secure American citizenship, there is also a sizable undocumented Dominican population in America. No reliable data has been published, but many researchers believe that there may be as many as 300,000 undocumented Dominicans in the United States.

Who are the retornados?

The *retornados*, or returned immigrants, are Dominicans who have spent some time in the United States and then have returned to the Dominican Republic either to establish businesses with capital earned abroad, or for personal reasons. There is no reliable data that shows just how many Dominicans have ventured to America and then returned to their homeland, but their number must be significant as businesses have cropped up in the Dominican Republic that serve the special needs of *retornados*.

How have Dominican Americans fared?

Dominican Americans are in many ways the invisible Latinos, especially in comparison to Mexican Americans, Puerto Ricans, and Cuban Americans. They have not yet carved a niche for themselves in American society and remain at the bottom of the Latino economic ladder.

Since many Americans of Dominican descent are of mixed

EVERYTHING YOU NEED TO KNOW ABOUT LATINO HISTORY

African and Spanish heritage, they have encountered the same prejudice and discrimination that African Americans have endured in America. Many Americans, who operate under the false belief that Dominican immigrants represent the poorest, most disenfranchised members of Dominican society, insist that these immigrants burden America's social service system. This could not be further from the truth. The majority of Dominican Americans have never been on welfare, or received food stamps or workers' compensation. What's more, as a group Dominicans who come to the United States are more highly educated than those who remain on the island, and a good number among them are professionals.

Unfortunately, most Dominican immigrants end up in low-wage, low-status blue-collar jobs, and many of their families live in poverty or just get by as a result. For instance, in New York City a large number of Dominican women make a meager living working in the garment industry (and enjoy little job protection), while Dominican men hold jobs in manufacturing, and the restaurant and hotel industry.

Little by little, Dominicans in New York are working their way up. Some have launched new small businesses or revamped preexisting ones, particularly *bodegas*, supermarkets, diners, family-style restaurants, travel agencies, and taxicab companies. As an example of just how invisible Dominican Americans are, many Dominican restaurateurs in New York City describe their food as Spanish and American, which is what Cuban and Puerto Rican cooking in America used to be called in the old days. Thus many of their patrons, both Latinos and non-Latinos, think they are getting dishes made by Cuban and Puerto Rican chefs. Dominican restaurateurs fear that if they told the "whole truth," Americans, who are unfamiliar with Dominican flavors, would shy away.

Who are some famous Dominican Americans?

One of the leading voices in American literature of the day is Dominican-born **Julia Alvarez,** who took the literary world by storm with the publication of her first novel, *How the García Girls Lost Their Accents,* in 1991. Her novels *In the Time of the Butterflies* (1994) and *¡Yo!* (1997) also earned kudos for the author.

Oscar de la Renta, one of the most recognizable names in the world of haute couture and ready-to-wear clothing, was born in the Dominican Republic in 1932. He later settled in New York City, where in the 1960s he created a billion-dollar international fashion business.

Tennis star **Mary Joe Fernández** was born in the Dominican Republic in 1971. She played at Wimbledon, her first Grand Slam tennis match, in 1986, at the tender age of fourteen, and then went on to become one of the world's leading doubles players, capturing the gold with **Gigi Fernández** at the 1992 Summer Olympics.

What is the favorite pastime of many Dominican Americans?

Dominican Americans are proud of their national music and dance, *merengue,* which is *número uno* among Latinos in New York, surpassing even Puerto Rican salsa. But the favorite pastime of many is not dancing but baseball, the national sport of the Dominican Republic.

What kinds of foods do Dominican Americans like?

Dominican Americans adore typical American fare, but they also have a love of traditional island cooking. The Dominican kitchen, like Puerto Rican and Cuban cooking, features chicken, pork, beef, and fish dishes mildly flavored with garlic, onion, and citrus juice. Rice, beans, fried plantains, and tropical tubers such as *yuca* and *yautía* are the usual accompaniments to main entrées.

Of the three Caribbean cuisines, Dominican cooking has the most pronounced African elements. The flavors of Africa are readily apparent in Dominican *sancocho*, a savory stew made with beef, chicken, or pork (and occasionally all three), to which chunks of West African yam, *yautía*, and *yuca* are added. A dish of *sancocho* adorned with slices of avocado is a quintessential Dominican meal in both Santo Domingo and Washington Heights. And a memorable one, too.

> To tell you the truth, the hardest thing coming to this country wasn't the winter everyone warned me about—it was the language. If you had to choose the most tongue-twisting way of saying you love somebody or how much a pound for the ground round, then say it in English. For the longest time I thought Americans must be smarter than us Latins—because how else could they speak such a difficult language . . . I guess for each one in the family it was different what was the hardest thing. For Carlos, it was having to start all over again at forty-five, getting a license, setting up a practice. My eldest Carla just couldn't bear that she wasn't the know-it-all anymore. Of course, the Americans knew their country better than she did. Sandi got more complicated, prettier, and I suppose that made it hard on her, discovering she was a princess just as she had lost her island kingdom. Baby Fifi took to this place like china in a china shop, so if anything, the hardest thing for her was hearing the rest of us moan and complain.
>
> Julia Alvarez, *¡Yo!* Chapel Hill, North Carolina:
> Algonquin Books of Chapel Hill, 1997.

SIETE

Americans of Central and South American Descent

Who are the Americans of Central and South American descent?

SALVADORAN AMERICANS

When did the Spanish conquer El Salvador?

When did El Salvador declare its sovereignty?

What is La Matanza?

Who was José Napoleón Duarte?

Why did civil war break out in El Salvador, and when was peace finally restored?

How many Salvadoran Americans are there, and
when did Salvadorans start coming to America in
large numbers?

What is the status of Salvadoran refugees in
America?

Where do Salvadoran Americans live, and how are
they doing?

GUATEMALAN AMERICANS

How resistant were the native peoples of Guatemala
to Spanish rule?

Who was Mariano Gálvez, and why was he such an
Anglophile?

How was coffee king in nineteenth-century
Guatemala?

What effect did the Depression have on
Guatemala?

Why did the United States invade Guatemala over
bananas?

When did Guatemalans start coming to America in
large numbers?

NICARAGUAN AMERICANS

How did Nicaragua make the transition from a
Spanish colony to a sovereign nation?

How did an American end up as Nicaragua's first president and English as the country's official language?

Why did the United States become embroiled in Nicaragua's affairs?

What was the Somoza dynasty?

What was the Sandinista National Liberation Front?

Who were the Contras?

How many Nicaraguan Americans are there and where do they live?

HONDURAN, COSTA RICAN, AND PANAMANIAN AMERICANS

How many Honduran Americans are there, and where do they live?

How are Costa Rican Americans different from other Americans of Central American ancestry?

What about Panamanian Americans?

COLOMBIAN AMERICANS

What were the Spanish seeking in Colombia?

Why did the United States pick a fight with Colombia?

What was "La Violencia"?

How did the drug trade engulf Colombia?

What brought Colombians to America, and where have they settled?

What is one of the biggest obstacles Colombian Americans have faced?

THE OTHER AMERICANS OF SOUTH AMERICAN DESCENT

What brought Ecuadorans to America?

Why are Peruvian Americans called "the children of success"?

What is the Argentinean Americans' secret to success?

What has motivated Chileans to come to America?

What about Venezuelan, Bolivian, Uruguayan, and Paraguayan Americans?

Who are the Americans of Central and South American descent?

Latinos with roots in Central America include Salvadoran Americans, Guatemalan Americans, Nicaraguan Americans, Honduran Americans, Costa Rican Americans, and Panamanian Americans. (Americans with roots in Belize, where Spanish is not the official language, are not counted as Latinos.) Immigration from Central America to the United States did not get under way, for the most part, until the late twentieth century, and so Americans of Central American ancestry are relative newcomers. Scourges of every kind, from military dictatorships, right-wing death squads, guerilla insurgencies, and poverty and hunger, are what triggered the movement north of peoples from most Central American countries. In the 1990s, with democracy in place in Central American nations, economic chaos has been the primary factor motivating Central Americans to come to America's shores.

Latinos of South American ancestry include Colombian Americans, Ecuadoran Americans, Peruvian Americans, Argentinean Americans, Chilean Americans, Venezuelan Americans, Bolivian Americans, Uruguayan Americans, and Paraguayan Americans. (Americans with roots in Guyana, French Guiana, Suriname, and Brazil—which were British, French, Dutch, and Portuguese colonies—are not considered Latinos.) Like Central Americans, South Americans are also new to the American scene. Americans of South American ancestry belong largely to the middle and upper-middle classes. Most groups came to America in search of better economic opportunity, although some, such as Colombians and Chileans, sought shelter from war and political instability.

SALVADORAN AMERICANS

When did the Spanish conquer El Salvador?

The Spanish conquest of El Salvador, which was launched in 1524, changed forever the course of the country's history. In the days when Spanish conquistador **Pedro de Alvarado** made landfall, El Salvador was inhabited by five Amerindian groups, one of which was the Pipil, an industrious people closely related to the Aztec, who called their homeland Cuscatlán, meaning "Land of the Jewel." The Pipil fought off the Spaniards with all their might, and Alvarado and his soldiers turned tail and retreated to Guatemala. Four years later, however, the Spanish invaders, who couldn't get precious metals off their minds, managed to subdue the Pipil. The Spanish christened their colony *El Salvador* ("The Savior") and made it part of the province of Guatemala.

The Spanish unearthed little silver and gold in El Salvador, and so they turned to agriculture and provided fourteen families, known as *los catorce grandes*, with enormous tracts of land. *Los catorce grandes* put the native peoples to work cultivating cacao, indigo, and later coffee. On September 15, 1821, the colonies of Central America announced an end to Spanish domination. Believing that strength lay in unity, the colonies created the United Provinces of Central America in 1823, but in 1838 the union completely fell apart. In the 1840s and 1850s each of the colonies declared itself a republic independent of Spain and the United Provinces of Central America, but expressed hope for Central American reunification. (Between 1838 and 1965 there were countless attempts at a reunion.)

Changes in the political status of El Salvador brought little relief to the native peoples and *mestizos*, and eventually they took matters into their own hands and rebelled. One of the most famous peasant uprisings took place in 1831, when **Anastasio Aquino** rallied thousands of natives and *mestizos* under the banner "Land for those who work it!" Conditions did not improve in the aftermath of the uprising, but the stage was set for events that would rip the nation apart at the seams.

When did El Salvador declare its sovereignty?

In 1856, El Salvador officially proclaimed itself a sovereign nation. The governments that would steer the country until the end of the nineteenth century were determined to develop a strong economy by supplying international markets with coffee. These governments were essentially oligarchies controlled by *los catorce grandes* (by this time they actually numbered around 200), a small aristocracy who by now possessed most of the land and wealth of El Salvador. *Los catorce grandes* were able to produce high yields of coffee by exploiting the native and *mestizo* workers. They forced the workers to labor on the plantations and prohibited them from owning parcels of their own to farm.

As the twentieth century dawned, El Salvador was one of the most prosperous nations in Central America, owing to its leading export crop: coffee. Coffee made it possible for railways to be built, highways to be paved, and the cities to grow. In this atmosphere of prosperity, the nation enjoyed relative stability, but it was only skin-deep. Discontent was growing among the exploited poor, and the tiny ruling oligarchy did nothing to diffuse the pressure that was building.

What is La Matanza?

La Matanza, meaning "The Slaughter" of 1932, marks one of the low points in El Salvador's tumultuous history. When the Great Depression rocked world markets, the price of coffee plummeted, and the already poor workers of El Salvador were forced to take wage cuts. Many lost their jobs altogether. As a result, the political situation became extremely unstable. In 1930 **Arturo Araujo,** who favored land reform and social democracy, was elected president to the great shock of the Salvadoran oligarchy and military. After Araujo announced that he would permit the communist party to take part in municipal elections, the military tossed him out of office and put a right-wing general, **Maximiliano Hernández Martínez,** in his place.

When Hernández Martínez did nothing to help the suffering peasants, rebel forces headed by university student **Agustín Farabundo Martí** formed a communist party called the Farabundo Martí National Liberation Front (FMLN). The FMLN exerted pressure on the Hernández Martínez government to change the system of land ownership that had left the people desperately poor, with power and wealth concentrated in the hands of a few. When their cries went unanswered, in 1932 the rebels organized a two-day revolt by the farmers. In response, the military, under orders from Hernández Martínez, executed Farabundo Martí and slaughtered 30,000 insurrectionists, many of them natives.

Who was José Napoleón Duarte?

For the next four decades, the people of El Salvador, who endured ever-worsening economic conditions, continued to cry for the fair redistribution of the land. But the government, which remained under the control of the coffee elite, refused to institute reform and called on the armed forces to suppress the masses. Finally, in 1972 it seemed that El Salvador was on the brink of change when **José Napoleón Duarte,** a moderate reformist candidate who had founded the Christian Democratic Party, appeared to have won a majority in the presidential election. Before a victory could be announced, however, the government had Duarte imprisoned, tortured, and exiled.

After Duarte was exiled, violence and repression became endemic in El Salvador. Civil disorder continued to rise as life got worse for the poor peasants, and guerilla groups grew in numbers and daring. The government's response to this increased dissent was to organize death squads that hunted down, tortured, and exterminated thousands of citizens thought to be sympathetic to the reform cause. (All women who wore blue jeans were highly suspect.) Those who perished came to be known as *los desaparecidos*, or "the disappeared ones," because military and paramilitary forces denied any involvement in their fate.

The situation came to a head in 1977 when government forces murdered Father **Rutilio Grande,** a rural pastor. San Salvador's archbishop **Oscar Romero,** a beloved religious leader, lashed out at the regime for its brutality, ushering the Catholic Church into the struggle. In 1979 reformist officers led a successful coup and installed a junta run by both the military and civilians that promised an end to the violence and sweeping land reforms. José Napoleón Duarte returned to El Salvador from exile, and the people thought that maybe, just maybe, change was just around the corner.

Why did civil war break out in El Salvador, and when was peace finally restored?

The civilians in the junta, which Duarte headed, objected to the military's unceasing efforts to crush dissent, and they soon threw up their hands and resigned. All power was once again concentrated in the hands of the military, which lashed out at the rebels with a vengeance—and at anyone suspected of belonging to the opposition. Countless Salvadorans were tortured or murdered by death squads. The FMLN fought back, and in 1980 a civil war erupted in El Salvador. One fateful event which sparked the war was the assassination, by government forces, of Archbishop **Romero,** who again openly criticized the Salvadoran government for its draconian rule.

The United States, fearful that a FMLN victory in the civil war might foster the spread of communism in Central America, lent massive economic and military aid to the Salvadoran government, ignoring its horrendous human rights violations. By the mid-1980s, the **Reagan** administration was dispatching a whopping $1.2 million a day to bolster the Salvadoran government in its fight. (Between 1978 and 1993 the United States would give El Salvador a grand total of $1.1 billion in military aid.) Although it did not go as far as sending American troops to El Salvador to fight the FMLN rebels, the United States supplied cutting-edge weapons, such as M60 machine guns and M16s, and also helped train and maintain Salvadoran army battalions.

One American-trained battalion, the Atlacatl Battalion, was responsible for one of the largest massacres in twentieth-century Latin American history. In "Operation Rescue," the Atlacatl Battalion slaughtered 1,000 civilians in an attempt to loosen the rebels' hold on the region of Morazan in late 1981. When the news broke, Salvadoran and American officials denied that any such massacre had occurred. The Reagan administration was in the middle of negotiating with Congress for continued aid to El Salvador, and verification of the massacre would have undermined its position that the Latin American nation had stepped up its efforts to protect human rights.

In 1984, **José Napoleón Duarte** was elected president of El Salvador, finally realizing his dream of leading the nation. He tried to restore harmony, but an ongoing civil war, economic hardship brought on by Duarte's austerity measures, and accusations of corruption on the part of his government left the door open for a wealthy coffee grower, **Alfredo Cristiani** of the right-wing National Republican Alliance (ARENA), to prevail in the presidential election of 1989.

In September 1989, the Cristiani government and FMLN rebels finally sat down at the negotiating table. At the last minute, the FMLN launched a final offensive, but failed to garner enough popular support to overthrow the government. During the fighting that ensued, an army-sponsored death squad broke into a Catholic university and brutally murdered six Jesuit priests, their housekeeper, and her daughter. This incident stunned the world, and the United States reacted by withdrawing aid from the Salvadoran government, forcing it to return to the negotiating table with the FMLN. A Truth Commission appointed by the United Nations in 1992 to get to the bottom of the most atrocious breaches of human rights in El Salvador revealed that the minister of defense, **General René Emilio Ponce,** had ordered the massacre of the Jesuit priests.

For two long years, the two sides negotiated under the supervision of the United Nations, and finally in January 1992, they signed historic peace accords. Under the accords, the government agreed to institute extensive reforms, which included the redistribution of land, the downsizing of the military, the creation of a civilian-controlled police force, and a purge of its most notorious human-rights violators. The government also guaranteed the FMLN political freedom. In return, the FMLN agreed to throw down its weapons.

The pace of reform was slow at first, and El Salvador struggled to resuscitate its economy. Twelve years of civil war had had a devastating effect on the nation; over 75,000 people lost their lives and hundreds of thousands were uprooted. But ARENA enthusiastically embraced democracy and the free market concept, and the FMLN dissolved its guerilla forces and became a legal political party. With democratic rule a reality, the World Bank and international investors were more than happy to aid El Salvador in its reconstruction, and by the late 1990s the nation's economy was percolating.

How many Salvadoran Americans are there, and when did Salvadorans start coming to America in large numbers?

According to the 1990 census, 565,000 people of Salvadoran descent make their home in the United States, but there are probably hundreds of thousands of undocumented Salvadoran refugees who went uncounted. About one out of every six Salvadoran Americans was born in the United States.

Emigration from El Salvador was just a trickle until the turbulent decade leading up to the civil war, when about 34,000 Salvadorans came to America. Once the civil war was unleashed in 1980, the pace of emigration picked up as terrorized Salvadorans without so much as a suitcase rushed for the border. Many had received death threats or orders to join the army, or had watched in horror as death squads killed family members and friends. In the 1980s alone, 214,000 Salvadorans entered the United States via legal channels. An unknown number of mostly poor Salvadoran peasants crossed into the United States illegally. They made their way to

American soil through Mexico by using counterfeit papers or by bribing officials manning control posts.

Some were also led or transported north and over the U.S.–Mexico border by smugglers, called coyotes, who demanded large sums of money for the risky trip. The coyotes were often abusive toward the Salvadorans in their keeping. In 1980, thirteen Salvadorans perished when their group was dumped somewhere in the middle of the Arizona desert, without food or water or directions on how to reach civilization. A good number of Americans, who deplored the United States' use of El Salvador as a battleground on which to fight the Soviet Union, sympathized with the plight of the Central Americans crossing the border. In the early 1980s, an American by the name of **Jim Corbett,** along with several others, aided by about three hundred religious congregations, organized the sanctuary movement, a network of safe houses for people escaping Central America. Their work shined the spotlight on the plight of Central Americans fleeing war and extreme hardship.

In the 1990s, even with civil war a thing of the past, Salvadorans have continued to face economic upheaval at home. The only way for many families to survive has been to send members north to work in the United States. These newer arrivals, and the immigrants who came before them, send payments of approximately one billion dollars (known as "remittances") back home annually, which makes them the largest source of foreign exchange revenue in El Salvador.

Like the refugees of the civil war, many Salvadoran immigrants of the 1990s (and those from other Central American countries) trekked through Mexico to the United States. In the 1990s, however, the trip has been especially fraught with danger. As they passed through Mexico, which they call "crossing the beast," many Central American immigrants were assaulted, raped, and robbed by hoodlums. Many would-be immigrants never made it to their final destination, but were taken into slavery or dumped back over the Mexico-Guatemala border. Some critics claim that the United States has fostered this situation because it expects Mexico to act as a filter for immigrants headed north from Central America. As a result, Mexican immigration agents are especially tough on Central Americans trying to squeeze through. In recent times, Mexico has taken steps to ameliorate the situation by setting up roadblocks along its southern border and along well-traveled corridors so that Central Americans do not even step foot on Mexican territory.

What is the status of Salvadoran refugees in America?

Most of the legal and undocumented Salvadoran refugees of the civil war period sought political asylum, but only about three percent of applicants were granted that status. The others were deemed ineligible for political asylum because they were unable to produce documents to prove "a well-founded fear of persecution." In fleeing for their lives, most had not paid any attention to gathering paperwork. But the truth of the matter is that no documentation in the world would suffice, because the refugees were pointing a finger at the Salvadoran government as the source of their anguish, the very government the United States had been nurturing with aid. (If the U.S. government granted the Salvadoran refugees political asylum, it would face the unsavory task of justifying the position it took in the civil war.)

Those considered ineligible for political asylum, or whose cases were still pending (that is, most Salvadorans), were stamped economic refugees, which meant that they could be deported at the drop of a hat. Fearing deportation, the Salvadoran refugees (along with refugees from Nicaragua, Guatemala, and Honduras who were in the same boat) filed a class action suit in 1985, alleging that the Immigration and Naturalization Service (INS) had discriminated against them and wrongly dismissed their appeal for political asylum. In 1990, the INS agreed to a settlement that guaranteed each refugee a fair hearing, and also permitted all members of the class to live and work legally in the United States while their asylum claims were pending.

Between 1986 and 1990, 100,000 undocumented Central Americans who had arrived before 1982 received the good news that their status had been changed to that of legal immigrants thanks to the amnesty provisions of the Immigration Reform and Control Act of 1986. But by 1997 the INS still had not addressed the remaining asylum claims of Salvadorans and other Central Americans. Many of the refugees whose status was still pending came to the conclusion that they were eligible for suspension of deportation (which leads to permanent residency) since enough time had passed for them to meet the requirement of seven years residency. (The other requirements were good moral character and proof that the refugee and his or her parents, spouse, or children who were legal U.S. residents would suffer exceptional hardship were the refugee deported.)

However, in 1997, the U.S. Congress passed a sweeping immigration law that makes it more difficult for refugees to be granted a suspension of deportation. To avoid deportation, a refugee must now show ten years of residency, as well as proof of good character and hardship to the family in the event that he or she is deported. (The refugee's hardship is no longer considered.) However, much of the time refugees rack up in the United States is not counted toward the ten years, and quotas have also been set on the number of refugees who can be granted suspension of deportation in any given year. As a result of these new laws, the approximately 300,000 Central American refugees whose status was still undecided in 1997 remain in limbo.

To make matters worse for the refugees, a provision of the new immigration law gives immigration officers the right to deport undocumented immigrants and prevent them from returning to the United States for several years even if they obtain the proper paperwork. The provision also called for the INS to ship as many as 93,000 foreigners across the border in 1997, one third more than in 1996. It should be noted, however, that a good number who have been returned are hardcore drug criminals or gang members with criminal records in the United States. In a six-month period spanning 1996 and 1997, 12 percent of those the INS sent home were from Central America, while 74 percent were from Mexico.

The INS and **President Clinton** assured Salvadorans and other Central Americans in the United States (and worried Central American leaders at a summit held in Costa Rica in May 1997) that the new law would not spark mass deportations of refugees, but still many Central Americans—undocumented and legal alike—live not knowing what the future will bring. Many fear that they will be separated from their American-born children. And so they live their lives in the shadows, hoping against hope that they won't cross paths with an INS agent.

Where do Salvadoran Americans live, and how are they doing?

According to a study released in 1997, Los Angeles boasts the largest Salvadoran population outside of El Salvador. Washington, D.C., and Houston have the second and third largest Salvadoran communities. About 83 percent of Salvadorans in America were born abroad, and because they have often felt like strangers in a strange land they have formed insular communities.

For the most part, Salvadoran Americans and Salvadoran refugees are forced to work long hours at low-paying jobs in the service sector due to a lack of education. They are extremely hard workers and they have been doing their utmost to forge a new life in the United States. About 65 percent of LA's Salvadorans are employed—the figure is 60 percent for other Latinos and 63 percent for whites. Still they are among the poorest of all Latinos, which is both a reflection of the humble life most led in rural parts of El Salvador and their undocumented status in the United States.

Salvadoran refugees, who once thought their stay abroad would be temporary, now feel at home in the United States and are eager to join mainstream society. In preparing for citizenship many have taken advantage of the English-language classes and American history lessons offered by a network of social service agencies such as the Central American Resource Center (formerly the Central American Refugee Center) in Los Angeles.

GUATEMALAN AMERICANS

How resistant were the native peoples of Guatemala to Spanish rule?

Extremely resistant. Spanish conquistadors led by **Pedro de Alvarado** set foot in what is present-day Guatemala in 1522. They ruthlessly pursued their mission to "bring light to those in darkness, and also to get rich," as one of Alvarado's men wrote. This mission directly involved the Maya of Guatemala, who, as is the case with the native peoples in Spain's other colonies, were forced to convert to Catholicism and were driven into slave labor. But of all the native peoples in Central America, the Maya put up the greatest resistance to subjugation. They fought tooth and nail to preserve their ancient ways. That many Guatemalans—and Guatemalan Americans— today partake of Mayan religious practices is testimony to their success. Still Spanish rule took its toll on the Maya. Before the sixteenth century was over, about 80 percent of the one million Maya who inhabited the Guatemalan highlands had lost their lives fighting the Spanish or their European diseases.

Who was Mariano Gálvez, and why was he such an Anglophile?

The colonies of Central America, Guatemala included, declared their independence from Spain in 1821, and two years later they formed a federation called the United Provinces of Central America. Just before the federation was dissolved in the early 1830s, a liberal named **Mariano Gálvez** emerged as the leader of Guatemala. Gálvez created an export-driven economy, and to fuel it he made room for the cultivation of more crops by auctioning off lands held by the church, groups of native peoples, and *mestizos*. The leading export was cochineal (a crimson dye derived from insects that thrive on the nopal cactus) and the major buyer was England, which had an expanding textile industry in the early nineteenth century. Consequently, ninety percent of the products Guatemala imported were British, and the Guatemalan economy became closely tied to Britain's. Gálvez turned out to be more of an Anglophile than anyone could have guessed. He lured English settlers to Guatemala with promises of land grants, and he attempted to replace the Spanish legal system with a British-inspired one.

How was coffee king in nineteenth-century Guatemala?

While **Mariano Gálvez**'s reforms made Guatemala richer, they inspired the wrath of the native and *mestizo* peasants, who saw little of the wealth and wanted their land back. In 1838, a poor *criollo* peasant by the name of **Rafael Carrera** led a guerilla insurgency that toppled the Gálvez government. Carrera would, for the most part, rule Guatemala from 1839 until his death in 1865. He gave the church back its real estate and its authority to dictate family life and education. A conservative ruler, Carrera also showed concern for the native and *mestizo* masses. When coffee took the place of cochineal as

Guatemala's major export, Carrera did not appropriate native and *mestizo* lands to grow coffee beans.

After Rafael Carrera's death, Guatemala experienced rebellion by **Serapio Cruz,** who had expected to succeed Carrera, and liberals and coffee planters in the western highlands setting the stage in 1873 for the rise to power of **Justo Rufino Barrios,** the first of several liberal military dictators to rule the country. In the name of economic growth and modernization, Barrios passed anticlerical legislation; expanded the public education system (to the benefit of the middle and upper classes); attracted foreign investors, especially English and German businessmen, to build the nation's infrastructure; and encouraged the formation of banks and other financial institutions. While he was most certainly a reformer, Barrios also expanded the coffee industry by expropriating native and *mestizo* lands and taking advantage of the workers. He also fortified the military, which became a tool of repression under his leadership.

What effect did the Depression have on Guatemala?

Two other liberal rulers followed **Justo Rufino Barrios**'s lead, then in 1898 **Manuel Estrada Cabrera** took office. During Estrada Cabrera's tenure, which lasted until 1920, Guatemala saw continued economic growth as coffee exports expanded. By the 1920s, the United States was heavily invested in Guatemala, replacing the Germans and the British, and thus exerted an enormous influence on Guatemalan internal affairs. The Great Depression caused the value of Guatemalan coffee beans to nosedive, which translated into increased unemployment and poverty. The people grew restless, and Guatemala was racked by a series of revolts.

A general by the name of **Jorge Ubico** managed to restore stability to the nation, and in 1930 he was overwhelmingly elected to the presidency. Ubico remained at the helm until 1944 by squelching all opposition, including the communist party, through the use of military force. During his years in office, he formulated many regulations that promoted the agenda of wealthy landowners and foreign investors, especially the United States. For instance, he forced the native peoples to carry passbooks which proved they had worked for at least 150 days in a given year. In order to obtain such proof, many natives had to go to work for wealthy landowners.

Why did the United States invade Guatemala over bananas?

During World War II, **General Ubico** in collaboration with the United States seized German property and permitted the U.S. military to station troops on Guatemalan soil. In so doing, Ubico lost the support of the coffee elite. Wartime inflation caused Guatemala's middle class great hardship, setting the stage for demonstrations against Ubico's dictatorship. In 1944 a reformist alliance of Guatemalans composed of students, professionals, and some soldiers, who wanted the Americans out of Guatemala and a better life for the people, forced Ubico, who got no help from the coffee elite, to relinquish the presidency. That same year **Juan José Arévalo,** a university professor who had been exiled to Argentina, was voted into office. Arévalo set to work building democracy in Guatemala, and his efforts were sustained by his successor, colonel **Jacobo Arbenz Guzmán,** who became president in 1950. Arbenz's greatest contribution was his agrarian reform program, which returned 1.5 million uncultivated acres belonging to large plantations to the native peoples and the *mestizos*. The big landowners who lost some acreage were reimbursed for their loss, but they were nonetheless infuriated.

One of them was the United Fruit Company (UFCO), an American enterprise that cultivated bananas on huge tracts of land in Guatemala. Thanks to the land reform program, about 234,000 acres of the UFCO's land were expropriated. The UFCO went kicking and screaming to **President Dwight**

Eisenhower. Several individuals in the Eisenhower administration had close links to the UFCO, and they beseeched the president to take action. So President Eisenhower, to protect the interests of American industry, announced that Guatemala had forged an alliance with the Soviet Union (Arbenz supported Guatemala's communist party) and thus was no friend of the Americans. On June 18, 1954, the United States traded bananas for bullets when two hundred troops and six aircraft, under the direction of the CIA, invaded Guatemala from Honduras. The U.S. government then promised to bomb Guatemala City if the Guatemalan military did not withdraw its support from Arbenz.

Arbenz fled the country, and the U.S. ambassador to Guatemala, **John Puerifoy,** handed the government over to **Colonel Carlos Castillo Armas,** who had the backing of Guatemalan businesses, the right wing, and the CIA. Armas reversed the agrarian reforms, handing acreage back to the big landowners, among them the United Fruit Company. He also reinstated military rule and had no qualms about using force to achieve his aims—which included demolishing any opposition from leftist organizations such as student groups, labor unions, and political parties. Soon Armas intensified his efforts to quell dissent by torturing, imprisoning, or condemning to death thousands of Guatemalans whom he considered suspect. But with so many enemies, Armas's days were numbered.

In 1957, a palace guard from the opposition killed the dictator. What followed was three decades of rule by American-backed military dictatorships which crushed popular resistance with violence. In the 1970s, the guerilla forces began to recruit native peoples of the highlands in large numbers. The Guatemalan government reacted by forming death squads, which combed the country in search of rebels whom they slaughtered by the thousands. In the 1980s, the situation worsened when the government gave villagers the choice to join the army and fight the rebels or be killed. Hundreds of thousands died, and many thousands fled to the highlands or across the border.

This cycle of violence continued virtually unchecked until the mid-1980s, when the United States, which could no longer reconcile all of the human rights abuses in Guatemala, withdrew much of its support from the Guatemalan government. In 1986, democracy was given another chance in Guatemala, when the military allowed **Marco Vinicio Cerezo Arévalo,** a civilian and the leader of the Christian Democratic Party, to take office. However, during his five-year rule, Cerezo's hands were tied, since he knew the military would do away with him if he strayed too far from its objectives. He did not dare negotiate with the guerillas who wanted lands returned to the natives and *mestizos,* better health care, higher wages, and a voice in politics for the people.

In 1993, a coup headed by **Jorge Serrano Elías,** a center-right businessman, seized control of the country, but the United States responded by cutting off economic aid, and within one month Serrano was history. Serrano had initiated peace talks with the major guerilla group, the Guatemalan National Revolutionary Unity (URNG), and his successor, **Ramiro de León Carpio,** took over where he left off. In 1996, the URNG and the government signed peace accords brokered by the United Nations, ending Guatemala's civil war, one of the bloodiest in Latin America. During the war, some 200,000 civilians, mostly native, were killed or "disappeared." By signing the accords, which make constitutional reforms internationally binding, Guatemalans prepared the ground for the first seeds of democracy to be sown.

When did Guatemalans start coming to America in large numbers?

The U.S. Bureau of the Census reported in 1990 that about 269,000 people of Guatemalan descent call America home. About 80 percent are foreign-born.

Most Guatemalans who left their homeland for the United States did so in the 1980s and 1990s when life in Guatemala became positively unbearable. As with Salvadorans, they either entered the United States through legal channels or made their way north through Mexico and over the border as undocumented aliens. *El Norte,* a film cowritten by **Gregory Nava, Anna Thomas,** and Guatemalan American **Arturo Arias**—nominated for an Academy Award for best screenplay in 1982—depicts the arduous journey north of a sister and brother who flee violence in Guatemala for refuge in Los Angeles. Nearly all who applied for political asylum were deemed ineligible for the same reasons as the Salvadoran refugees, and like Salvadorans in America, many live in fear of deportation due to the 1997 immigration law.

Los Angeles has the largest Guatemalan community outside of Guatemala, but other cities with sizable Latino communities, such as Houston, New York City, Washington, D.C., and Chicago have also attracted Guatemalans. Since many are in the United States illegally, Guatemalans try to blend into the Latino crowd in cities such as New York and Chicago, and so they risk losing touch with their roots. Like Salvadoran Americans and Salvadoran refugees, Guatemalans tend to toil at low-paying jobs, but they are optimistic that the future will be gentler and kinder.

NICARAGUAN AMERICANS

How did Nicaragua make the transition from a Spanish colony to a sovereign nation?

The first Spanish conquistador to step foot in what is present-day Nicaragua was **Francisco Fernández de Córdoba** who arrived there in 1523. Shortly after, he quite literally lost his head when he went against the wishes of his superior **Pedro Arias de Ávila** and tried to make Nicaragua a separate Spanish province. Arias de Ávila served as governor of Nicaragua from 1526 to 1531, and during this time he subdued the Nicarao Indians and other native tribes with a vengeance. The Spanish did not let up in their subjugation of the native peoples, and by 1650 the native population was reduced to one third of its original size. Just as in El Salvador and Guatemala, those who survived were forced to give up their traditions, relinquish any claim to the land, and labor for the Spanish.

When Central America declared its independence from Spain in 1821, Nicaragua became part of Mexico. This alliance lasted only a year, until Nicaragua joined the United Provinces of Central America. In 1838, Nicaragua left the United Provinces due to unreconcilable differences over whether an interoceanic canal should be built through the country. Although it declared itself a sovereign nation, Nicaragua lacked a national government and each village and city oversaw its own affairs. This worked to the advantage of those living in rural areas because their rights to the land were not interfered with and they were able to grow enough food to support their families.

How did an American end up as Nicaragua's first president and English as the country's official language?

Most Nicaraguan leaders agreed that if Nicaragua were to engage in international trade like a respectable nation, it would need a national government to regulate the use of the land and natural resources. However, they could not agree on how to set up the government. Two camps emerged: one based in León, which became known as the Liberal Party, and the other centered in Granada, called the Conservative Party. The Conservative Party, with **Fruto Chamorro** as its leader, established the Republic of Nicaragua in 1854 and was pretty much in charge. The liberals were intent on wresting control away from the conservatives, and so they invited an American by the name of **William Walker** to León to seek his counsel on how to accomplish this feat.

In 1855, Walker arrived in Nicaragua with his own notions about the country's future. Soon he took command of the liberal military, and thousands of Americans from the south, with Manifest Destiny on their minds, joined up with hopes of obtaining land grants and other perks in Nicaragua. In 1856, Walker went so far as to proclaim himself president of Nicaragua. He ruled the country for one year, during which he declared English the official language, sold or contributed parcels of land to American companies, made slavery legal, and even attempted to incorporate Nicaragua into the United States.

The armies of Central America united and battled Walker and his forces. The American admitted defeat in 1857 and left Nicaragua. A central government was then formed, and from 1857 to 1893 it was headed almost solely by conservatives. The conservative leaders created an atmosphere of political stability, but they also passed laws that made it easy for coffee planters, who by then had whole markets abroad to supply, to seize land from the native and *mestizo* peasants. With no parcels of their own to farm, the peasants were left with no means to support themselves and their families.

Why did the United States become embroiled in Nicaragua's affairs?

The United States wanted the rights to build a canal through Nicaragua to connect the Pacific and the Atlantic Oceans. **José Santos Zelaya,** an iron-fisted liberal dictator who took over Nicaragua in 1893, was not too keen about foreigners having any say about a canal on his turf. Zelaya was a tyrant who made lots of enemies among the conservatives. The United States, with its own interests very much at heart, encouraged the conservatives to stage a revolt against Zelaya. When Zelaya's forces executed two American adventurers who had tried to blow up two Nicaraguan ships, the U.S. government decided it had the perfect excuse to take matters into its own hands and sent in the marines.

Despite U.S. participation in the conservative revolt commandeered by **Juan Estrada,** Zelaya hung on to leadership until 1909, when another liberal, **José Madriz,** stepped into office. The U.S. government, in keeping with its role as "international police power" as spelled out in the 1904 Roosevelt Corollary to the Monroe Doctrine, forced Madriz to resign his post, and the Nicaraguan congress named Juan Estrada president in 1911. Estrada refused the leadership to protest the United States' extensive involvement in Nicaraguan affairs, and Vice President **Adolfo Díaz,** a conservative, assumed office. The U.S. government bankrolled Díaz $14 million (in the form of loans from American banks) to pay off European creditors banging at the door, but only after he agreed to allow the United States to supervise Nicaragua's financial matters until 1925, the year the debt was scheduled to be repaid.

Many Nicaraguans voiced their despair with this arrangement that essentially transformed their country into a U.S. protectorate, and the United States sent in the marines once again to restore peace. In 1916, the Nicaraguan government, which was now beholden to the Americans, granted the United States exclusive right to build a canal through its territory, but in the end the U.S. government found Panama more suitable for a canal. The United States was also given the go-ahead to set up military bases in Nicaragua, which it did, and the marines were a constant presence until 1933.

In the late 1920s, rebel forces banded together in opposition to the pervasive U.S. presence in Nicaragua and what they perceived as too much American meddling in their nation's affairs. They found a leader in **General Augusto César Sandino,** and called themselves Sandinistas in his honor. Although they were greatly outnumbered, the Sandinistas waged a successful guerilla campaign against the marines.

What was the Somoza dynasty?

In 1933, the United States abandoned its goal of keeping the peace in Nicaragua and withdrew its forces after Nicaraguan leaders promised to do their utmost to encourage order. Just to help matters along, the U.S. government arranged a presidential election in 1932, a year before American troops were pulled out. **Juan Bautista Sacasa,** a former rebel, was sworn in as president, and the United States organized a Nicaraguan National Guard to help him preserve order. A Nicaraguan by the name of **Anastasio Somoza García** was chosen to head the National Guard.

President Sacasa and General Somoza did not get along. They disagreed on many issues, one of them being what to do about **General Sandino** and the Sandinistas. In 1934, General Somoza took matters into his own hands and ordered the National Guard to assassinate General Sandino. Three hundred Sandinistas lost their lives as well. President Sacasa realized that the situation had spun out of control, and he tried to curb Somoza's powers, but it was too late. In 1936 Somoza swooped down on Sacasa, forcing him to resign. The next year found General Somoza president of Nicaragua.

The Somoza clan, which included family members and trusted friends, would rule Nicaragua for the next forty-two years. Wealth and control were concentrated in the hands of the Somozas, and those who challenged their absolute rule were intimidated or killed by the National Guard. In 1947 General Somoza handed the presidency over to a friend, but in 1950 he took the helm once again. By now the people of Nicaragua, who had lived so long in fear and poverty, were summoning their courage and social unrest grew.

In 1956 a young poet named **Rigoberto López Pérez** assassinated General Somoza at a ball in León. The reins of power were transferred to Somoza's eldest son **Luis Somoza Debayle,** who ruled Nicaragua until his death from a heart attack in 1963. A confidant of the Somoza family then assumed the presidency, but he died in office in 1966. Another of General Somoza's sons, **Anastasio Somoza Debayle,** subsequently took over as president and ruled with the same brutality as his father. While Somoza's riches multiplied, the people's situation grew more desperate. By the time Anastasio Somoza was reelected in 1974, 60 percent of Nicaraguans suffered from malnutrition and the middle and upper classes were in despair.

What was the Sandinista National Liberation Front?

In the early 1960s, the Sandinista National Liberation Front (FSLN), modeled after **General Augusto César Sandino's** guerilla forces, was founded. The FSLN aimed to bring an end to government corruption and to lift the people of Nicaragua out of grinding poverty and despair. Even though many FSLN leaders were imprisoned or murdered by the Somoza government over the years, the FSLN managed to become the largest and most influential opposition group in Nicaragua. In the 1970s, the FSLN brought many diverse groups into its fold, including student organizations and trade unions, and by 1978 it was clear that it had wrested control of the country away from its leader. But **Anastasio Somoza** would not let go of the last vestige of power until 1979, when he fled first to the United States and then on to Paraguay, where he was later assassinated.

Who were the Contras?

With **Somoza** out of the way, the FSLN set up a government with distinct Marxist components. A nine-member national directorate took over the decision-making, and the people voiced their opinions through the various organizations that were formed for peasants, workers, women, and so on. At first the FSLN turned to the United States and the West for financial support, but by 1980, the Sandinistas established close diplomatic and trade ties with the Soviet Union and Cuba.

The Cold War was still raging, and this alliance made the United States very nervous.

In 1980, the Republicans condemned the "Marxist Sandinista takeover of Nicaragua." To protect U.S. interests in the region and halt what it perceived as the spread of communism in Latin America, **President Ronald Reagan** cut off aid to Nicaragua and ensured that the World Bank and the International Monetary Fund followed suit. In 1981 the Reagan White House, certain that the Sandinistas would permit the USSR to erect military bases on Nicaraguan territory, secretly gave the CIA permission to fund opponents of the Sandinistas. These opponents, or counterrevolutionaries, who disagreed with the direction in which the FSLN was going, became known as the "Contras."

The Contras waged guerilla warfare throughout Nicaragua, forcing the Sandinistas to turn to the Soviet Union for military aid in the form of weapons, tanks, and aircraft. The International Court of Justice and the U.S. Congress condemned the fighting and the Reagan administration's support of the Contras, but the White House simply took the matter underground and diverted profits from the illegal sale of arms in Iran to the Contras. At the same time, President Reagan put the squeeze on the Sandinista government by imposing an economic and trade embargo on Nicaragua that would last until 1990 and would force the country to depend even more heavily on the Soviet bloc.

The actions of the United States and the Contras greatly weakened the FSLN and upset its social agenda. The FSLN had to channel enormous amounts of money, which had been earmarked for health care and education, into fighting a war against the Contras. The U.S.-imposed embargo only made the people's situation worse. By 1988 Nicaragua was in desperate financial straits. Unemployment skyrocketed to a whopping 35 percent and inflation soared to an unbelievable 33,000 percent. When the 1990 national elections rolled around, the people of Nicaragua voiced their despair at the polls. Sandinista **Daniel Ortega Saavedra,** who had been elected president in 1984, was defeated and **Violeta Barrios de Chamorro,** the leader of the opposition coalition, walked away the victor. Once she declared an end to the fighting and her intentions to establish a free market economy and democratize Nicaragua, **President George Bush** lifted the embargo and promised to lend financial support.

Even after its defeat, the FSLN remained the most popular party in Nicaragua and retained both strong representation in the national assembly and command of the labor unions and the armed forces, even though they were greatly reduced. Annoyed that Chamorro did not strip the FSLN of all its power and that the economy was not being privatized at a swift pace, Washington reduced its aid package to Nicaragua. As a result, the Chamorro government had trouble jump-starting the Nicaraguan economy. The Contras, by then called *recontras*, were also miffed about FSLN participation in the Chamorro government, and they reacted with outbursts of violence against demobilized Sandinistas, called *recampas*. Still, the two sides managed to sit down at the bargaining table and hammer out a peace agreement in the spring of 1994.

Though peaceful, Nicaragua remained politically polarized. In the 1996 presidential elections, **Arnoldo Alemán** of the coalition of the Liberal Alliance was declared the winner, but his opponent **Daniel Ortega Saavedra** of the FSLN accused Alemán of voter fraud. As long as the country remains deeply divided politically, critics say that it seems unlikely that its tattered economy will recover.

How many Nicaraguan Americans are there, and where do they live?

The U.S. Bureau of the Census counted 203,000 Americans of Nicaraguan descent in 1990. Four out of five were born in Nicaragua. Before 1980, the Nicaraguan American community was quite small. Then the war waged between the

Sandinista government and the Contras beginning in 1979 sent Nicaraguans fleeing across the border. Between 1982 and 1992, one out of ten Nicaraguans sought refuge in a foreign country. The majority of Nicaraguans who entered the United States did so illegally, typically by crossing Honduras, Guatemala, and Mexico to the U.S. border. In contrast to Guatemalan and Salvadoran refugees, Nicaraguans received preferential treatment when they applied for political asylum in the 1980s and early 1990s because they fled a communist government (not a U.S.-backed one), which the United States had tried desperately to topple. Nicaraguans continue to come to America to this day, but for economic reasons and in fewer numbers.

The majority of Nicaraguan Americans live in Miami, where they have formed a thriving enclave called Little Managua. Nicaraguan Americans as a group are more educated than Salvadoran and Guatemalan Americans, and thus the majority are not stuck in low-paying jobs. About one third of all Nicaraguan Americans hold white-collar positions, and another third are blue collar. Many Nicaraguan Americans send home a good chunk of their earnings.

HONDURAN, COSTA RICAN, AND PANAMANIAN AMERICANS

How many Honduran Americans are there, and where do they live?

The U.S. Bureau of the Census tallied 131,000 Honduran Americans in 1990. New York City has the largest Honduran American population, followed by Los Angeles and then Miami. A good number of Honduran Americans work as migrant farm laborers, many of whom are undocumented.

Hondurans ventured to the United States as early as the late 1700s. Since then there has been a very small but steady flow of Hondurans to America, though the number of immigrants rose in the 1980s and 1990s, when civil wars in neighboring countries created political unrest and economic hardship in Honduras. The borderlands of Honduras were a training ground for Nicaraguan Contras fighting the Sandinista government.

How are Costa Rican Americans different from other Americans of Central American ancestry?

Costa Rican Americans are one of the smaller Latino groups; in 1990 the U.S. census counted approximately 100,000 persons of Costa Rican descent. Ever since its birth as a nation in 1821, Costa Rica has known democracy for the most part (the only instability was a failed dictatorship in 1917–1918 and an attempted revolution in 1932). The Costa Rican people have never had cause to flee their homeland due to political oppression or economic hardship like other Central Americans. Since 1931, only about 57,500 Costa Ricans have taken up residence in the United States, and the rate of emigration remains slow. Most chose to settle in America either because they married a U.S. citizen, they attended an American university and then found a desirable job in the United States, they took advantage of research opportunities that are nonexistent in Costa Rica, or they desired a particular job.

Los Angeles boasts the largest concentration of Costa Rican Americans, followed by the New York–New Jersey metropolitan area, and south Florida. Rather than residing in their own neighborhoods, Costa Rican Americans are very much a part of the American mainstream, or they move in circles of other Latinos.

What about Panamanian Americans?

While there were many Panamanians among the Central Americans who made their home in the United States in the

1970s, they have come in much reduced numbers since then. In 1990, the U.S. Bureau of the Census counted only 92,000 Panamanian Americans. Most Americans of Panamanian descent reside in New England, New York, Florida, and California.

COLOMBIAN AMERICANS

What were the Spanish seeking in Colombia?

Christopher Columbus, who explored the mouth of the Orinoco River in 1498, was probably the first Spaniard to step on what is now Colombian soil. In the early 1500s, many Spanish conquistadors trekked through Colombia in their quest for the mythical city of El Dorado. While the Spanish never located El Dorado, they did found the city of Cartagena on Colombia's Caribbean coast, which evolved into a major port for ships sailing to Spain laden with gold and other treasures from the New World.

Why did the United States pick a fight with Colombia?

After 1740, a good deal of present-day Colombia belonged to New Granada, a territory which also encompassed Panama and Venezuela. In 1819, Spain relinquished its control of New Granada, which was then renamed New Colombia. Ecuador was annexed to New Colombia in 1822, but seceded in 1830, following in the footsteps of Venezuela, which broke off from the territory in 1829. In the 1830s, two rival political parties dominated the political scene in Colombia. The Conservative Party favored a strong central government, while the Liberal Party wanted power split between a weaker central government and regional governments. Their various attempts to consolidate power kindled unrest for most of the century, which culminated in a ferocious civil war waged from 1899 to 1902. By the time the civil war ended, 100,000 had died, the conservatives were in control, and Colombia was a wreck.

The United States took advantage of Colombia's vulnerability. In 1902, the U.S. government flexed its muscles in the region by laying claim to the zone where the Panama Canal was being constructed. The U.S. government tried to get Colombia to sign a treaty that officially gave the Americans full authority in the canal zone, but the Colombians refused. To make doubly sure that the United States understood their position, the Colombians sent troops to Panama to protect what was theirs. With a little nudging from the U.S. government, the Panamanians fought off the Colombian forces and declared their independence in 1903.

What was "La Violencia"?

For the next four decades, peace reigned supreme in Colombia. Then in 1948, the rivalry between the Conservative Party and the Liberal Party escalated again to civil war, which lasted until the mid-1960s in the countryside. Anywhere from 200,000 to 300,000 Colombians perished during this period, known as "*La Violencia*." In 1953 a military coup in Colombia brought the downfall of **Laureano Gómez,** who had tried to create a fascist state, and put **General Gustavo Rojas Pinilla** in command. When the economy worsened, liberals and conservatives banded together in opposition to Rojas, and in 1957 he fell from power. A year later, the two parties created a coalition government known as the National Front. With the National Front at the helm, the Colombian government began to put its shattered nation back together again. In 1966, **Carlos Lleras Restrepo** was named president, and until the end of his rule in 1970, he made efforts to diversify the economy, halt inflation, and institute land reforms.

How did the drug trade engulf Colombia?

Elections in 1974 heralded the end to a National Front–led government. The rift between the haves and have-nots had grown wide in Colombia, perfect conditions for a Marxist, antigovernment guerilla movement. During the late 1970s, the Colombian economy, which had known growth for many years, went into a tailspin due to a mountain of foreign debt. Colombia was besieged by guerilla unrest as well as violence from drug traffickers, who were consolidating their operations in cartels, and Colombians fled en masse over the border to safety in Venezuela. The Colombian government attempted to stop the drug trafficking, *el narcotrafico*, but they were met with incredible resistance, as the illegal drug trade supplied income to many Colombians. The drug cartels gradually took control of Colombian life, with acts of terrorism such as abductions and assassinations of public officials who refused to take bribes, as well as journalists, foreigners, and others; massacres; and car bombings, causing what acclaimed writer **Gabriel García Márquez** calls a "biblical holocaust" in *News of a Kidnapping* (1977), his nonfiction work about Colombian **Pablo Escobar,** kingpin of the Medellín cartel.

In 1989, with Colombia reeling out of control, President **Virgilio Barco Vargas** tried to crack down on the drug cartels, and again Colombia's drug lords responded with violence. During the 1990 election campaign, the drug cartels assassinated candidates it deemed a threat, but still **César Gaviria Trujillo,** a politician who just said no to drugs, managed to survive and win the election. Trujillo gave the drug cartels a bad time, encouraged pluralism, and made way for native peoples and former guerillas to participate in the nation's political life. He also revived the economy somewhat by negotiating with foreign creditors to bring down Colombia's debt.

Despite the efforts of Trujillo and other leaders, guerilla warfare and the drug trade have dominated the headlines in Colombia throughout the 1990s. The war between the guerillas and the Colombian armed forces, which are backed by private militias hired by big landowners and merchants, has displaced almost one million people since 1985. The guerillas are heavily involved in drug activities; they act as bodyguards for *los narcos*. With all the money the drug traffickers have brought in, they are fulfilling their objective of controlling the most lucrative territory. In 1997 they held sway in about half of the nation—the half with abundant oil and coca bushes. Since 1989, the United States has supplied Colombia with funds and equipment for its antidrug operations, and some critics have claimed that this aid has been rerouted for use against the guerillas, resulting in serious human rights abuses. But those who defend the program counter that guerilla revolutionaries and guerilla drug traffickers are often one and the same.

What brought Colombians to America, and where have they settled?

A handful of Colombians settled in the United States in the nineteenth century, along with other South Americans. Immigration picked up after World War I, when Colombian professionals came to America in a small but steady stream. Most settled a short subway ride away from their Manhattan work-places in the Jackson Heights section of Queens, a middle-class neighborhood which became known as "*El Chapinerito*." (Chapinero is a suburb of Bogotá.) The civil war of 1948 inspired Colombians to relocate to the United States in greater numbers in the 1950s, and this emigration continued unabated in the 1960s and 1970s, owing not to violence but to economic chaos in Colombia. Since the Immigration Act of 1965 established a strict quota for immigration (not political asylum) from the Western Hemisphere, very few Colombians, and only the most desirable, were allotted visas. Since they had little chance of establishing legal residency, most Colombians who came to the United States during these decades planned to remain only a short while to earn money. Of course, scores of Colombians stayed on without permanent residency. By 1990 the Colombian American population had risen to about 379,000, and in this decade more Colombians have reached American shores than any other South American group thanks to the drug trade and guerilla warfare in Colombia.

In the 1960s and 1970s, those with means settled in Jackson Heights, while others moved to burgeoning New York City enclaves in Rego Park, Flushing, Elmhurst, and Woodside. A small number chose Los Angeles, Houston, Washington, D.C., and Chicago. Miami, with its gentler climate, Latin flavor, and status as the business capital of Latin America, has attracted the majority of immigrating Colombians ever since the early 1980s.

What is one of the biggest obstacles Colombian Americans have faced?

Ever since the 1980s, Colombian Americans have had to fight the pervasive belief that they are a bunch of drug traffickers who have brought violence, corruption, and addiction to America's streets. The obvious truth is that almost all Colombian Americans are hard-working professionals, entrepreneurs, or workers in the service industries.

THE OTHER AMERICANS OF SOUTH AMERICAN DESCENT

What brought Ecuadorans to America?

Before the mid-1960s, only a scant number of Ecuadorans found their way to the United States. In 1964 Ecuador passed the Land Reform, Idle Lands, and Settlement Act, which called for the expropriation of land from absentee landlords and its distribution to the poor peasants. Many of the peasants, who had no experience as landowners and no credit, simply could not manage the land and they were forced to abandon it. Many left the rural areas altogether in search of opportunity in the cities, and some chose to immigrate to the United States. When these Ecuadorans sent money back home, others were encouraged by the economic prospects in America. Consequently, Ecuadorans have come to the United States in a steady stream since the 1960s. In 1990, the U.S. Bureau of the Census calculated that there are approximately 191,000 Ecuadoran Americans living in the United States.

Some Ecuadorans wait years to secure a visa to come to the United States. Others live in America illegally while waiting for their visa, and still others cross the border illegally from Mexico, or come by boat from Puerto Rico and live as undocumented aliens without ever applying for a visa. Most newcomers have one destination in mind: the New York metropolitan area, which in 1990 was home to about 60 percent of all Ecuadoran Americans. Another ten percent of Ecuadoran Americans reside in Los Angeles. The Ecuadoran American community is closeknit and resistant to assimilation, partly because many Ecuadorans swear allegiance to their home country and plan on returning, and thus see no point in wholeheartedly embracing the American way of life. As a result, only about 20 percent of those who are eligible for citizenship pursue it and many do not speak English fluently. While Argentinean Americans, Chilean Americans, and other Americans with roots in South America are mostly professionals and entrepreneurs, and Americans of Central American descent are largely working class, Ecuadoran Americans belong to both ranks.

Why are Peruvian Americans called "the children of success"?

Peruvians began immigrating to America in the early part of the twentieth century, but most arrived after World War II, in response to economic calamity and political violence and instability. The first to come were upper-class Peruvians. However, in the 1970s, the number of middle-class Peruvians entering the United States rose significantly. They put their education and business acumen to work and acculturated to the United States rather easily, which earned them the label "the children of success." The 1980s saw an increase in the numbers of lower-class Peruvians coming to America. Their assimilation has been the hardest due to a lack of formal education. In 1990 the U.S. Bureau of the Census calculated that there are approximately 175,000 Peruvian Americans.

What is the Argentinean Americans' secret to success?

In the 1990 U.S. census, 92,500 Argentinean Americans were counted. The first sizable group of Argentineans to immigrate to the United States were highly educated professionals seeking greater economic opportunities in the 1960s. Persecution during the "dirty war" that lasted from 1976 to 1983 sent more Argentineans, a good percentage of them Jews, to American shores. During this "war" the military overthrew the country's ineffectual leader **Isabel Perón,** destroyed the small guerilla movement, and incarcerated or killed 9,000 persons (*los desaparecidos*—the "disappeared") who supposedly were linked to the Left or terrorist groups. Thanks to their high educational attainment, the majority of Argentinean Americans are professionals, technicians, and skilled workers. They prefer urban areas with Latin spice. About 20 percent of all Argentinean Americans live in New York City, as it is a center of international business and retains an Italian flavor which Italo Argentinean Americans appreciate.

What has motivated Chileans to come to America?

First it was gold. The Gold Rush of 1848 brought Chileans to American shores in droves. After gold fever died down,

Chilean immigration almost came to a screeching halt, and many Chileans also returned home with stories of hardship rather than fortune. Those who stayed behind settled in San Francisco in a neighborhood called *Chilecito*, or "Little Chile," or in other enclaves in California known as "Chilitowns." Chileans did not come to America in significant numbers again until the mid-1960s. This second wave of Chilean immigration was comprised of mainly young, upper-class Chileans enrolled at American colleges and universities, professionals in search of opportunity, and the Chilean spouses of Americans doing business in Chile.

When Chilean president **Salvador Allende** was overthrown by dictator **Augusto Pinochet** in 1973, the modest flow of Chileans to America became a flood. One million citizens, particularly intellectuals, journalists and other professionals, ran for their very lives during Pinochet's violent military regime. They fled to other parts of Latin America, Europe, and Canada. A small percentage also went to the United States, where, without jobs, contacts, and housing, they had a tough time starting a new life. In 1990 Chilean president **Patricio Aylwin** encouraged Chileans in exile to return home with promises of financial aid. A good number went back to a more democratic Chile and to family members they had not seen in eons. Many took home children who had been born in the United States and spoke poor Spanish. The Chilean government responded by creating Spanish as a Second Language programs in schools. Despite all the Chilean immigrants who have gone home over the last two centuries, the U.S. Bureau of the Census tabulated 69,000 Chilean Americans in 1990, 55,600 of whom were born in Chile.

What about Venezuelan, Bolivian, Uruguayan, and Paraguayan Americans?

Add 48,000 Venezuelan Americans, 38,000 Bolivian Americans, 22,000 Uruguayan Americans, and 7,000 Paraguayan Americans to the Americans with roots in Colombia, Ecuador, Peru, Argentina, and Chile, and you get a marvelous mosaic called Americans of Spanish-speaking South American descent.

OCHO

La Política

LATINO VOTERS

What is the Voting Rights Act all about?

*Real power or paella in the sky: How much political
clout do Latinos really wield?*

*How much money do Latinos give to political
organizations?*

*Is it true that most Latino contributions go to the
Republican Party?*

Are there any Latino watchdog organizations?

LATINOS IN WASHINGTON

What do Latinos in Congress stand for?

Who are the Latinos in Congress?

Who are the high-profile Latinos in the U.S. government?

THE ISSUES

Why is proportional representation such a hot tamale?

Does bilingual education mean we'll all be speaking Spanish soon?

When was the first Latino studies program established?

What is Proposition 187, and how did it backfire on the Republicans who championed it?

LATINO VOTERS

What is the Voting Rights Act all about?

The civil rights movement launched by African Americans in the 1960s served as a model for Latino activists. For instance, the Brown Berets were modeled on the Black Berets, and African studies programs at institutions of higher learning gave rise to Latino studies programs. And, most important, the legal actions taken by African American leaders served as a blueprint for Latino leaders eager to rectify political and social injustice.

The first legal battles that Latinos fought to end discrimination took place in New York in the early 1970s, when a Puerto Rican group brought a lawsuit against the state alleging that it discriminated against Puerto Ricans at the polls by providing English-only ballots. The group argued that they had a legal right to ballots in Spanish since Puerto Ricans are Americans by birth whose mother tongue is Spanish. They won their case and all voting material was rendered bilingual.

On the heels of the Puerto Rican victory, the Mexican American Legal Defense and Education Fund (MALDEF) lobbied intensely for the passage of an amendment to the Voting Rights Act of 1965 which would give access to the voting booth to African Americans in places where it was denied (mainly in southern states). Congress passed the Voting Rights Act, which turned out to be quite effective; in many southern states the number of African American votes doubled in just a few years. MALDEF wanted the same consideration given to Latinos, particularly to Mexican Americans in Texas, where voter discrimination ran rampant. The 1975 amendments to the Voting Rights Act extended special provisions to Latino and other minorities for seven years. In 1982 those rights were extended for another seven years. As a result of these amendments, the Latino voter base is vastly larger.

Real power or paella in the sky: How much political clout do Latinos really wield?

If political power is measured by the number of elected representatives and federal and local posts held by Latinos, the answer to the question is *mucho*—at least as the twentieth century comes to a close—but not as much as the growing Latino population will undoubtedly wield by the year 2020.

The days of alienation and so-called "voter apathy" among Latinos are gone. The 1996 elections saw the highest Latino voter turnout in history thanks to an aggressive voter registration drive in Latino communities, get-out-the-vote efforts, and the raging immigration debate that instilled fear—and a desire for action—in many. On October 12, 1996, on the eve of the elections, 100,000 Latinos marched on Washington in what was called the first national Hispanic March for Justice, demanding an end to cutbacks in affirmative action programs, an increase in the federal minimum wage, and kinder amnesty programs for illegal immigrants.

In the 1996 elections Latinos were particularly impressed by the voter turnout in Texas, which was up an unprecedented 60 percent. In California it rose 40 percent, and in Florida 10 percent. Thus Latinos, who cast the swing vote in the 1992 presidential election in several states, played a decisive role in keeping **President Clinton** in office for a second term. In fact, while only 72 percent of Latinos are Democrats, an astonishing four out of five Latinos voted for Clinton—in part because the community was so enraged over immigrant bashing fueled by the Republicans. Many also voted for Clinton who might otherwise have gone with the Republicans because they felt he would appoint more Latinos to key positions than the GOP.

Just as soon as President Clinton won reelection, numerous influential Latinos voiced their concerns to the White House that the Clinton administration continue to name Latinos to key posts in the Cabinet, sub-Cabinet, and the judiciary. They also made it clear that their greatest wish would be for the president to appoint the first Latino to the Supreme Court, which they feel is well overdue.

Given the increase in the number of Latino immigrants applying for citizenship, most out of fear of deportation, the greater number of Latinos participating in the political process, and the continued rise in the Latino population, the possibility of a Latino Supreme Court justice—and even a president—does not look like paella in the sky anymore.

How much money do Latinos give to political organizations?

The Federal Election Commission (FEC) started issuing comprehensive data on political contributions in the United States in 1979. The data they have compiled shows that Latino contributions have risen twice as fast as the average in the last two decades. All told, it is estimated that Latino individuals and Latino businesses combined have contributed upward of $90 million to political parties and candidates since 1979.

Is it true that most Latino contributions go to the Republican Party?

Yes, even though 72 percent of Latino voters have aligned themselves with the Democrats.

The reason is that Cuban Americans, who are the most solvent Latino group and the one most involved in mainstream politics, are 70 percent Republican and vote 90 percent Republican in national elections. This also explains why a disproportionate amount of Latino political contributions comes from Florida, the home of over half a million Cuban Americans.

However, even Republican Cuban Americans have made contributions to both parties. It's called hedging your bets— and all powerful corporations do it. During the 1992 and 1996 elections, **Bill Clinton** benefited from Cuban American giving, both from big business and individual contributors.

The biggest individual contributor of all was Cuban American megamillionaire **Jorge Mas Canosa,** who was CEO of Church & Tower, a Miami construction company whose clients include Southern Bell and all of Dade County. From 1982 until his untimely death in 1997, he contributed in excess of $200,000 to candidates for national office. Mas Canosa is a true American success story. He fled Castro's regime in 1960 at age twenty-one and arrived in Miami a penniless refugee. After working as a stevedore, a shoe salesman, and a milkman, he purchased a faltering construction company and transformed it into an empire, amassing a personal fortune estimated to be worth over $9 million.

Jorge Mas Canosa was the leading light behind the Free Cuba Public Affairs Committee, whose agenda is to oust **Castro** and establish a democratic government in Cuba. Until his health suddenly deteriorated in 1997 due to a rare bone disorder, many observers in and outside of the Cuban American community were confident he would run for president of Cuba when (or if) Fidel Castro's regime toppled. In the 1990s, Mas Canosa was the most important lobbyist after Israel in America according to Washington insiders, and most believed that gave him enough political clout to succeed. Jorge Mas Canosa wielded so much power that in 1994, when the United States was in the midst of a Cuban refugee crisis, he was able to call Bill Clinton away from a birthday party celebration to have a chat about how to punish Castro. Clinton followed all of Mas Canosa's suggestions with the exception of imposing a naval blockade on Cuba.

Marife Hernández, a Puerto Rican and the former head of Cultural Communications, Inc., is the second biggest individual Latino political contributor and an active member of the Democratic Party. The third biggest contributor is Cuban American Republican **Alfonso Fanjul, Jr.,** the head of the Flo-Sun Corporation of Palm Beach, America's largest sugar producer. He contributed mucho bucks to Bob Dole's 1996 presidential campaign. Other important political contributors include Cuban American **Roberto G. Mendoza,** vice chairman of J. P. Morgan and Company, Inc., the fifth largest U.S. bank; **Arturo Díaz,** a Puerto Rican businessman affiliated with various companies in Rio Piedras and San Juan, Puerto Rico; Mexican American attorney **Earl Luna,** who is based in Dallas; and Cuban American **Roberto C. Goizueta,** who steered the Coca-Cola Company as CEO from 1981 until his death in 1997.

Are there any Latino watchdog organizations?

There are many such groups out there. Some represent Latinos as a whole, while others are devoted to a subgroup (Mexican Americans, Puerto Ricans, etc.). Among the most active are the League of United Latin American Citizens (LULAC), the Mexican American Legal Defense and Education Fund (MALDEF), the American GI Forum, the National Council of La Raza (NCLR), the Aspira Association, the National Association of Hispanic Publications (NAHP), the National Puerto Rican Coalition (NPRC), and the Cuban American National Foundation (CANF).

Some organizations are committed to addressing the concerns of Latinas who have suffered double discrimination based on gender and ethnicity. One such group is the National Council of Hispanic Women, which aims to open doors and minds so that Latinas may participate fully in all facets of American economic, political, and social life.

Besides these organizations that carefully monitor the political and social arenas, there is the Hispanic Association on Corporate Responsibility (HARC), whose principal directive is to watch the private sector closely so that large corporations "do the right thing" and reinvest a portion of the money spent by Latinos into Latino communities by way of higher-level jobs, franchise and dealership opportunities, and donations to philanthropies.

LATINOS IN WASHINGTON

What do Latinos in Congress stand for?

The overwhelming majority of Latinos in Congress are Democrats. Their priorities vary according to the states and districts they represent, and they stand on both sides of the issues. Most, however, are united under the banner of the Congressional Hispanic Caucus (CHC), a bipartisan group formed in 1976 by **Herman Badillo** and the four other Latino Democrats then in Congress. The CHC's mandate was to "voice and advance, through the legislative process, issues affecting Latino Americans," and much of its philosophy mirrors that of the dozens of Latino watchdog groups in America, such as LULAC, the American GI Forum, the Aspira Association, and La Raza Unida.

Not all Latino representatives, however, belong to the Congressional Hispanic Caucus. Seventeen-term Congressman **Henry B. González** (D-Texas) who still serves on the House Banking, Finance, and Urban Affairs Committee which he chaired for three terms, is not a member. However, his honorable efforts on behalf of the disadvantaged are certainly in line with the principles of the CHC.

Despite attempts on the part of Republicans to limit government's effective representation of minorities, the Congressional Hispanic Caucus has made great strides in the 1990s. It played an integral role in the passage of the Voters Assistance Act of 1992, also known as the "bilingual voting bill," which makes bilingual voting information readily available, thereby assuring that minorities who speak a language other than English have ready access to the ballot box. The CHC also pushed the 1991 Hispanic Access to Higher Education Bill, which called for establishing dropout prevention programs and encouraging higher education for Latinos.

Who are the Latinos in Congress?

The first Latinos in Congress were **Dennis Chávez** (D-New Mexico), **Edward Roybal** (D-California), **Eligio ("Kika") de la Garza** (D-Texas), and **Henry B. González** (D-Texas). They look like giant figures on Mount Rushmore to their Latino constituents.

Dennis Chávez, who died in 1962, was the first Latino ever elected to the U.S. Senate. Kika de la Garza, who enjoyed a distinguished career of thirty-two years in the U.S. House of

Representatives, stepped down from office in 1996. Edward Roybal retired from Congress in 1992 after thirty years of service to working-class voters of East Los Angeles. During his tenure, he introduced the first Bilingual Education Act and served as a member of the powerful House Appropriations Committee. His retirement also marked a new beginning, for that very same year his daughter, **Lucille Roybal-Allard,** was elected to Congress. Of the four Latino pioneers in government, only Henry B. González still serves in Congress. He was formerly chairman of the House Banking, Finance, and Urban Affairs Committee, and now he is the committee's highest-ranking Democrat.

The year 1992 was a banner year for Latinos in Washington. **Nydia Velazquez** (D-New York) became the first Puerto Rican woman to serve in the House. She is a member of the Banking, Finance, and Urban Affairs Committee and the Small Business Committee. Cuban-born Republican **Lincoln Díaz-Balart** (who is related to **Fidel Castro**) ran unopposed in Miami's 28th District, which is 80 percent Cuban American. He holds a seat on the Foreign Affairs Committee along with Cuban American **Robert Menendez** (D-New Jersey). Diaz-Balart joined yet another Cuban American Republican in the House, **Ileana Ros-Lehtinen,** who in 1989 became the first Latina in Congress after she was overwhelmingly elected to fill the seat of a popular Democratic congressman from Florida, **Claude Pepper,** after his death. In 1990, Ros-Lehtinen's seat came up for election, and she garnered 60 percent of the vote.

In 1997 Latinos and all Americans lost a heroic statesman when **Frank Tejeda** (D-Texas), another congressman from the "class of 1992," met an untimely death. Tejeda, who transformed himself from a high school dropout to a respected lawyer to the first congressman from the new Latino 28th District, is proof positive that no obstacle in life is insurmountable.

Other Latinos who are shaping policy in Washington include **Solomon Ortiz** (D-Texas), **Luis Gutiérrez** (D-Illinois),

José Serrano (D-New York), Ed Pastor (D-Arizona), and Loretta Sánchez (D-California). Sánchez, a congresswoman from Orange County, California, achieved a stunning victory in the 1996 election when she upset nine-term incumbent Republican Robert Dornan by a slim margin to become the nation's first Mexican American woman in Congress. Dornan contested the election and called for an investigation into possible voter fraud. A grand jury investigation into the allegations returned no indictments and in February 1998 a Congressional task force determined that Sánchez could retain her seat.

Who are the high-profile Latinos in the U.S. government?

In 1996 President Clinton appointed Bill Richardson, who served as U.S. Representative from New Mexico from 1983 to 1997, to the post of U.S. Representative to the United Nations, which he assumed in 1997. He also appointed former Transportation Secretary Federico Peña to head the Department of Energy, the first Latino to assume that post. Peña faces many challenges before him; he will have to reduce America's dependence on foreign oil, revamp the nuclear waste program, and battle legislators who wish to dismantle his department.

In 1996 the Clinton White House also named Aida Alvarez, who was previously director of the Office of Federal Housing Enterprise Oversight (which oversees the Fannie Mae and Freddie Mac programs), director of the Small Business Administration (SBA). As administrator of the SBA—an agency Clinton elevated to the Cabinet level—Alvarez seeks to provide more financing for minority businesses.

THE ISSUES

Why is proportional representation such a hot tamale?

Redistricting is drawing geographic and political boundaries to create new districts that give minorities majority power in neighborhoods where they are indeed the majority. This ensures that they carry enough weight to put candidates into office with a proven sensitivity to the needs of their community, thus ensuring that they receive fair representation in government. As the Latino population rises, new "proportional representation" districts emerge, which in turn brings a roster of new names—many Latino—to Congress.

The question of proportional representation is actually hotter than a habanero chile. Nowadays the tide is in favor of righting the past wrongs of underrepresentation by keeping the amendments to the Voting Rights Act on the books, and creating new apportionments.

Still many have questioned the wisdom of reapportionment. They belong to the melting pot school, which says that character and ability supersede ethnicity and that minorities should leave the ghetto and join the mainstream. They argue that the Garcias should be able to live in the same districts as the Cuomos, the Bloomsteins, the Tates, and the O'Shaughnessys, and not just next door to the Gonzalezes, and that they should all together be able to elect Ms. Schroeder or Mr. Perez to Congress, or whomever happens to be the best person for the job. That's the idea, anyway.

Linda Chavez belongs to the antireapportionment camp. In her 1991 book, *Out of the Barrio: Toward a New Politics of Hispanic Assimilation*, she argues that in order to maintain the political mandate that reapportionment has granted many Latinos, they are forced to stay in the *barrio* where they remain part of the poor underclass, which political clout was supposed to save them from in the first place. She asserts that at least reapportionment should be viewed as a transitory measure (which is how the Voting Rights Act was originally conceived) and not as a permanent legal fixture.

Advocates of reapportionment, such as representative **Nydia Velazquez** of New York, counter that the "melting pot" concept may be good in principle, but nonetheless many Latinos have been deprived of their constitutional rights to adequate housing, health care, social services, education, and economic opportunity. Unless they can elect politicians who are committed to their community, this situation will persist.

NINE LATINAS WHO HAVE MADE A DIFFERENCE

1. Joan Baez

Born in 1941, this folk singer and songwriter has worked hard for humanitarian causes for four decades. She founded the Institute for the Study of Nonviolence in 1965 and Humanitas International in 1979, and has served on the national advisory board of Amnesty International.

2. Fabiola Cabeza de Baca

Born in 1898, this pioneering Latina helped introduce modern food preparation systems to the people of New Mexico. She was the first Latina to receive a U.S. Government Superior Service Award.

3. Linda Chavez

In 1983 she became the first Latina to serve on the Civil Rights Commission after President Reagan appointed her to the post. In 1985 she ran the White House Office of Public Liaison, and in that capacity she was the highest-ranking woman in the White House.

4. Dolores Huerta — This great activist has fought for fair working conditions for America's minorities for many decades. She served as vice president of César Chávez's United Farm Workers from 1970–1973.

5. Virginia Musquiz — This top organizer of La Raza Unida Party fought hard to secure the protection of civil rights for farm workers in America.

6. Antonia Novello — In 1989, under the Bush administration, she became the first Latino and the first woman selected as U.S. surgeon general.

7. Helen Rodriguez — This doctor and activist, who is currently an attending physician at Lincoln Hospital in the Bronx, has been a leading spokesperson on issues regarding women's and children's health.

8. Josefina Sierro — In the 1930s she organized an underground railroad, similar to Harriet Tubman's, to bring home Mexican Americans who were taken to Mexico against their will during the U.S. government's draconian campaign to deport Mexicans en masse.

9. Emma Tenayuca — She organized the first successful strike of pecan shellers in San Antonio in the 1930s. Tenayuca served as a role model for César Chávez.

Does bilingual education mean we'll all be speaking Spanish soon?

Bilingual education got its start in Dade County, Florida, in 1960, when hundreds of thousands of newly arrived Cuban refugee children were enrolled in the county's public schools. Cuban refugees, holding fast to the belief that **Fidel Castro** would soon fall and they would return to their native land, felt that the children should be taught in both English and their mother tongue. They pushed for legislation that required the public schools to teach the kids a half day in Spanish and a half day in English. The Cuban-refugee children were mostly middle-class and quite motivated, and they did well in all their subjects. In fact, they achieved higher scores than English-speaking children in other schools in Florida.

Impressed with the achievements of the Cuban refugee children, politicians and teachers in the Southwest were chomping at the bit to try bilingual education out on their own Spanish-speaking students. And so Texas Senator **Ralph Yarborough** pushed a bill in 1967 that called for federal aid for bilingual education in schools that enrolled poor Mexican American children. Those who testified at the hearings insisted that these children, who were both linguistically and culturally disadvantaged, would learn more rapidly if they were taught in both Spanish and English, and that this in turn would build their self-esteem. They also argued that the children performed poorly in school in part because they were cut off from their roots and had a "damaged self-concept." To rectify this, they recommended that the schools instruct the children about Mexican American culture. In 1968 the bill was made into law as the Bilingual Education Act.

Before long, a group of high school students in Los Angeles, enraged that they had been taught little about their cultural traditions, staged a massive walkout demanding compulsory bilingual and bicultural education for all Mexican American children. One by one schools in states such as Massachusetts, Texas, and New Jersey developed bilingual education programs for Latino children, and eventually they broadened the scope of their programs to include all children whose first language was not English. In 1978, further amendments to the Bilingual Education Act allowed for children who already spoke English to be put in bilingual, bicultural programs.

Much debate has raged over how best to structure bilingual education. Some bilingual educators and politicians favor the immersion method, where students are placed in English-only classes and then given special instruction in their native language or in English on the side. Others prefer the late-exit method, where students learn in their native language for three to five years and then are slowly taught English. Some opt for the far less common double-immersion method, where English speakers learn Spanish and Spanish speakers learn English side by side in one classroom. This method has caused quite an uproar, as some have interpreted it as a desire to make everyone Spanish-speaking. A 1996 study conducted by George Mason University on the long-term success of students in bilingual education programs nationwide found that those who were taught by the double-immersion method did the best academically, followed by those taught by the late-exit method.

The biggest debate now is not how to shape bilingual programs but whether they should exist at all. Opponents argue that bilingual education merely serves as a stumbling block in the path to English-language proficiency. This argument has been voiced by influential members of the Latino community, including Mexican American **Richard Rodriguez,** author of *Days of Obligation: An Argument with My Mexican Father*. Opponents of bilingual education also insist that students who receive bilingual instruction end up doing poorly in school and are consequently held to a lower standard. This practice, they contend, puts the students' futures in jeopardy, since potential employers may decide that those educated in bilingual programs are not as well prepared for the work force as their peers. Some who are against bilingual education have even argued that bilingual programs are a form of insidious discrimination, since many immigrant Latino kids wind up in separate classrooms and, eventually, in a separate world.

Many who oppose bilingual education are as much concerned about the larger question of America's fate as they are the futures of immigrant children. English-only proponents argue that the great influx of Spanish speakers into the United States who are neither immersed entirely in English nor encouraged to acculturate to the mainstream (and who have no need to do so thanks to federal and state-sponsored bilingual programs), has created an undeniable Spanish-speaking atmosphere that threatens the unity of the nation. They insist that without English to hold it together, the nation will break into political and social factions, each vying for its own interests.

In response to growing concern over the fate of the nation, **Senator S. I. Hayakawa** of California introduced a joint Senate resolution to amend the U.S. Constitution in 1981 so that it would read, "The English language shall be the official language of the United States," but the bill went to sleep during the Ninety-seventh Congress. What motivated Hayawaka to introduce such a resolution were invariably those "*Se Habla Español*" signs found everywhere on the American landscape—from classrooms to storefronts. Fifteen years later politicians had still not laid this issue to rest. In 1996 a bill to make English the official language passed the House but was not taken up in the Senate. English-only organizations, such as U.S. English, as well as some states and municipalities, share the federal government's concerns over the sound of "so much Spanish." In fact, since 1986 eighteen states have passed laws recognizing English as their official language.

The arguments put forth by bilingual education proponents gained strength in 1997, when the results of a five-year study of the educational progress of immigrant children in bilingual programs in San Diego were released. The study found that the children became fluent in English quickly and that they actually favored English over their native tongue. The study also showed that they got better grades and dropped out with less frequency than fellow students whose parents were born in the United States. However, opponents to bilingual education quickly underscored the study's findings that a high percentage of immigrant students favored an ethnic label such as Mexican American over simply American, which shows that the country is indeed in the process of breaking up into factions. And so the debate rages on.

Two things are clear in all this. We will not all be speaking Spanish like natives soon, but many of us English-only speakers will know a smattering of Spanish (just visit any dentist's office in southern California and listen to the Anglo dentists pepper their speech with Spanish words when they converse with their Spanish-speaking patients). And secondly, more and more of us will be speaking both Spanish and English as we move into the twenty-first century.

When was the first Latino studies program established?

Universities and colleges also responded to the call for bilingual and bicultural education by integrating courses on Chicanos, Puerto Ricans, or all Latinos into the curriculum. In 1968 the first Mexican American studies program was put in place at Los Angeles State College. A year later a historic Chicano conference was held in Santa Barbara, California, where Latino educators drew up a declaration calling for the formation of Chicano studies programs in California. Soon colleges and universities around the nation were establishing entire departments devoted to the study of Latinos. Some later made it a requirement that all students take one or more multicultural courses. For instance, at the University of Maryland students must enroll in at least one course devoted to women or a minority group, be it Latinos, African Americans, Native Americans, Asian Americans, or gays and lesbians.

THE TOP 15 UNIVERSITIES THAT GRADUATED THE MOST LATINOS IN 1993

1. Florida International University (1,612)

2. University of Texas at El Paso (840)

3. University of Texas at Austin (835)

4. University of California, Los Angeles (812)

5. University of California, Berkeley (772)

6. California State University, Los Angeles (702)

7. University of Texas Pan American at Edinburg (682)

8. University of Texas at San Antonio (561)

9. University of New Mexico, Main Campus (550)

10. San Diego State University (543)

11. Texas A & M University (509)

12. California State University, Fullerton (469)

13. California State University, Northridge (445)

14. University of Arizona (437)

15. Southwest Texas State University (431)

This shift in college and university curricula and a greater awareness of Latinos have resulted in the establishment of countless corporate grants and fellowships for Latino students and departments. They also led to the creation of a federal program that contributes in excess of $750 million a year to bilingual and bicultural secondary and higher education—a far cry from the meager sums given to enhance the education of Latinos just thirty years ago.

What is Proposition 187, and how did it backfire on the Republicans who championed it?

In 1994 California Republicans led by **Governor Pete Wilson** (who was looking for a way to get reelected) decided that they had to put a stop to what they called the "browning" of the state, by giving illegal immigrants a good reason to leave the country and discouraging others from coming. To achieve this end, they championed Proposition 187, a measure aimed at making life really tough for illegal immigrants in California, most of whom are Mexican, by excluding them from many federal programs including Medicaid, welfare, and food stamps, and by denying their children citizenship even if they were born on American soil, as well as access to public schools and government-sponsored health care, including immunization programs. California Republicans also championed a lesser-known measure called Proposition 209, which would end affirmative action.

Proponents of Prop 187 vilified Mexicans at their rallies to whip up support for the measure among Anglo Californians. They also grossly exaggerated the number of illegal aliens in the state and forgot to mention that 50 percent of illegal aliens were legal aliens who simply overstayed their visas. California voters bought their arguments hook, line, and sinker, and approved Prop 187 at the polls, but there was strong opposition from the state's registered Latinos, 57 percent of whom turned out to vote. Even though California voters approved Prop 187 and Prop 209, their implementation is still tied up in the courts.

The voters' approval of Prop 187 created grave concern among California's two million permanent resident aliens (most of whom are of Mexican descent), who feared that they were next in line for demonization by the state's Republicans. Overnight, the number of students of Mexican origin enrolled in citizenship classes rose exponentially, and the number of applications for citizenship in California climbed 500 percent from 1992 levels. This activity has hardly tapered off. In the late 1990s, the Los Angeles district office of the Immigration and Naturalization Service was receiving approximately 25,000 applications for citizenship per month.

The passage of Prop 187 also gave unregistered Mexican Americans, many newly naturalized, the impetus to register to vote. Before Prop 187 many were not sure which party to join. Not surprisingly, most have gone with the Democratic Party. This marks a real shift in allegiance, since before Prop 187, the Republicans captured up to two fifths of the Latino vote.

Thanks to these trends in naturalization and voter registration among Americans of Mexican descent, Latino political power in California is increasing at a fast rate. And so in the end Prop 187 backfired on California's Republicans. However, the fact is that the Republicans were misled. Even if Prop 187 had sent illegal aliens fleeing over the border, the "browning" of California would not have been stemmed. Illegal aliens or no illegal aliens, the disparity between Latino and Anglo birthrates in California ensures that the state will have a Latino majority by the year 2040.

NUEVE

Famous Latinos

RITMO LATINO

What is Latin rhythm all about?

Is the tango considered Latin rhythm?

Was Desi Arnaz responsible for bringing Latin rhythm to the U.S.?

Who are the Latino music stars of the 1980s and 1990s?

Is Plácido Domingo the only Latino opera star?

What about classical musicians?

ON THE STAGE AND THE SILVER SCREEN

*Who were the first Latino actors, and what roles did
they play?*

Why do Latinos hate Tonto?

*Who are some other famous Latino actors and
directors?*

Who are the Latino dancers?

Is Mickey Mouse a Latino?

*Who are some well-known Latino talk show hosts
and commentators?*

WRITERS AND ARTISTS

Who's writing the books?

Who's painting the pictures?

A PASSION FOR FASHION

Who are some Latino fashion designers?

Who is César Pelli?

ON THE CUTTING EDGE OF SCIENCE AND
TECHNOLOGY

Who are the great Latino scientists?

TAKE ME OUT TO THE BALL GAME ... BOXING RING ... TENNIS COURT

Is soccer número uno among Latinos?

Who are the Latino baseball legends, and who are the great players of today?

Who are the Latino stars on the tennis court?

Who are some Latinos in the world of golf?

Who are the Latino football players?

Who are some Latinos in other sports?

RITMO LATINO

What is Latin rhythm all about?

Mambo, salsa, samba, conga, son, son montuno, guaracha, merengue, cumbia, bugalu, danzón, bolero, Afro-Cuban Latin jazz, and even cha-cha (called *cha cha cha* in Spanish) are all part of what Americans call the Latin beat. Its foundation is African, since the tambour, the conga and the bongo drums, brought over by African slaves, are the heart and soul of this contagious music.

Over the centuries, the Spanish guitar, fiddle, accordion, trumpet, and saxophone were added to the African and Amerindian instruments—such as the marimba (xylophone), the maraca and other rattles, bells, the *guiro* (a serrated gourd that is played by scraping it with a stick), and the *claves*, wooden sticks that keep the beat. The result: a distinctive sound that defies even the tin-eared to sit still.

In the United States where Latin music thrives, hardly a nightclub, a ballroom, a disco, a television show, a TV commercial, an ice-skating rink, or a dance company has not felt the impact of that irrepressible Latin beat. It seems that the rhythm has gotten the whole world, as nowadays Latin music has fans all around the globe. *Salsa, conga, guaracha, merengue,* and Latin jazz bands play to full houses in Amsterdam, Paris, London, Moscow, and Montevideo. Even Japan boasts an all-Japanese *salsa* band called Orquesta de la Luz.

The Latin beat is but one of many Latino sounds heard in America. Another important style that is just beginning to cross over to mainstream America, thanks to Mexican American music legend **Selena,** is *tejano,* a blend of Mexican *ranchera,* country, polka, pop, Colombian *cumbia,* and reggae, which is especially popular in Texas. Tragically, Selena was murdered by the president of her fan club in 1995, on the eve of her English-language debut. Her death shocked the entire nation, Anglos and Latinos alike, and also fostered a greater appreciation of the richness of Mexican American culture.

Is the tango considered Latin rhythm?

Not really. The tango is a Latin dance and song style. It became popular in Buenos Aires at the beginning of the twentieth century, and twenty years later it had spread throughout Latin America, Europe, and the United States. The tango is derived from the *milonga,* a sexy Argentinean dance, and the *habanera,* a graceful dance that originated in Cuba during the Spanish colonial period. (There's a *habanera* song in Bizet's opera *Carmen.*) By the 1920s, the tango had evolved into an elegant, stylized dance with long, gliding steps and dips, accompanied by melancholic music and songs. Singer **Carlos Gardel** popularized tango songs in the World War I era and put Argentina on the musical map. **Evita Perón** (of *Evita* fame) is said to have been a very big tango *aficionada.*

Was Desi Arnaz responsible for bringing Latin rhythm to the U.S.?

I Love Lucy's **Desi Arnaz,** a Cuban-born actor and musician, was certainly responsible for introducing mainstream television-watching America to the sounds of African Cuban drums with his famous "Babaloo," which incidentally is a song to the Yoruban deity Babalú, a much beloved *santo* of the *Santería* religion.

But even before Desi played and sang with his band in the 1950s and 1960s, **Xavier Cugat,** a Spanish violinist, band leader, and composer, who had once lived in Cuba and Mexico, had introduced African Cuban music to Hollywood. After being named leader of the band at the Waldorf-Astoria Hotel in New York City in 1933, Cugat was much sought after by Tinseltown, and his band starred in many popular films of the 1930s and 1940s. Cugat also worked his Latin magic behind the scenes as a sound mixer and film producer for several of **Charlie Chaplin**'s pictures.

Another musician who made a huge splash among Anglo audiences in the 1950s was **Damaso Pérez Prado,** who caught the musical imagination of Americans with his *mambo* tunes. **Ritchie Valens,** the first Latino rock star, was just starting to make waves with 1950s Anglo audiences with songs like "That's My Little Suzie" when he perished in a plane crash in early 1959. His life is chronicled in the 1987 motion picture *La Bamba.* After the film came out, the traditional Mexican folk song Valens popularized was on everybody's lips: even those who couldn't say *"para bailar la bamba se necesita . . ."* would hum *"La la la la la Bamba la la la la la . . ."*

In the 1960s, **Joe Cuba**'s *bugalu* tune "Bang Bang" was an overnight hit and crossed over from the Latin to the Anglo charts. By then Mexican American singer **Trini López** was skyrocketing to fame with his single "If I Had a Hammer," and the "king of Latin music," **Tito Puente,** the great Puerto Rican bongo player, orchestra leader, and composer, was catching on among Anglos. Puente's performance in the 1992 film *The Mambo Kings* brought him Hollywood fame and broad recognition. A winner of numerous Grammy Awards, Puente had recorded 108 albums by 1997.

Some of those albums he recorded with singer and composer **Celia Cruz,** the "queen of salsa," who came to the United States from Cuba in 1961. Before long she was the idol of Latinos all over America, but her strong, metallic, very African rhythms did not catch on in the Anglo community until much later. In 1995 **President Bill Clinton** presented Celia Cruz with the National Medal for the Arts, making her the first Latino pop singer to be awarded the honor.

Three Mexican American performers whose careers were launched in the mainstream in the 1960s eventually made it into the pantheon of America's greatest performers of the twentieth century. The first is entertainer **Vicki Carr,** who sang on the nightclub and variety show circuits before millions of fans in the sixties, and acted on stage as well. In 1992 she won a Grammy for Best Latin Pop for her album *Cosas del amor.* The second is "queen of folk" **Joan Baez,** who is also a great humanitarian and was actively involved in the civil rights movement and the Vietnam War protest. In the early seventies young Americans sang along to her smash hit "The Night They Drove Old Dixie Down." The third is **Linda Ronstadt,** whom everyone thought was Anglo until she crossed over (or back) to her Mexican roots and recorded an album in Spanish. Her versions of **Roy Orbison**'s "Blue Bayou" and **Buddy Holly**'s "It's So Easy" made her America's greatest female pop rock star in the 1970s.

In the late 1960s Puerto Rican crooner **José Feliciano** wooed audiences with his suggestive "Light My Fire," a single he included on his 1968 album *Feliciano!*, and Mexican American **Carlos Santana** hypnotized millions with his *"Oye como va,"* from his album *Abraxas.* In the 1970s along came Mexican American **Freddie Fender,** the son of migrant workers, who captivated audiences with his country-style songs, such as his 1975 hit "Before the Next Teardrop Falls." Spanish and Greek American **Tony Orlando** won a huge following that decade with numbers such as "Tie a Yellow Ribbon 'Round the Ole Oak Tree," which Billboard proclaimed a top song of the year.

In those early days *congero* (conga player) **Ramon "Mongo" Santamaría,** flutist **Dave Valentin,** pianist **Hilton Ruiz,** saxophonist **Paquito D'Rivera,** and bassist **Andy González** helped shape the Latin sound. Other great Latin performers and bandleaders of the era among many more were **Eddie Palmieri, Machito, José Curbelo, Pupi Campo, Miguelito Valdéz, Marcelino Guerra,** and **Frank Martí.**

Who are the Latino music stars of the 1980s and 1990s?

Many of the performers of the 1960s, including **Joan Baez, Linda Ronstadt, Celia Cruz,** and **Tito Puente,** are as popular today as they were decades ago.

In addition, the 1980s and 1990s have seen new generations of talented singers. One of the greatest is **Gloria Estefan,** who warned America in one of her songs that "the rhythm is gonna get you"—and it has. By blending the Latin beat with rhythm and blues and pop, and singing in both English and Spanish, Gloria Estefan and the **Miami Sound Machine** have singlehandedly ushered Latin music into the mainstream in a big way, selling over 20 million copies of their albums. Estefan's popularity is so tremendous that when she nearly severed her spinal cord in an accident in 1990 while traveling with her band, her husband and manager **Emilio Estefan, Jr.,** and her son **Nayib** in their tour bus, the people of Miami held a candlelight vigil for her all night long on *Calle Ocho*, Eighth Street, in the heart of Little Havana. After making a miraculous recovery, the singer launched an international comeback tour and performed before cheering crowds at sold-out concerts all over the world.

Her lyrics may often be in English, but Gloria Estefan's

soul is purely Latin, and this combination has inspired many Latino musicians. Among them is fellow Cuban American **Jon Secada,** who under the guidance of producer Emilio Estefan, Jr., went from being a backup vocalist for Gloria Estefan in 1989 to an international pop superstar in 1992 after the release of his multiplatinum album *Jon Secada.*

Another singer who has benefited from the genius of producer Emilio Estefan, Jr., is Cuban newcomer **Albita.** Called the Latin **k.d. lang** because of her androgynous looks, Albita arrived in Miami in 1993, and ever since she has been delighting listeners with old numbers from prerevolutionary Cuba as well as new sounds with rock and jazz elements.

Latino pop idol **Julio Iglesias,** who has Spanish, Cuban, and Puerto Rican roots, achieved celebrity in the early 1980s. By 1983 he was the best-selling singer in the world, having sold over 100 million albums. Nowadays he shares the limelight with his son **Enrique Iglesias,** who released a debut album bearing his own name in 1995 and rose swiftly to stardom. Some music critics have predicted that Enrique Iglesias will emerge as the most important recording artist of the next two decades.

Mariah Carey, who has Venezuelan roots, achieved stardom in the music world with the release of her very first album in 1990, which hit number one on the Billboard pop album chart and earned the singer Grammy Awards for Best Pop Female Vocalist and Best New Artist.

Other Latino singers who enjoy quite a following include the hard-hitting Puerto Rican group **Barrio Boyzz;** the Mexican American group **Menudo;** the Mexican American folk/rock group **Los Lobos,** which won a Grammy for "Mariachi Suite," on the soundtrack album to the film *Desperado*; Mexican American **Flaco Jimenez,** who also won a Grammy for his self-titled album; **The Cover Girls; The Triplets; Lisa Lisa;** and Southwest artists **Little Joe Hernandez,** brassmen **Charlie Sepulveda** and **Humberto Ramirez, Judy Torres,** and **Angelica.**

Is Plácido Domingo the only Latino opera star?

Plácido Domingo, born in Spain, raised in Mexico, and residing in New York City, is certainly the Latino superstar of opera. But other Latinos have a place in the pantheon of great opera singers, among them Puerto Rican basso cantante **Justino Diaz,** who debuted at the Metropolitan Opera in 1963 and has been singing in major opera houses ever since. Mezzo-soprano **Dulce Reyes** and tenor **César Hernandez** have also made their mark in the world of opera.

What about classical musicians?

Cellist **Andres Diaz** and flutist **Viviana Guzman,** who has worked with **Plácido Domingo** and **Mikhail Baryshnikov,** are among the most noteworthy Latino classical musicians. World-famous Chilean pianist **Claudio Arrao,** lauded for his interpretations of Beethoven's piano music, resided in New York City from 1941 until his death in 1991. In 1995 **Santiago Rodriguez,** the first Cuban American classical musician to achieve prominence, garnered critical applause for his first recording *Rachmaninoff Edition, Volumes 1, 2, and 3.*

Among the world-class conducters are Chilean American **Juan Pablo Tzyuierdo,** who conducts for the Pittsburgh Symphony Orchestra, and Uruguayan American **Gisèle Ben-Dor,** music director and conductor of the Boston ProArte Chamber Orchestra, the Annapolis Symphony, and the Santa Barbara Symphony.

ON THE STAGE AND THE SILVER SCREEN

Who were the first Latino actors, and what roles did they play?

Ever since Mexican American heartthrobs **Ramón Novarro** and **Gilbert Roland** seduced moviegoers with their artful expressions and dashing good looks in the 1920s and 1930s; Mexican American actresses **Dolores Del Río** and **Lupe Vélez** captivated audiences in both silent films and talkies; Cuban American **César Romero** played both villain and Latin lover in the 1930s, '40s, and '50s; and Spanish American **Rita Hayworth** (born Rita Cansino) sang, danced, and acted opposite the likes of **Fred Astaire, Gene Kelly, Gary Cooper,** and **Glenn Ford,** Latino actors have been romancing the silver screen.

In fact, early Hollywood pictures capitalized on the myth of the Latin lover—the notion that Latinos are more sensual, sultry, and sexy than Anglos. Of course, Hollywood also exploited other myths—that of the dirty, devious, lazy, or stupid Mexican in countless cowboy movies, and of the shifty Latin with the thick Spanish accent who finds himself in exotic places like Argentina, Uruguay, and the South Pacific. While Latinos were often cast in these roles (which **Ricardo Montalbán** once summed up as the "laggard, lover, or bandit"), they also went to non-Latino actors, whose hair was dyed shoe-polish black and whose pencil-thin mustaches were made to look particularly suspect. (For example, take a look at **Paul Newman** as a Mexican renegade in the 1964 film *The Outrage*.)

Although such overt typecasting has gone the way of the silent screen, Hollywood continues to cast Latinos in stereotypical roles. Early in her career, Cuban American actress **Elizabeth Peña,** who played an abused wife in the 1987 motion picture *La Bamba*, told the *Los Angeles Times*, "I'm usually offered the roles of the prostitute, the mother with seventeen children, or the screaming wife getting beaten up." Tired of such typecasting, Peña turned down **Robert Redford**'s invitation to play a Mexican in the 1988 feature film *The Milagro Beanfield War*.

Latinos have faced much discrimination on the stage, as well. Until **Joseph Papp** invited minorities to act in productions of his New York Shakespeare Festival in Central Park and his classical plays at the Public Theater, very few audiences had ever seen a Latino like **Raúl Julia** or **Martin Sheen** play a serious dramatic part, let alone one as monumental as Hamlet.

Why do Latinos hate Tonto?

The Lone Ranger's sidekick, Tonto, is portrayed as a dimwit. In fact, his name is Spanish for "dopey" or "slow-witted." To add insult to injury this (we assume) Pueblo Indian (of mixed Native American and Mexican heritage?) calls his boss "Kimasabe," which is a corruption of the Spanish phrase *quien más sabe*, literally "he who knows best." This movie and comic book duo emblematize the prejudice and insensitivity that Latino groups have been laboring to abolish for years, both in Hollywood and mainstream society.

Who are some other famous Latino actors and directors?

Actor, writer, and director **Anthony Quinn,** who was born in Chihuahua, Mexico, on April 15, 1915, has enjoyed a long and distinguished stage and screen career. In the early days, **Cecil B. De Mille** (whose daughter Quinn married) cast the actor as a "bad guy" or Indian, but later he landed memorable roles in films such as *Viva Zapata!* (1952), *La Strada* (1954), *Lust for Life* (1956), *Lawrence of Arabia* (1962), and *Zorba the Greek* (1964). After six decades of acting, Anthony Quinn is still delighting audiences with his performances in such films as *Only the Lonely* (1991) and *The Last Action Hero* (1993).

Mexican American **Ricardo Montalbán,** who starred as Mr. Roarke in the 1978–83 television series *Fantasy Island*, as well as in scores of other TV shows and films, is also credited with being among the first Latinos to land nonethnic roles in national TV commercials. Remember his Chrysler commercials and his "Corinthian leather" lines? As it turns out, typecasting is what got the actor that first job with Chrysler Motors. The company hired him because they needed a person with Spanish roots to fit the name of their luxury car, the Cordoba. Montalbán proved so talented that he served as a Chrysler spokesman for two decades, shedding the Latin image along the way.

The 1970s saw the rise of Mexican American comedian and actor **Freddie Prinze.** Prinze costarred as Chico in one of the first TV sitcoms with a Latino bent, *Chico and the Man*, which first aired in 1974. Tragically he ended his life three years later. Mexican American comedian and actor **Richard "Cheech" Marín,** who with **Tommy Chong** was awarded a Grammy for the Cheech and Chong comedy album *The Wedding Album*, also cowrote and starred in a handful of highly successful Cheech and Chong movies in the 1980s. Another Mexican American actor, **Edward James Olmos,** whose tough-cop role as Lieutenant Castillo in the popular 1980s television series *Miami Vice* made him an overnight success, is one of the busiest actors and directors in Tinseltown. On the big screen, Olmos has starred in such films as *Stand and Deliver* (1988), and *Selena* (1997), about slain Mexican American tejano music star **Selena Quintanilla Pérez.** *Selena* was written and directed by **Gregory Nava,** a Mexican American who also directed *El Norte* (1983) and *Mi Familia* (1995). *Selena* also saw the big-screen debut of Puerto Rican actress **Jennifer Lopez.** Lopez gave such a convincing performance as Selena that she is now a much sought-after Hollywood actress.

Puerto Rican actress **Rita Moreno** made history as the first performer to receive all four of the most coveted awards in American entertainment: the Oscar, the Tony, the Grammy, and the Emmy. Her career skyrocketed in 1961 when she played Anita in the screen version of *West Side Story*, and she has been dazzling audiences ever since. Dynamic stage actress **Chita Rivera,** who is also Puerto Rican, was honored with a Tony Award for Best Actress for her performance in 1984 in *The Rink* and in 1993 in the Broadway hit *Kiss of the Spider Woman*. Puerto Rican actress and director **Miriam Colón** has done much on behalf of Latino actors. In 1967 she founded the world-famous Puerto Rican Traveling Theater, a bilingual company that stages plays by Latinos as well as the classics.

Puerto Rican **José Ferrer** was a much-revered star of the stage and screen. He was awarded a Tony for his acting in a 1946 stage production of *Cyrano de Bergerac*, and then became the first Latino to win an Oscar—for Best Actor for his performance in the 1950 film version of *Cyrano*. Highlights of his later career include roles in **Woody Allen**'s *A Midsummer Night's Sex Comedy* (1982) and appearances in the television series *Columbo*. Puerto Rican actor **Raúl Julia** is remembered not only for his marvelous stage performances with the New York Shakespeare Festival, but also for his spectacular acting in such films as *The Eyes of Laura Mars* (1978), *Kiss of the Spider Woman* (1985), and *Presumed Innocent* (1990). Millions mourned the actor's untimely death in 1993. Puerto Rican actor **Jimmy Smits** garnered great popularity with his performances in the television series *L.A. Law* and *NYPD Blue*, and on the big screen in such films as *Mi Familia* (1995).

A Puerto Rican actress and choreographer who catapulted to fame rather recently is **Rosie Pérez,** who has starred in such motion pictures as *Do the Right Thing* (1989) and *White Men Can't Jump* (1992). She was nominated for an Academy Award for Best Supporting Actress in 1994 for her performance in the 1993 film *Fearless*.

Ofelia González was honored with six awards for best actress for her performance in theater, film, and television, before coming to America from Cuba in 1971. A year after her arrival she joined the Spanish-language New York theater company *Repertorio Español*, where she has remained since. In

1992 González was awarded an Obie for sustained excellence of performance. Actress and singer **Maria Conchita Alonso,** who was born in Cuba in 1957, played in *Moscow on the Hudson* (1984) and *The House of the Spirits* (1994), a highly acclaimed film based on the novel of the same name by Chilean American writer **Isabel Allende.** Another actor born in Cuba in the 1950s is **Andy García,** who earned great applause for his performances in such films as *The Untouchables* (1987), *The Godfather, Part III* (1990), and *Steal Big, Steal Little* (1996). One of his latest projects is the film *The Lost City*, which explores the world of a cabaret owner in 1950s Havana. The screenplay was written by the prominent Cuban novelist **Guillermo Cabrera Infante,** who resides in London.

Martin Sheen, whose father immigrated to America from Spain by way of Cuba, and who was born **Ramón Estévez,** is a Hollywood legend. Highlights of his career, that began on the stage in 1959, include lead roles in **Francis Ford Coppola**'s 1979 film *Apocalypse Now* and *Gandhi* (1982). Martin Sheen should also be credited for spawning a whole new generation of Latino actors—his own sons, **Charlie Sheen** and **Emilio Estevez,** both of whom are top box-office draws and critically acclaimed directors in their own rights.

Bolivian American **Raquel Welch,** who was born Raquel Tejada, was America's premier sex symbol in the 1960s and 1970s when she starred in numerous movies and television shows that capitalized on her physical features. In the early 1980s, she was finally lauded for her talent as an actor when she appeared in the Broadway musical *Woman of the Year*. Panamanian American singer, songwriter, and actor **Rubén Blades** has made appearances in such motion pictures as *Crossover Dreams* (1985) and *The Milagro Beanfield War* (1988). Colombian American actor, comedian, writer, and director **John Leguizamo** earned an Obie and an Outer Critics Circle Award for his one-man comedy *Spic-o-rama* that ran in New York in the early 1990s. His performances in the 1993 motion pictures *Super Mario Brothers* and *Carlito's Way* have made Leguizamo a household word.

Panamanian American theater director **José Quintero** founded with others the Circle in the Square in New York City, which would emerge as Off Broadway's most important theater before it moved to Broadway in 1972. At the Circle in the Square, Quintero staged many of **Eugene O'Neill**'s plays, including *Long Day's Journey into Night*, which opened on Broadway in 1956 and garnered a Tony Award and the *Variety* Award for director.

Among the hundreds of other Latinos and Latinas who have left their mark in Hollywood or are just now taking Tinseltown by storm are **Esai Morales,** who starred as **Ritchie Valens**' half-brother in *La Bamba* (1987); **Irene Cara,** who appeared in the 1980s films *Fame* and *Flashdance*; and **Lupe Ontiveros,** who played Yolanda Saldívar in the film *Selena* (1997).

Who are the Latino dancers?

Some of the scores of Latino dancers are Cuban American **Fernando Bujones,** one of the finest classical dancers of the twentieth century; **Lourdes Lopez,** who performs with the New York City Ballet; the Joffrey Ballet's **Beatriz Rodriguez, Nicole Marie Duffy,** and **Lissette Salgado; Cristina Gonzalez,** with the Alvin Ailey Repertory Ensemble; the American Ballet Theater's **Paloma Herrera;** and Ballet Hispanico's **Pedro Ruiz, Tina Ramirez,** and **José Costas.**

All of these dancers follow in the footsteps of two great Latino masters who had their own dance companies: Spanish American **José Greco,** who popularized Spanish and Latin American dance in America, and Mexican American **José Limón,** one of the world's greatest modern dancers and choreographers. These dancers also follow in the footsteps of Argentine Mexican American ballerina **Lupe Serrano,** who in 1953 became the first Latino to serve as principal dancer for the American Ballet Theater, a company with which she performed for almost twenty years.

Is Mickey Mouse a Latino?

Rumor has it that **Walt Disney,** the creator of **Mickey Mouse** and the Disney Empire, was born **José Luis Guirao** in a village in Spain, and was later adopted by Elias and Flora Disney of Chicago. The circumstances surrounding his birth were apparently kept from Walt, who learned of his lineage when he tried to obtain a copy of his birth certificate. The story goes that he told no one of his true ethnicity since there was so much hatred against Latinos in those days. Latinos have come a long way. In 1997 Walt Disney World got a little Latin flavor when **Gloria Estefan** and **Emilio Estefan** opened Bongos Cuban Cafe in Florida's Magic Kingdom.

Who are some well-known Latino talk show hosts and commentators?

Puerto Rican **Geraldo Rivera** is one of the most-recognized faces in the media. He got his start as a reporter for WABC-TV in New York in 1970 and later served as a chief reporter on *20/20.* In 1987 Rivera launched his own nationally syndicated daytime talk show, *Geraldo,* which he hosts to this day (in 1996 the name was changed to *The Geraldo Rivera Show*). Since 1994 he has also hosted *Rivera Live,* a nighttime program on CNBC that deals with issues in the news.

Cuban American talk show host **Cristina Saralegui** is a household name among 6.5 million Spanish speakers in the United States and Latin America who tune in to her television program *El Show de Cristina,* and her radio show *Cristina Opina.* In 1991 *El Show de Cristina* became the first Spanish-language talk show to capture an Emmy.

The 1990s have seen a sharp rise in the number of Latinas in the news room. **Jackie Nespral** and **Elizabeth Vargas** at NBC, and **Giselle Fernandez** at CBS, are perhaps the three most prominent Latina news correspondents of the day.

WRITERS AND ARTISTS

Who's writing the books?

Latino writers did not catch the attention of mainstream America until rather recently. It all started when Colombian writer **Gabriel García Márquez** stunned readers worldwide with his *One Hundred Years of Solitude* (1970), written in a surrealistic style labeled "magical realism." This style had been established years before in Latin America by my father, **Lino Novas Calvo,** author of *El negrero*, a novel about the African slave trade in the Americas, among others.

Once acquainted with the Latin spirit, mainstream American readers wanted more. It did not take them long to find the Latino writers in their midst, such as **Carlos Castaneda,** the Peruvian-born anthropologist who has penned nine books based on the hallucinatory states of consciousness he experienced with a sorcerer named Don Juan Matus, including *The Teachings of Don Juan: A Yaqui Way of Knowledge* (1968), *A Separate Reality: Further Conversations with Don Juan* (1971), and *Journey to Ixtlan: The Lessons of Don Juan* (1972). Castaneda, who captivated American readers (especially the antiestablishment) in the 1960s and 1970s, vanished into thin air in the 1980s (few know what he looks like), but his books are still selling well (by 1996 he had sold eight million copies in seventeen countries).

The publication of **Oscar Hijuelos**'s Pulitzer prize-winning first novel, *The Mambo Kings Play Songs of Love*, in 1989, and its transformation into the Hollywood film *The Mambo Kings* in 1992, ushered in an era of widespread recognition for Latino writers that continues to this day. Many works by Latinos crowd the shelves in libraries and bookstores, large and small, across America.

Among the Latina novelists, short story writers, and poets (and their most celebrated works) are **Isabel Allende,** author of *The House of the Spirits* (1985), which was made into a 1994 motion picture and has been translated into about twenty-seven languages, and *Paula* (1994); **Helena María Viramontes,** who penned *The Moths and Other Stories* (1985); **Judith Ortíz Cofer,** who wrote *The Line of the Sun* (1989) and the poetry collections *The Latin Deli* (1993) and *Reaching for the Mainland & Selected New Poems* (1996); **Sandra Cisneros,** author of *The House on Mango Street* (1989) and *Woman Hollering Creek and Other Stories* (1991); **Cristina Garcia,** who wrote *Dreaming in Cuban* (1992), which was chosen as one of the best novels of that year by the *New York Times* and *The Agüero Sisters* (1997); poet and novelist **Ana Castillo,** who penned *The Mixquiahuala Letters* (1986) and *Loverboys* (1996); **Julia Alvarez,** who wrote *How the García Girls Lost Their Accents* (1991); *In the Time of the Butterflies* (1994) and *¡Yo!* (1997); **Himilce Novas,** author of *Mangos, Bananas and Coconuts: A Cuban Love Story* (1996) and *Princess Papaya* (1999); **Demetria Martinez,** who wrote *Mother Tongue* (1994); and **Montserrat Fontes,** who penned *Dreams of the Centaur* (1996).

Among the Latino novelists, short story writers, and poets (and their most celebrated works) are **John Rechy,** author of *City of Night* (1963); **Piri Thomas,** who penned *Down These Mean Streets* (1967); **José Antonio Villarreal,** author of *Pocho* (1970); **Tomás Rivera,** who wrote *And the Earth Did Not Devour Him* (1971); **Ernesto Galarza,** who wrote *Barrio Boy* (1971); **Rudolfo Anaya,** author of *Bless Me, Ultima* (1972); **Carlos Castaneda,** who penned *Journey to Ixtlan: The Lessons of Don Juan* (1972); **Oscar "Zeta" Acosta,** author of *The Autobiography of a Brown Buffalo* (1972); **Juan Soto,** who wrote *Spiks* (1973); **Miguel Piñero,** who penned *Short Eyes* (1974); **Ed Vega,** author of *Mendoza's Dreams* (1987); **Oscar Hijuelos,** who wrote *The Mambo Kings Play Songs of Love* (1989) and *Mr. Ives' Christmas* (1995); **Guy Garcia,** author of *Skin Deep* (1988) and *Obsidian Sky* (1994); **Alejandro Morales,** who penned *The Brick People* (1988); **Victor Villaseñor,** author of *Rain of Gold* (1991); and **Jaime Manrique,** author of *Latin Moon in Manhattan* (1992) and *Twilight at the Equator* (1997).

TWENTY-FIVE IMPORTANT BOOKS WRITTEN BY LATINOS

1. John Rechy, *City of Night* (1963)

2. Piri Thomas, *Down These Mean Streets* (1967)

3. José Antonio Villarreal, *Pocho* (1970)

4. Tomás Rivera, *And the Earth Did Not Devour Him* (1971)

5. Rudolfo Anaya, *Bless Me, Ultima* (1972)

6. Carlos Castaneda, *Journey to Ixtlan: The Lessons of Don Juan* (1972)

7. Oscar "Zeta" Acosta, *The Autobiography of a Brown Buffalo* (1972)

8. Juan Soto, *Spiks* (1973)

9. Miguel Piñero, *Short Eyes* (1974)

10. Gloria Anzaldúa and Cherríe Moraga, eds., *The Bridge Called My Back: Writings by Radical Women of Color* (1981)

11. Edward Rivera, *Family Installments: Memories of Growing Up Hispanic* (1982)

12. Cherríe Moraga, *Loving in the War Years* (1983)

13. Sandra Cisneros, *The House on Mango Street* (1984)

14. Helena María Viramontes, *The Moths and Other Stories* (1985)

15. Isabel Allende, *The House of the Spirits* (1985)

16. Ana Castillo, *The Mixquiahuala Letters* (1986)

17. Oscar Hijuelos, *The Mambo Kings Play Songs of Love* (1989)

18. Julia Alvarez, *How the García Girls Lost Their Accents* (1991)

19. Sandra Cisneros, *Woman Hollering Creek and Other Stories* (1991)

20. Victor Villaseñor, *Rain of Gold* (1991)

21. Richard Rodriguez, *Days of Obligation: An Argument with My Mexican Father* (1992)

22. Cristina Garcia, *Dreaming in Cuban* (1992)

23. Esmeralda Santiago, *When I Was Puerto Rican* (1993)

24. Demetria Martinez, *Mother Tongue* (1994)

25. Montserrat Fontes, *Dreams of the Centaur* (1996)

Who's painting the pictures?

Nowadays Latino artists, imbued with the traditions of the past, are exhibiting their works in museums and galleries, and at street festivals and church fairs in virtually every large metropolis in America. **Pablo Picasso, Joan Miró, Salvador Dalí, Diego Rivera, Alfonso Osorio,** and **Rufino Tamayo** are only a handful of the hundreds of twentieth-century artists whose genius they draw upon.

One of the greatest Latino artists is Venezuelan-born sculptor **Marisol (Marisol Escobar),** who attained great notoriety in the 1970s. A friend and kindred spirit of **Andy**

Warhol, Marisol has exhibited her sculptures at the Museum of Modern Art in New York and many other museums around the world. She has served as an inspiration to the new crop of Latino artists working in America today.

Among the Latino artists who have more recently received recognition at top New York and Los Angeles galleries, as well as the *Museo del Barrio* in New York and other Latino museums, are **Juan Sánchez,** through whose mixed-media works the theme of Puerto Rican independence runs; **Arturo Cuenca,** who before defecting to the United States was considered one of Cuba's most prominent young artists; **Pepon Osorio,** whose multimedia installations explore Latino culture; **German Perez,** a Dominican American artist whose canvases vibrate with primary colors and the flavor of the Caribbean in New York; Peruvian-born **Alberto Insua,** whose works evoke those of **Salvador Dalí;** Argentine American **Susana Jaime Mena,** whose works combine painting and sculpture; **Jorge Tacla,** a Chilean-born artist whose landscape paintings are much sought after; Mexican American **Charlie Carrillo,** who is considered the leading contemporary New Mexican *santero*, or maker of religious artifacts (that are nowadays collected as art); Mexican American **Jaime Palacios,** whose androgynous, disjointed, and compelling figures have made him a popular New York artist; and **Kukuli Velarde,** originally from Peru, who works in clay.

A PASSION FOR FASHION

Who are some Latino fashion designers?

Oscar de la Renta, who was born in the Dominican Republic, created a billion-dollar international clothing business headquartered in New York in the 1960s that now runs the gamut from haute couture to ready-to-wear, and from ties to fragrances. In 1993 he became the first American designer to take over a French couture business when he took the helm of the classic house of Pierre Balmain.

Cuban-born **Adolfo Sardina** (known to the world simply as Adolfo) opened his own New York salon in 1962, and early on designed hats for **Betsy Bloomingdale, Gloria Vanderbilt Cooper, Babe Paley,** and **Lady Bird Johnson.** In the 1980s he was the favorite designer of First Lady **Nancy Reagan.**

Isabel Toledo, who came from Cuba to the United States in the 1960s at age five, took the fashion scene by storm in the mid-1980s. She has won applause for her remarkable designs that combine fabrics and shapes to create an air of elegant whimsy. Her designs are for sale at exclusive stores such as Bergdorf Goodman and Barneys in New York.

Who is César Pelli?

A designer too—but of buildings not clothing. In 1991 the American Institute of Architects named **César Pelli** one of ten of the nation's most influential living architects. Pelli, an Argentine American, was the first Latino to earn such a distinction. Some of his works include the United States Embassy in Toyko, the Pacific Design Center in Los Angeles, and the World Financial Center and Winter Garden at Battery Park in New York City—deemed one of the top ten examples of American architecture designed since 1980. In 1995 the American Institute of Architects awarded Pelli a gold medal for these and other contributions.

ON THE CUTTING EDGE OF SCIENCE AND TECHNOLOGY

Who are the great Latino scientists?

Puerto Rican **Antonia Novello,** a specialist in pediatric nephrology, held one of the highest posts in the National Institutes of Health before President **George Bush** appointed her U.S.

Surgeon General in 1990, As surgeon general she did much to draw attention to the health issues of the country's constituencies who have historically been neglected—namely, women, children, and minorities.

Luis Alvarez was one of the world's leading scientists in the field of elementary particle physics. In 1968 he was honored with the Nobel Prize in physics for constructing a bubble chamber that allowed scientists to observe more subnuclear particles than ever before. During World War II, Alvarez took part in the Manhattan Project, which developed and then constructed the atomic bombs dropped on Japan, and also worked on the development of radar. Called the "wild idea man," he holds over forty patents. In the 1970s, Luis Alvarez formulated the impact theory of dinosaur extinction with his son **Walter Alvarez,** a respected geologist.

Mexican American physicist **Alberto Baez** helped advance the field of X-ray imaging optics. His contributions include an instrument that bears his name—the Kirkpatrick–Baez X-ray microscope—which is in use at laser fusion labs around the globe. Another leading Latino physicist is Guatemalan American **Victor Pérez-Mendez,** who is an expert in the field of experimental heavy ion physics.

While working with leading primatologist **Richard Wrangham** in the rain forests of Africa, Mexican American biochemist **Eloy Rodríguez** discovered that sick chimpanzees forage for plants with an unpleasant taste. He concluded that these plants must possess healing properties and that they might be useful in the treatment of humans. With that discovery, Dr. Rodríguez pioneered a whole new field: zoopharmacognosy. Rodríguez is also one of few Latinos to earn the distinction of having an endowed chair in science at an American university.

The first Latino to travel into the cosmos was Costa Rican American **Franklin Chang-Díaz,** a physical scientist who by 1994 had taken part in four of NASA's space shuttle missions. The first Latina in space was Mexican American **Ellen Ochoa,** who was aboard the space shuttle *Discovery* on its April 1993 mission. Another Latino astronaut for NASA is Mexican American **Sidney Gutiérrez**, who served as commander for the Shuttle Avionics Integration Laboratory and was also a pilot on the STS-40 Spacelab Life Sciences aircraft, which completed a nine-day mission in June 1991.

Argentine American **Adriana Ocampo,** a planetary geologist, has been involved in NASA's *Viking* mission to explore Mars, and is also a science coordinator for the *Galileo* mission to Jupiter. As the chief scientist at NASA from 1993 to 1996, **France Anne Córdova** worked on various satellite projects, including the Hubble Space Telescope. She is the recipient of NASA's highest honor—the Distinguished Service Medal.

TAKE ME OUT TO THE BALL GAME . . . BOXING RING . . . TENNIS COURT

Latinos love sports. Doesn't everybody? you may ask. According to American Sports Data, Inc., Latinos engage in sports activities or watch professional sports on TV more than the average American. Just as an example, 12 percent of Latinos play tennis, while only 9 percent of non-Latino whites and 7 percent of African Americans engage in the sport. And 26 percent of Latinos watch tennis on television, more than any other group. Soccer, football, baseball, softball, basketball, bicycling, hiking, running, racquetball, tennis, skiing, aerobics, and weight training are favorite Latino pastimes.

Is soccer número uno among Latinos?

Of all professional sports, baseball is the all-time Latino favorite. But soccer runs a close second. Latin Americans who immigrated to America after World War II brought with them their love of soccer, or *fútbol*, and the sport grew in popularity in Latino neighborhoods across the country. Nowadays many Latinos, young and not so young, play in weekend soccer leagues, organized games in their neighborhoods, and the occasional *cascarita* (pick-up game). Newer immigrants especially love to watch international matches on television and cheer for the old country and their favorite players.

Thanks to Latinos (and newer immigrants from Europe), soccer is slowly catching on in mainstream America. And thanks also to Latinos, the U.S. soccer team is garnering more respect abroad. Five Latinos, **Marcelo Balboa, Fernando Clavijo, Hugo Perez, Tab Ramos,** and **Claudio Reyna,** helped steer the U.S. team to the second round in World Cup play in 1994, a feat which stunned the international soccer world.

Who are the Latino baseball legends, and who are the great players of today?

Latinos' love of baseball dates all the way back to pre-Colombian times, when the native Taino and Siboney peoples who inhabited the Caribbean played a similar game with a wooden stick and a ball, which became popular among the Spanish colonizers and Africans. The game of baseball as we know it today is based on cricket and rounders, two British games, and became popular in America in the 1800s.

Perhaps the greatest Latino baseball legend is **Roberto Walker Clemente.** Born August 18, 1934, in Carolina, Puerto Rico, Clemente joined the Pittsburgh Pirates in 1955 and spent his entire eighteen-year major league career with the team. He is considered one of baseball's finest outfielders and won National League batting titles in 1961, 1964, 1965, and 1967. Among his other distinctions, Clemente played in every All Star Game from 1960 to 1972, and led the Pirates to world championships in 1960 and 1971. Roberto Clemente was as great a humanitarian as he was a baseball player. After a catastrophic earthquake shook Managua, Nicaragua, in December 1972, Clemente loaded up a cargo plane with supplies and set off to help in the relief effort. Shortly after takeoff, the plane crashed, killing all on board. In homage to the great player, the Baseball Writers Association of America waived the usual five-year wait for induction and voted Roberto Clemente into the Baseball Hall of Fame in 1973. He was the first Latino to earn that distinction.

Orlando Cepeda was named Rookie of the Year in 1958, his first year with the San Francisco Giants. With the St. Louis Cardinals in 1967, he became one of only four players to be selected the National League's Most Valuable Player by a unanimous vote. Another baseball great is Cuban American outfielder **Tony Oliva,** who won the American League batting title three times while with Minnesota from 1962 to 1976. **Lou Piniella,** who had a stellar decade-long career with the Yankees before retiring from play in 1984, has been manager of the Seattle Mariners since 1993. In 1995 Piniella was named the American League Manager of the Year. Cuban American infielder **Tony Perez,** who played mostly with the Cincinnati Reds from 1964 to 1986, was a National League All-Star seven times.

Roberto Clemente was an inspiration to future generations of Latino professional baseball players, such as Mexican American pitcher **Fernando Valenzuela,** who in 1981 as a rookie pitcher helped the Los Angeles Dodgers capture their first world championship since 1965. "Fernandomania" hit Los Angeles and the nation. For his efforts that season, he was awarded the Cy Young Award, the first rookie to receive pitching's highest honor. Valenzuela was selected for the All-Star team from 1981 to 1986, and in 1986 the Dodgers issued him a $5.5 million contract, making him the highest-paid Latino in baseball at the time. In 1993 the pitcher was signed by the Baltimore Orioles, but 1994 found him with the Philadelphia Phillies.

Other players who were inspired by Clemente include **Keith Hernández,** who won eleven consecutive Gold Glove Awards and had a lifetime batting average of .296; **Bobby Bonilla,** who was voted a member of the National League All-Star team every year from 1988 to 1991 and now plays for the Florida Marlins; and Cuban-born **José Canseco** of the Oakland Athletics, who was Rookie of the Year in 1986, and two years later became the first player to hit forty home runs and steal forty bases in a single season.

With each passing year the number of Latinos sporting major league baseball uniforms rises. The majority of Latinos in baseball today are foreign-born with roots in the Dominican Republic, Puerto Rico, Venezuela, Cuba, and Mexico. Among the top players in 1996 and 1997 were Panamanian American **Mariano Rivera;** Puerto Rican **Bernie Williams,** who led the Yankees to victory in the World Series in 1996; and Puerto Rican **Juan González** of the Texas Rangers, who won the American League's MVP Award in 1996.

Who are the Latino stars on the tennis court?

Tennis is another sport in which Latinos shine. Latino men were the first to break down ethnic barriers in tennis, and Mexican American **Richard "Pancho" Gonzáles,** who never took formal tennis lessons, was the first to gain fame on the court. He caught the attention of tennis fans in 1948 when he defeated **Eric Sturgess** in the U.S. National Championships at Forest Hills. Gonzáles captured the same title again in 1949 the year he turned pro. Open tennis (professional tennis) was brand new, and some tournaments, such as Wimbledon, were against it and did not allow pros to mix with amateurs. As a result, Gonzáles was barred from playing in the world's premier tennis tournament while he was in his prime. Many believe that had he been allowed to play Wimbledon he would have captured many titles. He did manage to win one. In 1969, a year after open tennis came to Wimbledon, a forty-one-year-old Gonzáles amazed the tennis world by capturing the singles title in what was then the tournament's longest match in history. When he died on July 3, 1995, all of tennis mourned the passing of a hero.

Another tennis hero is Ecuadoran American **Pancho Segura,** whose legs were deformed by premature birth and diseases he suffered as a child. Despite the odds, Segura excelled in tennis, turning pro in 1947. From 1950 to 1952 he captured the U.S. Pro Championships, defeating Pancho Gonzáles in the finals in 1951 and 1952. Open tennis arrived too late for Pancho Segura, and he played in only one open tournament, the men's doubles of the first open Wimbledon. From the late 1960s to the mid-1970s Segura coached **Jimmy Connors,** helping him capture his first Wimbledon title in 1974. In 1984 Pancho Segura was elected to the Tennis Hall of Fame.

Among the top Latina tennis players is Salvadoran American **Rosemary Casals,** who won over ninety tournaments in a career that began in 1966. She and **Billie Jean King** dominated women's doubles in the late 1960s and early 1970s, winning five Wimbledon women's doubles titles (1967–68, 1970–71, and 1973), the U.S. Championships doubles title in 1967, and the U.S. Open doubles title in 1971 and 1974, among others. Rosemary Casals was instrumental in ridding tennis of sexism and gender inequality, which would enable women's tennis to flourish as a popular sport in the 1980s and 1990s.

Among Latina players currently on the professional circuit is Puerto Rican **Gigi Fernández,** one of the world's best doubles tennis players. She has won many Grand Slam women's doubles titles, including the U.S. Open in 1990 and 1992. Another is **Mary Joe Fernández** (of no relation to Gigi), who made her first appearance at Wimbledon in 1986 at the tender age of fourteen and has been a dynamo on the court ever since. At the 1992 Summer Olympics, she and partner Gigi Fernández captured a gold medal in women's doubles.

Who are some Latinos in the world of golf?

Mention the name **Lee Treviño,** one of the greatest players in the history of golf, and sports fans smile. That's because the Mexican American player loves to crack jokes and chatter on the green, and because he has a heart of gold, rarely leaving a tournament he has won without donating a large sum of the prize to charity. Despite his humor, Lee Treviño has never forgotten those rough early days. Born on December 1, 1939, in Dallas, Treviño rose from abject poverty to stun the golfing world at the U.S. Open in 1968, where he defeated **Jack Nicklaus.** In spite of his talent, when he played in the Masters he had to change his spikes outside the doors of country clubs, which looked down upon the minority player. Lee Treviño has won many titles and trophies in his illustrious career and continues to amaze the crowds at Senior tournaments.

Back in the days when Lee Treviño turned pro, virtually the only other Latino on the green was **Juan "Chi Chi" Rodríguez,** who was born on October 23, 1935, in Río Piedras, Puerto Rico. In 1963, Rodríguez won his first PGA title at the Denver Open, but his career really peaked after he joined the Senior Tour in 1985. By 1993 he had won so many tournaments that he belonged to the $5 million club for overall earnings, whose members include golf legends Lee Treviño, Jack Nicklaus, and others. Rodríguez has also contributed to many philanthropies. In 1979 he founded the Chi Chi Rodríguez Youth Foundation, which provides children in need with tutoring, vocational training, and a little bit of golf. He also underwrites college tuition for many high school graduates each year, and much more.

Mexican American **Nancy López** would later follow in the footsteps of Lee Treviño and Chi Chi Rodríguez and master a sport dominated by Anglos—as well as break new ground for women athletes. López has shattered many records in her illustrious career. In 1978 she won a record five consecutive LPGA events and was named LPGA Rookie of the Year and Player of the Year, the only golfer to enjoy both distinctions in a single year. Thanks to her spectacular performance, attendance tripled for the LPGA Tour, and along with the fans came the media and corporate sponsorship that women's golf so desperately needed. In 1989 López was inducted into the PGA/World Golf Hall of Fame. A great humanitarian, Nancy López is committed to many causes on behalf of children.

TWENTY-ONE GREAT LATINO ATHLETES

1. Bobby Bonilla — This outfielder and slugger for the New York Mets made the National League All-Star Team in 1988 and 1989 and was the highest paid player in 1993.

2. José Canseco — This outfielder with the Texas Rangers is one of the highest paid players in baseball today. He was the American League's Most Valuable Player in 1988.

3. Rosemary Casals — This tennis legend won over ninety tournaments, including five Wimbledon doubles titles in the 1960s and 1970s with Billie Jean King.

4. Roberto Clemente — One of the greatest players in baseball history and a humanitarian, Clemente played for the Pittsburgh Pirates from 1955–72 and earned twelve Golden Glove Awards.

5. Angel Cordero, Jr. — This top jockey broke a record by winning the Kentucky Derby for the third time in 1985. In 1988 he became the first Puerto Rican to be inducted into the Thoroughbred Racing Hall of Fame.

6. Oscar de la Hoya — This boxer won the only gold medal in boxing for America at the 1992 Summer Olympics and captured the world welterweight boxing championship in 1996 by defeating Mexican great Julio César Chávez.

7. Donna De Varona   This swimmer became the first Latino to win a gold medal in her sport when she captured gold in two events at the 1964 Summer Olympics in Tokyo.

8. Trent Dimas   This gymnast captured a gold medal at the 1992 Olympics in Barcelona.

9. Mary Joe Fernández   This tennis great played in her first Wimbledon tournament in 1986 at the age of fourteen. She won a gold medal in doubles with Gigi Fernández at the 1992 Summer Olympics.

10. Gigi Fernández   This tennis star won many Grand Slam doubles titles, including the U.S. Open title in 1988, 1990, and 1992. She took the gold in doubles at the 1992 Summer Olympics.

11. Tom Flores   This football player, who quarterbacked for the Oakland Raiders in the 1960s, ranks among the most successful NFL coaches, winning NFL Coach of the Year in 1982.

12. Pancho Gonzáles   This tennis legend won the U.S. National Championships and the U.S. Clay Court Championships in 1948 and 1949; in 1969, at age 41 he stunned the tennis world by winning the Wimbledon singles title.

13. Nancy López   This golf great was LPGA Rookie of the Year and the Player of the Year in 1978, and was inducted into the PGA/World Golf Hall of Fame in 1989; López

opened the door for both Latinas and all women in golf.

14. Pedro Pablo Morales

This swimmer won gold at the 1984 and 1992 Summer Olympics.

15. Lou Piniella

This baseball great was Rookie of the Year in 1969 and helped the Yankees win the 1977 World Series by batting .333 in the Series; he managed the Yanks after retiring in 1984 and now manages the Cincinnati Reds.

16. Chi Chi Rodríguez

One of the first Latino pro golfers, Rodríguez's real success began in 1985 at age fifty when he joined the Senior Tour; his career earnings have surpassed $5 million.

17. Alberto Salazar

This distance runner won the New York Marathon from 1981 to 1983, and the Boston Marathon in 1982.

18. Pancho Segura

This tennis legend won the U.S. Pro Championships singles from 1950–1952 and the doubles in 1954 and 1956; he coached Jimmy Connors to his first Wimbledon title in 1974.

19. Lee Treviño

This legendary golfer who won the U.S. Open, the British Open, and the Canadian Open in 1971, a feat for which he was given many honors, had earned over $7 million by the end of 1993.

20. Fernando Valenzuela

This baseball player became the first rookie to win the Cy Young Award in

1981 and was on the All-Star Team from 1981 to 1986.

21. Tony Zendejas — One of five members of the Zendejas family to play in the National Football League as a kicker, Tony is currently with the Rams.

Who are the Latino football players?

Football, a great American sport, has not attracted many Latinos, since most are smaller and slighter than the average football player. Still, there are a few exceptions. **Tom Flores,** the son of Mexican American farm workers, is one of them. As a quarterback, Flores steered the Kansas City Chiefs to a Super Bowl victory in 1967. As an assistant coach of the Oakland Raiders in 1980 and head coach of the Los Angeles Raiders in 1984, he garnered two more wins at the Super Bowl. Tom Flores has had a great impact on the world of football; in fact, his autobiography *Fire in the Iceman* is considered a classic.

Mexican American **Jim Plunkett** is another exception. Drafted by the Boston Patriots in 1971, Plunkett earned the title of NFL Rookie of the Year for his skills as a quarterback. With the superior coaching of Tom Flores, Plunkett led the Oakland Raiders to victory in Super Bowl XV in 1980, and was named Most Valuable Player for his effort. He repeated his stellar performance in 1982 by helping the Raiders defeat the Washington Redskins in Super Bowl XVII. In 1988 a shoulder condition forced Jim Plunkett to retire from football.

Lyle Azado, the former All-Pro linesman for the Los Angeles Raiders, enjoyed scores of victories. He tragically succumbed to brain cancer in 1992, at the age of 43.

The **Zendejas** family launched a whole dynasty of pro kickers in the 1980s. Five Zendejas family members made it into the National Football League. The most famous is probably **Tony Zendejas,** who is currently a kicker for the Rams. His brother **Marty** and cousins **Luis, Max,** and **Joaquin** have all retired from successful careers in the sport.

Who are some Latinos in other sports?

Boxing boasts several Latino greats. Puerto Rican **Carlos Ortiz** is a boxing legend. He won the lightweight title in 1962 and held on to it for the most part until 1968. Ortiz was inducted into the International Boxing Hall of Fame in 1991. Today Mexican American boxer **Oscar de la Hoya,** who won gold at the 1992 Summer Olympics in Barcelona and the world welterweight boxing championship in 1997, is a role model for many young Latinos all across America who dream of fame in the ring.

The 1992 Summer Olympics in Barcelona, Spain, proved a fertile ground for other Latino athletes. Cuban American **Pedro Pablo Morales** captured gold in swimming (just as he did in 1984); **Mary Joe Fernández** won a gold medal in tennis; and **Trent Dimas** won a gold medal in gymnastics. It was a proud moment when Americans of Spanish descent won gold right in the heart of Spain. In the 1996 Summer Olympics in Atlanta **Lisa Fernández** pitched the women's softball team to a gold medal, and **Rebecca Lobo** became the first Latina to capture a gold medal in basketball.

In other sports, Cuban American distance runner **Alberto Salazar** won the New York Marathon in 1980, 1982, and 1983, and the Boston Marathon in 1982. **Angel Cordero, Jr.,** a top jockey, broke a record by winning the Kentucky Derby for a third time in 1985. When his career spanning three decades came to an end in 1992 after a riding accident, Cordero had won over 7,000 races. In 1988 he earned the distinction of being the first Puerto Rican inducted into the Thoroughbred Hall of Fame. Mexican American figure skating champion **Rudy Galindo** captured the National Championships in 1996 after the judges awarded him a 6.0, the first perfect score in a national competition since 1988. That year he also became the first Latino to medal in the World Figure Skating Championships when he captured the bronze. Galindo is not only the first Mexican American to achieve prominence in his sport, he is also the first openly gay American figure skating champion.

What's on the Web?

There are as many Latino-related websites in cyberspace as there are fish in the sea. Here are a few general interest sites that serve as a great starting point for exploring Latino topics on the Web:

http://www.amarillas.com
This site is a Latino mini-yellow pages with a directory of links to Latino places of interest on the Web.

http://www.latinoweb.com
This page explores Latino and Latin American culture, art, music, film, and much more.

http://www.latinolink.com
This site contains Latino-oriented chat forums, and also fo-

cuses on Latino literature, art, entertainment, politics, business, travel, and more.

http://www.hisp.com
This site houses *Hispanic*, the magazine for those who want to stay current on Latino affairs.

http://www.hispanstar.com
This site belongs to *Hispanic Business*, the magazine for Latino professionals, entrepreneurs, and CEOs.

http://www.mundolatino.org
The Mundo Latino website houses real-time chatrooms. (Peru, Argentina, etc.), allowing Latins around the world to interact in cyberspace.

http://ladb.unm.edu/www/retanet
This site—geared toward teachers—is packed with information about Latin America. It includes databases of resource material, lesson plans, a photo archive, and a list of links to other sites devoted to Latin America.

http://www.lamusica.com
This page of links to websites is a good launching point for finding Latino music sites on the Web. It also has original content on Latino music.

http://www.shopculture.com
This is the official Himilce Novas home page.

Selected Readings

GENERAL WORKS

Abalos, David T. *Latinos in the United States: The Sacred and the Political.* Notre Dame, IN: University of Notre Dame Press, 1986.

Acosta-Belén, Edna, and Barbara R. Sjostrom, eds. *The Hispanic Experience in the United States: Contemporary Issues and Perspectives.* New York: Praeger, 1988.

Alarcón, Norma, and Sylvia Kossnar. *Bibliography of Hispanic Women Writers.* Bloomington, IN: Chicano-Riqueño Studies, 1980.

Augenbraum, Harold, and Ilan Stavans, eds. *Growing Up Latino: Memoirs and Stories.* New York: Houghton Mifflin, 1993.

Bodnar, John. *The Transplanted: A History of Immigrants in Urban America.* Bloomington: Indiana University Press, 1985.

Borjas, George J. *Friends or Strangers: The Impact of Immigrants on the U.S. Economy.* New York: Basic Books, 1990.

Cafferty, Pastora San Juan, Barry R. Chiswick, Andrew M. Greeley, and Teresa A. Sullivan. *The Dilemma of American Immigration: Beyond the Golden Door.* New Brunswick, NJ: Transaction Books, 1983.

Canto, Leandro. *Todos fuimos a Miami.* Caracas: SEDECO, 1986.

Chavez, Linda. *Out of the Barrio: Toward a New Politics of Hispanic Assimilation.* New York: Basic Books, 1991.

Christensen, Thomas, and Carol Christensen, eds. *The Discovery of America & Other Myths: A New World Reader.* San Francisco: Chronicle, 1992.

Cockcraft, James D. *The Hispanic Struggle for Social Justice: The Hispanic Experience in the Americas.* New York: Franklin Watts, 1994.

Collier, Simon, Thomas E. Skidmore, and Harold Blakemore, eds. *The Cambridge Encyclopedia of Latin America and the Caribbean.* New York: Cambridge University Press, 1992.

Contreras, Carlos Alberto, and James W. Wilkie, eds. *Statistical Abstract of Latin America.* Los Angeles: UCLA Latin American Center Publications, 1991.

Crawford, James. *Bilingual Education: History, Politics, Theory, and Practice.* Trenton, NJ: Crane, 1989.

DeFreitas, Gregory. *Inequality at Work: Hispanics in the U.S. Labor Force.* New York: Oxford University Press, 1991.

Dinnerstein, Leonard, and David M. Reimers. *Ethnic Americans: A History of Immigration.* New York: Harper & Row, 1988.

Fernández-Shaw, Carlos M. *Presencia española en los Estados Unidos.* New York: Facts on File, 1992.

Foner, Nancy, ed. *New Immigrants in New York.* New York: Columbia University Press, 1987.

Ford Foundation. *Los hispanos: problemas y oportunidades.* New York: Ford Foundation, 1984.

Fox, Geoffrey. *Hispanic Nation: Culture, Politics, and the Constructing of Identity.* Secaucus, NJ: Carol, 1996.

Gann, Lewis H., and Peter J. Duignan. *The Hispanics in the United States: A History.* Boulder, CO: Westview, 1986.

Garcia, F. Chris. *Pursuing Power: Latinos and the Political System.* Notre Dame, IN: University of Notre Dame Press, 1997.

Glazer, Nathan, ed. *Clamor at the Gates: The New American Immigration.* San Francisco: ICS Press, 1985.

González, Ray, ed. *After Aztlan: Latino Poets of the Nineties.* Boston: David R. Godine, 1992.

González-Wippler, Migene. *The Santería Experience.* Englewood Cliffs, NJ: Prentice-Hall, 1982.

González Echevarría, Roberto, and Enrique Pupo-Walker, eds. *The Cambridge History of Latin American Literature.* Cambridge, England: Cambridge University Press, 1996.

Hadley-Garcia, George. *Hispanic Hollywood: The Latins in Motion Pictures.* New York: Carol, 1990.

Hague, Eleanor. *Latin American Music: Past and Present.* Detroit: B. Etheridge, 1982.

Handlin, Oscar. *A Pictorial History of Immigration.* New York: Crown, 1972.

Haslip-Viera, Gabriel, and Sherrie L. Baver. *Latinos in New York: Communities in Transition.* Notre Dame, IN: University of Notre Dame Press, 1996.

Henderson, James D., and Linda Roddy Henderson. *Ten Notable Women of Latin America.* Chicago: Nelson-Hall, 1978.

Hernández-Chávez, Eduardo. "Language Maintenance, Bilingual Education, and Philosophies of Bilingualism in the United States," in James A. Alatis, ed., *International Dimensions of Bilingual Education.* Washington, DC: Georgetown University Press, 1978.

Higham, John. *Strangers in the Land: Patterns of American Nativism, 1860–1925.* New Brunswick, NJ: Rutgers University Press, 1988.

Hispanic. Washington, DC: Hispanic Publishing, April 1990– February 1998.

Hispanic Business. Santa Barbara, CA: Hispanic Business Publications, February 1990–June 1997.

Kanellos, Nicolás. *The Hispanic Almanac: From Columbus to Corporate America.* Detroit: Visible Ink, 1994.

Kanellos, Nicolás, with Cristelia Pérez. *Chronology of Hispanic-American History.* New York: Gale Research, 1995.

Lachaga, José María de. *El pueblo hispano en USA: minorías étnicas y la Iglesia Católica.* Bilbao: Desclée de Brouwer, 1982.

Lamm, Richard D., and Gary Imhoff. *The Immigration Time Bomb: The Fragmenting of America.* New York: Truman Talley, 1985.

Lockhart, James, and Stuart B. Schwartz. *Early Latin America: A*

History of Colonial Spanish America and Brazil. Cambridge, England: Cambridge University Press, 1983.

Moncada, Alberto. *La americanización de los hispanos.* Barcelona: Plaza & Janes, 1986.

Moore, Joan, and Harry Pachon. *Hispanics in the United States.* Englewood Cliffs, NJ: Prentice-Hall, 1985.

Moreno Fraginals, Manuel, Frank Moya Pons, and Stanley L. Engerman, eds. *Between Slavery and Free Labor: The Spanish-Speaking Caribbean in the Nineteenth Century.* Baltimore: Johns Hopkins University Press, 1985.

Muller, Thomas, and Thomas J. Espenshade. *The Fourth Wave: California's Newest Immigrants.* Washington, DC: Urban Institute Press, 1985.

Natella, Arthur A., Jr. *The Spanish in America, 1513–1974: A Chronology and Fact Book.* Dobbs Ferry, NY: Oceana, 1975.

Novas, Himilce. *The Hispanic 100: A Ranking of the Latino Men and Women Who Have Most Influenced American Thought and Culture.* New York: Carol, 1995.

Novas, Himilce, and Rosemary Silva. *Latin American Cooking Across the U.S.A.* New York: Alfred A. Knopf, 1997.

Ortiz, Elizabeth Lambert. *The Book of Latin American Cooking.* New York: Alfred A. Knopf, 1979.

O'Shaughnessy, Hugh. *Latin Americans.* London: BBC Books, 1988.

Pachon, Harry, and Louis DeSipio. *New Americans by Choice: Political Perspectives of Latino Immigrants.* Boulder, CO: Westview, 1994.

Poey, Delia, and Virgil Suarez, eds. *Iguana Dreams: New Latino Fiction.* New York: Harper Perennial, 1992.

Porter, Rosalie Pedalino. *Forked Tongue: The Politics of Bilingual Education.* New York: Basic Books, 1990.

Ratliff, William E. *Castroism and Communism in Latin America, 1959–1976: The Varieties of Marxist-Leninist Experience.* Washington, DC: American Enterprise Institute for Public Policy Research, 1976.

Reimers, David M. *Still the Golden Door: The Third World Comes to America.* New York: Columbia University Press, 1992.

Richard, Alfred Charles, Jr. *The Hispanic Image on the Silver Screen: An Interpretive Filmography from Silents into Sound, 1898–1935.* New York: Greenwood, 1992.

Roberts, John Storm. *The Latin Tinge: The Impact of Latin American*

Music on the United States. New York: Oxford University Press, 1979.

Rochín, Refugio I., ed. *Immigration and Ethnic Communities: A Focus on Latinos.* East Lansing, MI: Julian Samora Research Institute, 1996.

Sandoval, Moises. *On the Move: A History of the Hispanic Church in the United States.* Maryknoll, NY: Orbis, 1990.

Santoli, Al. *New Americans: An Oral History.* New York: Viking, 1988.

Shorris, Earl. *Latinos: A Biography of the People.* New York: W.W. Norton, 1992.

Simon, Julian Lincoln. *The Economic Consequences of Immigration.* Cambridge, England: B. Blackwell, 1989.

Smith, Peter H. *Talons of the Eagle: Dynamics of U.S.–Latin American Relations.* New York: Oxford University Press, 1996.

Sotomayor, Marta, ed. *Empowering Hispanic Families: A Critical Issue for the '90s.* Milwaukee: Family Service America, 1991.

Sutton, Constance R., and Elisa M. Chaney, eds. *Caribbean Life in New York City: Sociocultural Dimensions.* New York: Center for Migration Studies of New York, 1987.

Valdés, M. Isabel, and Martha H. Seoane. *Hispanic Market Handbook.* Detroit: Gale Research, 1995.

Vigil, Maurilio E. *Hispanics in American Politics: The Search for Political Power.* Lanham, MD: University Press of America, 1987.

Villarreal, Roberto E., and Norma G. Hernandez, eds. *Latinos and Political Coalitions: Political Empowerment for the 1990s.* New York: Greenwood, 1991.

Weyr, Thomas. *Hispanic U.S.A.: Breaking the Melting Pot.* New York: Harper & Row, 1988.

Williamson, Edwin. *The Penguin History of Latin America.* London: Penguin, 1992.

Zucker, Norman L., and Naomi Flink Zucker. *The Guarded Gate: The Reality of American Refugee Policy.* San Diego: Harcourt, Brace, Jovanovich, 1987.

THE SPANISH CONQUEST

Bernaldez, Andres. *Historia de los reyes catolicos Don Fernando y Doña Isabel.* Granada: Imprenta y libreria de D. J. M. Zamora, 1856.

English translation: *Selected Documents Illustrating the Four Voyages of Columbus,* vol. 1. London: Hakluyt Society, 1930.

Cabeza de Vaca, A. N. *Naufragios y comentarios.* Madrid: Taurus, 1969. English translation: *Adventures in the Unknown Interior of America.* New York: Collier, 1961.

Casas, Bartolome de las. *Opusculos, cartas y memoriales,* vol. 110. Madrid: Biblioteca de Autores Españoles, 1958. English translation: *The Devastation of the Indies.* New York: Seabury, 1974.

Colón, C. *Raccolta colombiana, I,* vols. 1 and 2. Rome, 1892–94. English translation: *Journals and Other Documents.* New York: Heritage, 1963.

Díaz del Castillo, Bernal. *Historia verdadera de la conquista de la Nueva España.* 2 vols. Mexico: Porrua, 1955. English translation: *The True History of the Conquest of New Spain.* 5 vols. London: Hakluyt Society, 1908–16.

Duran, Diego. *Historia de las Indias de Nueva-España y islas de tierra firme.* 2 vols. Mexico: Porrua, 1967. English translation: *Book of the Gods and Rites and the Ancient Calendar.* Norman: University of Oklahoma Press, 1971.

Godoy, Diego. "Relación a H. Cortés." In *Historiadores primitivos de Indias,* vol. 1. Madrid: Biblioteca de Autores Españoles, 1877.

Lockhart, James. *Spanish Peru, 1532–1560.* Madison: University of Wisconsin Press, 1968.

Todorov, Tzvetan. *The Conquest of America: The Question of the Other.* New York: Harper & Row, 1984.

MEXICAN AMERICANS

Acuña, Rodolfo F. *Anything but Mexican: Chicanos in Contemporary Los Angeles.* London: Verso, 1996.

———. *Occupied America: A History of Chicanos.* New York: HarperCollins, 1988.

Bayless, Rick, with Deann Groen Bayless. *Authentic Mexican: Regional Cooking from the Heart of Mexico.* New York: William Morrow, 1987.

Binder, Wolfgang, ed. *Partial Autobiographies: Interviews with Twenty Chicano Poets.* Erlangen, Germany: Palm & Enke, 1985.

Blea, Irene I. *La Chicana and the Intersection of Race, Class, and Gender.* New York: Praeger, 1992.

Bruce-Novoa. *RetroSpace: Collected Essays on Chicano Literature: Theory and History.* Houston: Arte Público, 1990.

Calderón, Héctor, and José David Saldívar, eds. *Criticism in the Borderlands: Studies in Chicano Literature, Culture, and Ideology.* Durham, NC: Duke University Press, 1991.

Commission on Civil Rights. *The Excluded Student: Educational Practices Affecting Mexican-Americans in the Southwest.* Washington, DC: Government Printing Office, 1972.

De Anda, Roberto M., ed. *Chicanas and Chicanos in Contemporary Society.* Boston: Allyn and Bacon, 1996.

Elizondo, Virgilio P. *The Future is Mestizo: Life Where Cultures Meet.* Oak Park, IL: Meyer-Stone, 1988.

Galarza, Ernesto. *Barrio Boy.* Notre Dame, IN: University of Notre Dame Press, 1971.

García, Mario T. *Memories of Chicano History: The Life and Narrative of Bert Corona.* Berkeley: University of California Press, 1994.

Glazer, Mark. *A Dictionary of Mexican American Proverbs.* New York: Greenwood, 1987.

Graham, Joe S., ed. *Hecho en Tejas: Texas-Mexican Folk Arts and Crafts.* Denton: University of North Texas Press, 1991.

Herrera-Sobek, María. *The Bracero Experience: Elitelore Versus Folklore.* Los Angeles: UCLA Latin American Center Publications, 1979.

Iglesias Prieto, Norma. *Medios de communicación en la frontera norte.* Mexico: Fundación Manuel Buendia; Programa Cultural de las Fronteras, 1990.

Jussawalla, Feroza, and Reed Way Dasenbrock, eds. *Interviews with Writers of the Post-Colonial World.* Jackson: University Press of Mississippi, 1992.

Kanellos, Nicolás. *Understanding the Chicano Experience Through Literature.* Houston: University of Texas Press, 1981.

Langley, Lester D. *MexAmerica: Two Countries, One Future.* New York: Crown, 1988.

Lattin, Vernon E., ed. *Contemporary Chicano Fiction: A Critical Survey.* Binghamton, NY: Bilingual Press/Editorial Bilingüe, 1986.

Limón, José Eduardo. *Mexican Ballads, Chicano Poems: History and*

Influence in Mexican-American Social Poetry. Berkeley: University of California Press, 1992.

Long, Haniel. *The Marvelous Adventure of Cabeza de Vaca.* Clearlake, CA: Dawn Horse, 1992.

López de Gómara, Francisco. *Historia de la conquista de Mexico.* Mexico: Editorial Pedro Robredo, 1943. English translation: *Cortés: The Life of the Conqueror by His Secretary.* Berkeley: University of California, 1964.

Maciel, David R., and Isidro D. Ortiz, eds. *Chicanas/Chicanos at the Crossroads: Social, Economic, and Political Change.* Tucson: The University of Arizona Press, 1996.

Mayberry, Jodine. *Mexicans.* New York: Franklin Watts, 1990.

McWilliams, Carey. *North from Mexico: The Spanish-Speaking People of the United States.* New York: Greenwood, 1990.

Meier, Matt S., and Feliciano Ribera. *Mexican-Americans/American Mexicans: From Conquistadors to Chicanos.* New York: Hill and Wang, 1993.

Miller, Tom. *On the Border: Portraits of America's Southwestern Frontier.* Tucson: University of Arizona Press, 1981.

Moquin, Wayne, with Charles Van Doren, eds. *A Documentary History of the Mexican Americans.* New York: Praeger, 1971.

Paz, Octavio. *The Labyrinth of Solitude.* New York: Grove, 1985.

Peñuelas, Marcelino C. *Cultura hispanica en Estados Unidos: los chicanos.* Madrid: Ediciones Cultura Hispanica del Centro Iberoamericano de Cooperación, 1978.

Pettit, Arthus G. *Images of the Mexican-American in Fiction and Film.* College Station: Texas A&M University Press, 1980.

Pierri, Ettore. *Chicanos, el poder mestizo.* Mexico City: Mexicanos Unidos, 1979.

Samora, Julian, and Patricia Vandel Simon. *A History of the Mexican-American People.* Notre Dame, IN: University of Notre Dame Press, 1977.

Sánchez, George J. *Becoming Mexican American: Ethnicity, Culture and Identity in Chicano Los Angeles, 1900–1945.* New York: Oxford University Press, 1993.

Sewell, Dorita. *Knowing People: A Mexican-American Community's Concept of a Person.* New York: AMS, 1989.

Skerry, Peter. *Mexican Americans: The Ambivalent Minority.* New York: Macmillan, 1993.

Tafolla, Carmen. *To Split a Human: Mitos, Machos y la Mujer Chicana.* San Antonio: TX: Mexican American Cultural Center, 1985.

Tatum, Charles M., ed. *New Chicana/Chicano Writing.* Tucson: The University of Arizona Press, 1992.

Time-Life Books, eds. *Mexico.* Alexandria, VA: Time-Life Books, 1986.

Trujillo, Carla, ed. *Chicana Lesbians: The Girls Our Mothers Warned Us About.* Berkeley, CA: Third Woman, 1991.

Weigle, Marta, ed. *Two Guadalupes: Hispanic Legends and Magic Tales from Northern New Mexico.* Santa Fe: Ancient City, 1987.

Weigle, Marta, and Peter White. *The Lore of New Mexico.* Albuquerque: University of New Mexico Press, 1988.

West, John O., ed. *Mexican-American Folklore: Legends, Songs, Festivals, Proverbs, Crafts, Tales of Saints, of Revolutionaries, and More.* Little Rock, AR: August House, 1988.

PUERTO RICANS

Aliotta, Jerome J. *The Puerto Ricans.* New York: Chelsea House, 1991.

Bothwell Gonzalez, Reece B. *La cuidadania en Puerto Rico.* Rio Piedras: Editorial Universitaria, Universidad de Puerto Rico, 1980.

Carr, Raymond. *Puerto Rico: A Colonial Experiment.* New York: New York University Press, 1984.

Carrion, Arturo Morales, ed. *Puerto Rico: A Political and Cultural History.* New York: W.W. Norton, 1984.

Coll y Toste, Cayetano. *Puertorriqueños ilustres.* Rio Piedras, PR: Editorial Cultural, 1971.

Dietz, James L. *Economic History of Puerto Rico: Institutional Change and Capital Development.* Princeton, NJ: Princeton University Press, 1986.

Fitzpatrick, Joseph P. *Puerto Rican Americans: The Meaning of Migration to the Mainland.* Englewood Cliffs, NJ: Prentice-Hall, 1987.

Flores, Juan. *Divided Borders: Essays on Puerto Rican Identity.* Houston: Arte Público, 1991.

Hauberg, Clifford A. *Puerto Rico and the Puerto Ricans.* New York: Twayne, 1975.

Hauptly, Denis J. *Puerto Rico: An Unfinished Story.* New York: Atheneum, 1991.

Larsen, Ronald J. *The Puerto Ricans in America.* Minneapolis: Lerner, 1989.

Lopez, Adalberto, and James F. Petras, eds. *Puerto Rico and the Puerto Ricans: Studies in History and Society.* Cambridge, MA: Schenkman, 1974.

Melendez, Edwin, and Edgardo Melendez, eds. *Colonial Dilemma: Critical Perspectives on Contemporary Puerto Rico.* Boston: South End, 1993.

Mohr, Eugene V. *The Nuyorican Experience: Literature of the Puerto Rican Minority.* Westport, CT: Greenwood, 1982.

Perez y Mena, Andres Isidoro. *Speaking with the Dead: Development of Afro-Latin Religion Among Puerto Ricans in the United States, A Study into the Interpenetration of Civilizations in the New World.* New York: AMS Press, 1991.

Samoiloff, Louise Cripps. *A Portrait of Puerto Rico.* New York: Cornwall, 1984.

Sánchez Korrol, Virginia. *From Colonia to Community: The History of Puerto Ricans in New York City.* Berkeley: University of California Press, 1994.

Turner, Faythe. *Puerto Ricans at Home in the USA: An Anthology.* Seattle: Open Hand Publishing, 1991.

CUBAN AMERICANS

Blight, James G. *The Shattered Crystal Ball: Fear and Learning in the Cuban Missile Crisis.* Savage, MD: Rowman & Littlefield, 1990.

Bonachea, Ramon L., and Marta San Martin. *The Cuban Insurrection, 1952–1959.* New Brunswick, NJ: Transaction, 1974.

Boswell, Thomas D., and James R. Curtis. *The Cuban-American Experience: Culture, Images, and Perspectives.* Totowa, NJ: Rowman & Allanheld, 1984.

Cortes, Carlos E., ed. *The Cuban Experience in the United States.* New York: Arno, 1980.

Del Aguila, Juan M. *Cuba: Dilemmas of a Revolution.* Boulder, CO: Westview, 1994.

Del Mar, Marcia. *A Cuban Story*. Winston-Salem, NC: John F. Blair, 1979.

Duncan, Walter Raymond. *The Soviet Union and Cuba: Interests and Influence*. New York: Praeger, 1985.

García, María Cristina. *Havana USA: Cuban Exiles and Cuban Americans in South Florida, 1959–1994*. Berkeley: University of California Press, 1996.

Geyer, Georgie Anne. *Guerrilla Prince: The Untold Story of Fidel Castro*. Boston: Little, Brown, 1991.

Grupo Areíto. *Contra viento y marea: jóvenes cubanos hablan desde su exilio en Estados Unidos*. La Habana, Cuba: Casa de las Americas, 1978.

Kiple, Kenneth F. *Blacks in Colonial Cuba, 1774–1899*. Gainesville: University Presses of Florida, 1976.

Llanes, José. *Cuban Americans: Masters of Survival*. Cambridge, MA: Abt, 1982.

Medina, Pablo. *Exiled Memories: A Cuban Childhood*. Austin: University of Texas Press, 1990.

Mesa-Lago, Carmelo. *The Economy of Socialist Cuba: A Two-Decade Appraisal*. Albuquerque: University of New Mexico Press, 1981.

Murphy, Joseph M. *Santería: An African Religion in America*. New York: Original Publications, 1989.

Olson, James S., and Judith E. Olson. *Cuban Americans: From Trauma to Triumph*. New York: Twayne, 1995.

Padilla, Herberto. *Self-Portrait of the Other: A Memoir*. New York: Farrar, Straus & Giroux, 1990.

Pérez, Louis A., Jr. *Cuba: Between Reform and Revolution*. New York: Oxford University Press, 1988.

Perez-Firmat, Gustavo. *Life on the Hyphen: The Cuban-American Way*. Austin: University of Texas Press, 1994.

Rieff, David. *The Exile: Cuban in the Heart of Miami*. New York: Simon & Schuster, 1993.

Rogg, Eleanor. *The Assimilation of Cuban Exiles: The Role of the Community and Class*. New York: Aberdeen, 1974.

Scott, Rebecca J. *Slave Emancipation in Cuba: The Transition to Free Labor, 1860–1899*. Princeton, NJ: Princeton University Press, 1985.

Suchlicki, Jaime. Cuba: *From Columbus to Castro*. Washington, DC: Pergamon-Brassey's, 1986.

Timerman, Jacobo. *Cuba: A Journey*. New York: Alfred A. Knopf, 1990.

DOMINICAN AMERICANS

Betances, Emelio. *State and Society in the Dominican Republic.* Boulder, CO: Westview, 1995.

Bogen, Elizabeth. *Caribbean Immigrants in New York City: A Demographic Summary.* New York: Department of City Planning/Office of Immigrant Affairs and Population Analysis Division, 1988.

Cambeira, Alan. *Quisqueya la Bella: The Dominican Republic in Historical and Cultural Perspective.* Armonk, NY: M.E. Sharpe, 1997.

Grasmuck, Sherri, and Patricia R. Pessar. *Between Two Islands: Dominican International Migration.* Berkeley: University of California Press, 1991.

Haggerty, Richard A., ed. *Dominican Republic and Haiti: Country Studies.* Washington, DC: Federal Research Division, Library of Congress, 1991.

Hendricks, Glenn. *The Dominican Diaspora: From the Dominican Republic to New York City—Villagers in Transition.* New York: Teachers College Press, 1974.

Klein, Alan M. *Sugarball: The American Game, the Dominican Dream.* New Haven, CT: Yale University Press, 1991.

AMERICANS OF CENTRAL AND SOUTH AMERICAN DESCENT

Anderson, Thomas P. *Politics in Central America: Guatemala, El Salvador, Honduras, and Nicaragua.* New York: Praeger, 1982.

Barry, Tom. *Roots of Rebellion: Land and Hunger in Central America.* Boston: South End, 1987.

Biesanz, Richard, Karen Zubris Biesanz, and Mavis Hiltunen Biesanz. *The Costa Ricans.* Englewood Cliffs, NJ: Prentice-Hall, 1982.

Black, George. *The Good Neighbor: How the United States Wrote the History of Central America and the Caribbean.* New York: Pantheon, 1988.

Buckley, Kevin. *Panama: The Whole Story.* New York: Simon & Schuster, 1991.

Buckley, Tom. *Violent Neighbors: El Salvador, Central America, and the United States.* New York: Times Books, 1984.

Child, Jack, ed. *Conflict in Central America: Approaches to Peace and Security.* London: C. Hurst, 1986.

Crawley, Eduardo. *Nicaragua in Perspective.* New York: St. Martin's, 1984.

Didion, Joan. *Salvador.* New York: Simon & Schuster, 1983.

Faugsted, George E., Jr. *Chilenos in the California Gold Rush.* San Francisco: R & E Research Associates, 1973.

Hamilton, Nora, Jeffry A. Frieden, Linda Fuller, and Manuel Pastor, Jr., eds. *Crisis in Central America: Regional Dynamics and U.S. Policy in the 1980s.* Boulder, CO: Westview, 1988.

Krauss, Clifford. *Inside Central America: Its People, Politics, and History.* New York: Summit, 1991.

Lopez, Carlos U. *Chilenos in California: A Study of the 1850, 1852 and 1860 Censuses.* San Francisco: R & E Research Associates, 1973.

McNeil, Frank. *War and Peace in Central America.* New York: Scribner's, 1988.

Monaghan, Jay. *Chile, Peru, and the California Gold Rush of 1849.* Berkeley: University of California Press, 1973.

Painter, James. *Guatemala: False Hope, False Freedom: The Rich, the Poor and the Christian Democrats.* London: Catholic Institute for International Relations, 1987.

Simon, Jean-Marie. *Guatemala: Eternal Spring, Eternal Tyranny.* New York: W.W. Norton, 1987.

Williams, Robert G. *Export Agriculture and the Crisis in Central America.* Chapel Hill: University of North Carolina Press, 1986.

Woodward, Ralph Lee. *Central America: A Nation Divided.* New York: Oxford University Press, 1985.

Index

California:
  Bear Flag Revolt, 81–82
  Gold Rush, 29, 82–86, 266
  mining, Latinos' role in, 83–84
  missions, Spanish, 29
  Proposition 187, 287–88
  Spanish settlement of, 65
Californios, 65, 81–82, 85–86
Campbell, Jack, 112
Campeche, José, 139
Campo, Pupi, 295
Campos, Albizu, 150
Canary Islands, 35
Candel Miranda, Rafael, 153
Canseco, José, 314–15, 318
Capac, Manco, 32
Cara, Irene, 160, 303
Cárdenas, Lázaro, 96
Carey, Mariah, xii, 160, 296
Carib, 21–22
Caribbean Islands, 18–19, 21–22
Carrillo, José Antonio, 82
Carmen, Julie, 160
Carr, Vikki, 160, 294
Carranza, Venustiano, 88
Carrera, Rafael, 245–46
Carrillo, Charlie, 309
Carter, Jimmy, 155, 201–2
Casals, Rosemary, xii, 316, 318
Castaneda, Carlos, 305, 306, 307
Castilian Spanish, 35, 37
Castillo, Ana, 119, 306, 308
Castillo Armas, Carlos, 248
Castillo de San Marcos National
  Monument, 28–29
Castro, Fidel:
  background of, 191–92
  Marielitos and, 201–2
  revolution led by, 184–85, 187,
    190–94
  rule of Cuba, 191–206, 274
Castro, Raúl, 191, 192
Castro Díaz-Balart, Fidel, 191
Catalonia, 35, 36
Catholicism:
  conversion of natives to, 26, 42,
    55–56

Mexican Revolution and, 89
  in Spain, 39–42
  see also Santería
Caucasian Race Resolution, 98–99
Central America, 12–13, 229–64
  see also specific countries
Central American Resource Center,
  244
Cepeda, Orlando, 314
Cerezo Arévalo, Marco Vinicio, 249
Céspedes, Carlos Manuel de, 174,
  186
Chamorro, Fruto, 251
Chamorro, Violeta Barrios de,
  257
Chang-Díaz, Franklin, 311
Chapinerito, El, 263
Charles V, King of Spain, 60
Charo, xii, 160
Charreada, 123–24
Chávez, César Estrada, 52, 54, 102,
  108–11, 121
Chávez, Denise, 119
Chávez, Dennis, 276
Chavez, Linda, 158, 279–81
Chayanne, 160
Chibcha Indians, 34
Chicano movement, 111–14, 117
Chicanos, 18, 52
  see also Mexican Americans
Chile, 13, 266–67
Chile peppers, 127–28
China, Emperor of (Grand Khan),
  19, 20
Chocolate, 126
Chong, Tommy, 300
Christianity, spread of, 19, 39–42,
  55–56
  see also Catholicism
Cinco De Mayo, 123
Cisneros, Henry, xii, 64
Cisneros, Sandra, 4, 119, 306, 307,
  308
Clavijo, Fernando, 313
Clemente, Roberto Walker, 313–14,
  318
Clifford, George, 137–38

Fender, Freddie, 294
Ferdinand, King of Spain, xii, 18, 19, 40–41, 134, 135
Fernández Enrique, 4
Fernández, Gigi, 227, 316, 318
Fernandez, Giselle, 304
Fernández, Leonel, 224
Fernández, Mary Joe, xii, 227, 316, 318, 322
Fernández, de Cordoba, Francisco, 250
Ferré, Luis, 155
Ferrer, José, xii, 301
Films about Latinos, 203
Flores, Tom, 319, 321
Fontes, Montserrat, 119, 306, 308
Food, *see* Cuisine
Foraker Act, 148–49
1492, 42
Free Cuba Public Affairs Committee, 274
Freedom Flotilla, 201
Frémont, John Charles, 81
French Guiana, 233

Gadsden, James, 80
Gadsden Treaty, 80–81
Galarza, Ernesto, 306
Galicia, 35, 36
Galindo, Rudy, 322–23
Gálvez, Bernardo de, 66
Gálvez, Mariano, 245
Gandhi, Mahatma, 110
García, Andy, 161, 302
Garcia, Cristina, 306, 308
Garcia, Guy, 306
García Márquez, Gabriel, 262, 305
Gardel, Carlos, 292
Giancana, Sam, 196
Gillespie, Archibald, 82
Goizueta, Roberto C., xii, 183, 274
Gold, 19, 29, 30
  California Gold Rush, 82–86, 266
Goldberg, Arthur, 99
Gómez, Laureano, 261
Gómez, Máximo, 174

Gonzáles, Richard "Pancho," 315, 319
Gonzáles, Rodolfo "Corky," 112–13, 118, 119
González, Andy, 295
Gonzalez, Cristina, 161, 303
González, Henry B., xii, 91, 276–77
González, Juan, 315
González, Ofelia, 301–2
Granada, 42
Grande, Father Rutilio, 236
Grau San Martín, Ramón, 185, 187
Greco, José, 303
Grijalba, Juan de, 27
Gringos, 53
Grito de Dolores, El, 54, 68–69, 117, 122
Grito de Lares, El, 140–41
Grito de Yara, El, 177–78
Gronk (artist), 120
Guadelete, Battle of, 38
Guam, 182
"Guantanamera," 180
Guantánamo Bay, 186, 204
Guatemala, xiii, 13, 22, 244–50
Guatemalan Americans, 249–50
Guerra, Marcelino, 295
Guevara, Ernesto "Che," 191, 192, 194–95
Gusanos, 194
Gutiérrez, José Ángel, 113
Gutiérrez, Luis, 277–78
Gutiérrez, Sidney, 312
Guyana, 233
Guzmán Fernández, Silvestre Antonio, 223
Guzman, Viviana, 297

Haiti, 20, 216
Ha-Levi, Juda, 39
Havana, Cuba, 171
Hayakawa, S. I., 284
Hay, John, 144–45
Hayworth, Rita, xii, 161, 298
Healers (*curanderas*), 115

Index